AMERICAN CATHOLIC
TRADITIONS

AMERICAN CATHOLIC TRADITIONS

Resources for Renewal

Sandra Yocum Mize
William L. Portier

Editors

THE ANNUAL PUBLICATION
OF THE COLLEGE THEOLOGY SOCIETY
1996
VOLUME 42

ORBIS BOOKS

Maryknoll, New York 10545

The Catholic Foreign Mission Society of America (Maryknoll) recruits and trains people for overseas missionary service. Through Orbis Books, Maryknoll aims to foster the international dialogue that is essential to mission. The books published, however, reflect the opinions of their authors and are not meant to represent the official position of the society.

Co-published by the College Theology Society and Orbis Books, Maryknoll, NY 10545-0308
Manufactured in the United States of America

Orbis/ISBN 1-57075-109-9

To

Christopher Kauffman
and
David O'Brien,

historians who wear their learning gracefully
and share it abundantly—even with theologians.

Contents

PART II
AESTHETICS

PART III
LOCAL THEOLOGIES

Acknowledgments

The editors are grateful to our colleagues who served as readers. Their careful reports were indispensable to us in putting this volume together. We also wish to thank Brenda Fox, Meredith Moore, Beth Mayer, and Beth Buckley for their assistance in preparing the manuscript. Thanks too to our families for their support. Special thanks to Bryan Mize and Bonnie Portier, and to Susan Perry for keeping us on track.

Introduction

In the aftermath of the second Vatican Council, Catholic theology exploded with new vitality. Some of its effervescence bubbled into unexpected places. The ground shifted. People had to reorient themselves on new theological terrain. While still home to the familiar clerical voices of old Europe, the theological landscape now included women, laity, and voices from other continents and cultures.

Though variously situated and juxtaposed on this new landscape, most of its inhabitants would agree that renewal in Catholic theology has generally enriched the church's life even as it has made it more complex and sometimes more painful. Most importantly, they would also agree that theological renewal was made possible by the decades of historical scholarship that preceded it. This movement of historical scholarship is known as *ressourcement*, a return to biblical, patristic, and liturgical sources.

In the United States, the decades since the council have seen a veritable *ressourcement* in American Catholic studies. It has happened in an interdisciplinary flurry on the back roads and the borders between history and theology and cultural studies. In a return to the sources comparable to the one that preceded Vatican II and energized subsequent theological renewal, new generations of scholars have begun to recover the American Catholic past and to reconstruct it along the lines of current historiography. *American Catholic Traditions* makes some of this new scholarship accessible to a wider audience. Teachers and scholars who want to situate their reflections in and address them to the lives of contemporary American Catholics have much to learn from the new historiography.

Most of the essays in this book were presented at the forty-second annual meeting of the College Theology Society, May 30-June 2, 1996, at the University of Dayton. This meeting ranged widely over the theme of "Religious Intellectual Traditions in the United States." Grouping the essays under the three headings of "Praxis," "Aesthetics," and

"Local Theologies," we have focused this volume more sharply on American Catholic traditions.

Sandra Yocum Mize sets the tone for Part I, "Praxis," with a look at how narrowly construed understandings of what makes an "intellectual" have too often consigned Catholics to the back roads. On a programmatic tour of these byways, she locates five Catholic sites, networks of conversations and practices, that have served as traditions or homes for intellectuals understood in a more organic sense. Careful attention to these sites or traditions tends to destabilize and enrich our understandings of the title's other two key terms, *American* and *Catholic*. Roberto Goizueta's response further explores the Hispanic/Latino site at which Mize had time for only a brief stop. Goizueta highlights the potential contributions of praxis-based Latino theologies.

Reflecting on his experience in the Catholic community at the Pine Ridge Reservation in South Dakota, Michael Steltenkamp offers an important challenge to the often sloppy ideology that surrounds the question of the evangelization of Native peoples. In its treatment of Black Elk (c.1863-1950) and other Catholic Indians as active agents in their own histories, Steltenkamp's anthropologically informed approach to Lakota Catholicism is comparable to Lamin Sanneh's interpretation of Christianity's impact on the cultures of West Africa.[1]

The culture created by the immigrants was another site briefly visited by Sandra Yocum Mize. The assimilationist approach of most Catholic immigrants led to the democratization of Catholic culture among the second and third generations of middle-class Catholics. This democratization extended to movements of "socially engaged holiness," such as the U.S. Grail and the Catholic Worker. Drawing upon his active participation in the Worker tradition, Michael Baxter sketches a "radicalist" alternative to what he sees as the prevailing "Americanist" tradition in Catholic social ethics. James Fisher responds with a cautionary reminder about just how "American" Dorothy Day really was.

Continuing this exploration of the Worker tradition, Frederick Bauerschmidt offers an insightful interpretation of St. Thérèse of Lisieux's "Little Way" and Dorothy Day's appropriation of it. Showing the politically engaged Day legitimately espousing the "Little Way," he sheds light on the peculiarities of Catholic Worker spirituality and political engagement. In her discussion of the vision of Jacques van Ginniken and its appropriation by the women of the U.S. Grail, Patricia DeFerrari performs a similar service for the Grail Movement in the United States and its theologies of work.

Any proposed deepening of the category of "intellectual" must come eventually to the imagination. In retrieving American Catholic aesthetic traditions, it would be difficult to avoid the "analogical imagination" as both a descriptive and an analytical category. In Part II's opening essay, Anthony Smith illuminates immigrant Catholic engagement with the symbols of American popular culture in the first half of this century. He shows director John Ford's Catholic sensibility at work in three of his classic films: "Stagecoach" (1939), "Fort Apache" (1948), and "The Sun Shines Bright" (1953).

The 1996 annual meeting at Dayton featured two symposia devoted to exploring the analogical imagination. The first considered "The Contributions of William F. Lynch, S.J. to American Catholic Intellectual Life." The second offered two critical appraisals of Paul Giles's *American Catholic Arts and Fictions: Culture, Ideology, Aesthetics* (1992).

William F. Lynch (1908-1987) is not widely remembered today. He is perhaps most likely to be known for the early 1960s Mentor editions of some of his books. As a college student in 1964, I recall reading *Christ and Apollo: The Dimensions of the Literary Imagination.* But one might argue the case, apart from questions of direct influence, that David Tracy's theological classic *The Analogical Imagination: Christian Theology and the Culture of Pluralism* could not have been written in 1981 if Lynch's corpus had not preceded it. Regardless of how that argument might turn out, however, Lynch's time appears to have come. Widespread disenchantment with Enlightenment notions of rationality signals a turn to the imagination. Blending David Toolan's personal reminiscences with the tight exposition and analysis of Gerald Bednar and John Kane, these essays provide both enticement for the logos-weary and a bibliographical map to guide them through Lynch's work on the imagination.

Paul Giles has argued that the Catholic analogical imagination gives rise to an alternative intellectual style, and further, in its secularized form, to an alternative literary tradition. Una Cadegan and Peter Huff engage these claims in spirited fashion. Appreciative of the conception and sheer scope of his project, they nevertheless take issue with Giles's interpretations of both literature and Catholicism.

Part III explores some of the Catholic intellectual traditions that might have been devalued in what Mize has identified as an American tradition of "the intellectual." As "local theologies," they might now serve as both inspiration and resource. In Jon Roberts's contribution, we leave the back roads and travel down some of the more familiar highways of American intellectual history. Revisiting the theme of secularization, Roberts charts the eclipse of God-talk in the cultural spaces of the nineteenth-century natural world and twentieth-century moral and social worlds. Utilizing anthropologist Clifford Geertz's notion of "local knowldege," Elizabeth McKeown's response returns our attention to the back roads. She suggests that the sciences and social sciences, whose discourses Roberts analyzes, are, in Geertz's phrase, "crafts of place." As if to illustrate this, McKeown's own contribution to this volume chronicles a modest Catholic presence at the beginning of the discipline of anthropology in this country.

Patricia McDonald turns a contemporary biblical scholar's careful eye to Francis Gigot's (1859-1920) *New York Review* articles from early in this century. Readers will be surprised at the advanced state of biblical scholarship practiced by Gigot on the eve of the papal censure of modernism in 1907.

In Part III's final contribution, Patrick Carey breaks new ground with his account of the emergence of college theology as a discipline in American Catholic undergraduate institutions. Carey's conclusion challenges contemporary teachers of theology and religious studies to develop definitions of the discipline and coherent programs. These programs, he urges, should mirror the healthy pluralism of the first half of the twentieth century and address the needs, both spiritual and intellectual, of contemporary students.

As you consider Carey's challenges, we invite you to listen to the forgotten voices of William F. Lynch and Francis Gigot. Listen as their chorus is joined and enriched by a host of others from Dorothy Day and the Grail women to Black Elk and John Ford's sinners and cavalrymen. The history of American Catholic life and thought, understood inclusively, holds the kinds of intellectual and spiritual resources needed to renew American Catholic theology and rescue it from abstraction and dependency. We hope that *American Catholic Traditions* will stimulate such renewal by putting American Catholic theologians and teachers in better contact with their historical roots.

William L. Portier

Notes

[1] See Lamin Sanneh, *Translating the Message, The Missionary Impact on African Culture* (Maryknoll, N.Y.: Orbis Books, 1989).

Part I

PRAXIS

On the Back Roads:
Searching for American Catholic
Intellectual Traditions

Sandra Yocum Mize

The title, "On the Back Roads: Searching for American Catholic Intellectual Traditions," suggests two things. First, "back roads" connotes at the very least a slow-going journey through a minimally charted landscape where one might encounter dead-ends, detours, and other unknown quantities. The second part of the title, "Searching for American Catholic Intellectual Traditions," suggests clear destinations, as if such traditions might actually exist if one searches diligently enough. I have spent about twelve years now travelling these "back roads."[1] I use that image advisedly because in fact my dissertation focused upon the public discourse of three bishops and two male converts, five prominent American Catholic men of the nineteenth century. From the perspective of those who study American Catholicism, I opted for a study of the elite within the U.S. Catholic community. Yet in perusing general histories of American intellectual life, none of these five, with the exception of Orestes Brownson, is ever mentioned. Even discussions of Brownson usually end with his conversion to Catholicism, which suggests that the historians conclude that conversion marks the end of his intellectual life. In fact, without extra-textual evidence, I would find it difficult to defend the existence of Catholics, intellectual and otherwise, in the United States based upon these general histories.[2]

When I first agreed to write this essay, I had envisioned a simple task of demonstrating that Catholic intellectuals did exist even prior to 1965. Somewhat like Abraham, if I could convince a rather skeptical audience of the existence of just ten American Catholic intellectuals, then you might spare the whole community from intellectual oblivion.

3

After all, most intellectual histories present the same select group of men and women as the heroes of their narratives; so why couldn't the same be done for American Catholics? Yet to identify a few Catholic intellectuals currently absent from textbooks hardly satisfies my alleged goal of locating "American Catholic intellectual traditions." Even though many of my students attempt to convince me otherwise, a single person does not constitute a tradition. Identifying an "intellectual tradition" requires locating networks of conversations and practices that operate in a community as interpretive guides embedded in particular questions and particular conclusions concerning a whole host of issues. To further complicate the issue, within the study of American Catholicism, "tradition" is often associated with ethnic identities or ecclesially regulated practices and beliefs. The closest to a discussion of an acculturated intellectual tradition concerns the Americanists.[3] The other academic movement that has received some attention is neo-Thomism, whose participants serve alternately as villains and heroes depending on the narrative one reads.[4]

Neither these two movements nor any others will receive extensive analysis in this paper, though many will receive mention. This essay is more like the introductory paragraphs of chapters in a travelogue. In some cases, I will point out the locations of a few of these networks of conversations and practices that have taken up questions concerning the world mediated through "United States" or "American" and "church" or "Catholic," the Catholic's place in that world, and how that place serves as the context for relationship with God. In other cases, I will simply point to persons whom I suspect may lead into networks of conversations and practices that will eventually prove to be alternate routes into American Catholic intellectual traditions. I offer no guarantees that some of these avenues are not dead-ends or detours; such risks are unavoidable on this particular journey.

To announce all these destinations indicates that I do not share the conclusions of those other students of American intellectual traditions. Proclaiming this difference does not exempt me from their influence, indicated by my locating this essay's content on the back roads of the academic study of U.S. intellectual life, even in its religious variants. To understand these cartographers' assumptions in locating "the intellectual" can help clarify not only their exclusion of Catholics but also many Catholics' unease in claiming the existence of American Catholic intellectual traditions. This essay, therefore, has two major divisions reflecting both my concern to understand the tradition of "the intellectual" in the United States and my desire to identify American Catholic intellectual traditions. The first section will briefly sketch conceptions of "the intellectual" that have dominated historiography since the turn of the century and how these conceptions almost invariably exclude the majority of American Catholics. The second part will explore the roads less travelled in search of American Catholic intellectual traditions.

"The Intellectual": An American Tradition

The identity of the "intellectual" has its own complicated history in the United States. The tradition of the "intellectual" which I find most pertinent to the present discussion came to fruition in the nineteenth century. The quintessential example of this figure is the agnostic, as James Turner describes in his remarkable book, *Without God, Without Creed: The Origins of Unbelief in America.*[5] This American intellectual stands alone—the descendent of no tradition and the toady of no external authority. The intellectual hero or heroine rejects traditional interpretative frameworks, suspends all beliefs except in his or her ability to forge new and truer insights into the way things really are. He or she is a sort of gnostic with a streamlined cosmology who arrives at these new insights through empirical evidence discovered through observations and even better, experimentation. In other words, science as practiced in the laboratory provides a near univocal model for all intellectual pursuits. The intellectual's burden is to use newly discovered knowledge to free the individual from a burdensome past and open up a future of infinite progress. Obviously, not all persons designated as intellectuals fit this description, but I do think that sufficient evidence exists to acclaim this set of referents as embedded certainly in the "modern" discourses on "the intellectual" and, with some variation concerning science, "postmodern" discourses on "the intellectual."

This persona of the "self-made intellectual" manifests one of many guises of "the autonomous self," a figure who appears throughout American literature. Examples abound in historical accounts from brave religious reformers—much to the chagrin of the more tradition-bound Martin Luther and John Calvin—to the founding fathers, the premier example being Thomas Jefferson. They also appear in our tales of economic success, as the frontiersmen Davy Crockett or Daniel Boone, and later, transformed for the capitalist's consumption, the rags-to-riches entrepreneur, Andrew Carnegie. Yet, the "intellectual" occupies a unique position in this pantheon of "selves" since he or she generates "the intellectual" and in so doing becomes "the intellectual." The designation of "intellectual" as a profession actually solidified the unique social position of the self-made intellectual. Some of these professional intellectuals earned income as journalists like the churlish H. L. Mencken, others as novelists and free-lance writers, but the majority located themselves in the rapidly changing colleges and universities. In the academy, as in many other U.S. institutions at the turn of the century, these changes mirrored those in the economy ordered by divisions of labor. Intellectuals quite naturally became the specialists on what constituted an "authentic intellectual" since they were defining their own kind.

Some of these intellectuals then composed histories of their predecessors: brave men and an occasional woman who stood against the traditions of their own times to think new thoughts and act upon them. One could easily identify predecessors in the United States as William Clebsch does in *American Religious Thought*.[6] James Turner provides a typical example of such historical assessments. "What [Charles Elliot] Norton valued above all in Emerson was his 'fidelity to his own ideals,' his 'unflinching assertion of the supreme right of private judgment; of the wrong done to human nature by "authority" in matters of religion.'"[7] The intellectual's moral obligation lay in continuing this task in the service of human progress.

Many "modern" intellectual histories presented intellectuals from the past, not to reappropriate their intellectual insights but to measure their contributions to intellectual progress and to inspire others in undertaking the mission of progress on the behalf of the future. Postmodern intellectuals have exchanged power for progress as the defining purpose of their intellectual endeavors. Corresponding to this exchange in purpose, the postmodern embraces the ever-changing present moment as the location of power just as the modern's beloved progress resided in the future. The commitment to stand against authority and tradition seems even more pressing even if more futile.

I must note, however, that certain postmodern theorists have actually included Catholics in their discussions of American intellectuals. In *Roads to Rome* Jenny Franchot analyzed the intricate influence of "Catholicism" as the "Other" in Protestant literature from Maria Monk to Nathaniel Hawthorne, and the impact of that discourse on four Catholic converts: Elizabeth Seton, Orestes Brownson, Isaac Hecker, and

Sophia Ripley. Of course, her primary focus was upon the aesthetic appeal of "Catholicism" among disaffected New England Calvinists rather than a study of literature generated within a Catholic tradition.[8] More apropos for this discussion is Paul Giles's *American Catholic Arts and Fictions: Culture, Ideology, Aesthetics*. Giles offers a sophisticated analysis of varied expressions and points of view among artists from Catholic backgrounds.[9] One response I have to this attention is simply "hurrah!" I feel somewhat like Binx Bolling, the protagonist of Walker Percy's *The Moviegoer*, who talks of a New Orleans neighborhood as being certified because it appears in a movie.[10] In the case of American Catholics, their certification comes with appearance on the pages of a critical theorist's text. Why, after over five hundred pages of analysis, Paul Giles is even willing to concede that "in an American context at least, the notion that a Catholic cast of mind must infallibly be associated with dogmatism in one form or another is simply a popular misconception."[11] Like Binx Bolling's appraisal of that New Orleans neighborhood whose authentic existence is somehow heightened by its projection on the screen, so American Catholicism receives legitimation as the location for potential intellectuals by their being objectified (or is it subjectified?) with all the deconstructive prowess that a postmodern critical theorist can muster. I suppose that I am now engaging in what Paul Giles identifies as "Catholic skepticism."

My purpose in mentioning Giles is not to dismiss his work, though my flippancy may suggest otherwise. Paul Giles does in fact have to deal with an audience that has embraced the popular misconception that the synonym for Catholicism is dogmatism. Yet, I have this uneasy feeling that Giles himself still remains under the spell of that popular misconception insofar as those whom he studies remain intellectual when Catholicism lies more in their background than foreground. So Flannery O'Connor "is, to be sure, a 'Catholic' writer, but not just along the lines of narrower neo-scholastic orthodoxies, for the grotesque forms of her texts are charged also with the multiple uncertainties and discontinuities of postmodernist literary and theological thought."[12] While on the one hand I cannot disagree with his assessment, on the other hand I get the uneasy feeling that Giles views O'Connor as someone who overcame her Catholicism as much as she drew from it.

His coining the phrase "Catholic skepticism" as an umbrella under which he fits a wide variety of American Catholic artists feeds my unease even as it clarifies. In good Catholic fashion, he does cite historical precedents for this attitude in the work of Erasmus, Pascal, and Montaigne. My central question is "skeptical of what"? Giles quotes, for example, a Flannery O'Connor letter responding to the disillusionment that poet Alfred Corn felt about his Catholicism. She writes, "What kept me a skeptic in college was precisely my Christian faith."[13] How does her skepticism compare with her peer Mary McCarthy, who serves as another of Giles's subjects? Anyone familiar with Flannery O'Connor's comment to Mary McCarthy concerning the Eucharist as a mere symbol has to wonder if their skepticisms share a common location within the American Catholic discourse.[14]

At the risk of playing with fire, let me be a little postmodern myself. Giles has done little to alter the narrative of the intellectual hero formulated in the late nineteenth century except to show that even some Catholics qualify for the honor of a self who had overcome dogmatism, the death knell of intellectual life. Those whom Giles includes as genuine artists, even those with a more or less amicable relationship to the Catholic institution, "displayed no crabbed narrowness of spirit, as among the orthodox, but a spirit of exploration, a fresh openness to the human adventure." The quote comes not from Giles but from Turner's description of the "agnostic."[15] Giles's Catholic skeptics seem to have a great deal in common with Turner's agnostics and so remain with the bounds of the tradition of the "intellectual."

While I remain in awe of Giles's comprehensive treatment and juxtaposition of Catholics as diverse as John Powers and Robert Mapplethorpe, I admit to a lingering dissatisfaction, even frustration, with a discourse that persists in dismissing or ignoring what the majority of Catholics, including Flannery O'Connor, took seriously and recognized as their primary intellectual inspiration. They were heirs of a tradition that brought them into whole networks of conversations and practices that predate and exceed the United States. Their primary responsibility was to avoid squandering that inheritance, either by ignoring its ability to mediate the American experience or by reducing it to that culture. Most viewed this responsibility as one not primarily to the "authentic self" but to the whole Catholic community, past, present, and future. While I admit that few display the artistry of a Flannery O'Connor, I am not sure that those of a more didactic or overtly pious persuasion should be automatically excluded from consideration as intellectuals. Of course, I share with these pious didactic types an engagement with that multivalent tradition that from my perspective continues to evade even the best deconstructionist's efforts and serves as a constructive resource for my own identity as a faithful, sometimes pious, and other times didactic Catholic skeptic.

Of course, other American Catholics have long been aware of these judgments against the quality of their community's intellectual contributions in the United States. One can find all sorts of indicators that Catholics attempted to gain credibility according to at least some of the rules for intellectual engagement that emerged at the end of the nineteenth century. Identifying neo-scholastic method as the "science of theology" serves as a notable example. In the 1939 conference, "Man and Modern Secularism," the Reverend Gerald B. Phelan makes the point very clear.

College students are given an insight into the *sciences* of material and living things, the *science* of history, the *science* of philosophy, the *science* of literary and artistic appreciation and criticism, while they are not given a corresponding training in the *science* of theology.

He then goes on to argue "that theology is entitled to a place in the curriculum of the Catholic college and entitled also to scientific treatment proportionate to the capacities of college students and analogous to the scientific treatment commonly given to other subjects in the curriculum."[16] Phelan's appeal to "science" only serves to highlight the gap between the Catholic intellectual endeavor and that of almost every other intellectual in the United States who found little in theology to warrant the designation "scientific." The use of a philosophical-theological system developed as *scientia* in the thirteenth century, not modern science, served only to widen that gap.

I cannot help but note, however, that Phelan also invokes that ubiquitous Catholic term "analogous to." The term has no equivalent in the traditions of plain speech, empiricism, positivism, or pragmatism and remains always under the suspicion of those who operate out of those other networks of conversations and practices. It simultaneously connotes absolute difference and unity, and served the didactic Phelan as much as the artistic O'Connor in shaping their self-conscious ordering of their world. Its frequent use is suggestive of an alternative epistemology drawn not so much from sacramental theology but from sacramental practices. There seems to be no equivalent practice in the logocentric epistemology of "the intellectual" previously described.

Phelan, of course, identifies the Catholic university and college as the site of Catholic intellectual endeavors. Certainly, the founders of these institutions intended to emulate their secular counterparts in academic excellence. Yet, the similarity serves once again to highlight the significant gap between Catholic intellectuals and their secular peers. The Catholic university or college remained under the purview of clergy or women religious who could hardly be revered as models of breaking free from all traditions and external authorities. They conceived of their work as a "vocation" even as they strove to become more "professional." Such a self-description within the context of the communal life in a religious order places intellectual life in a land quite foreign to Turner's independent, self-validating agnostic.

Even John Tracy Ellis, in his trenchant criticism of Catholics' failure to engage in American intellectual life, remains in that foreign land. He describes the intellectual in terms of a "vocation" that arises from "the love of scholarship for its own sake."[17] The article then proceeds to chide American Catholics for their failure to live up to this ideal and their inability to produce any intellectual tradition.[18]

He then proceeds with a historical sketch that names nascent intellectual traditions aborted first through immigration and later through the Modernist condemnation. These events, along with the effects of anti-Catholicism, stifle Catholic intellectual life and therefore the formation of traditions. To heap insult onto injury, Ellis then cites study after study as proof of Catholics' lack of engagement in scientific and other graduate-level research. This gentleman scholar minces no words in his indictment of American Catholics.

> The chief blame, I firmly believe, lies with Catholics themselves. It lies in their frequently self-imposed ghetto mentality which prevents them from mingling as they should with their non-Catholic colleagues, and in their lack of industry and the habits of work. . . . It lies in their failure to have measured up to their responsibilities to the incomparable tradition of Catholic learning of which they are the direct heirs.[19]

This final phrase in Ellis's last remark reveals that even his noble "intellectual" practices his or her craft in a realm quite unlike that of "the intellectual" of the secular academy.

Ellis's article lays out the dilemma of the American Catholic intellectual at least prior to 1965. The dilemma to which I refer is not one of those alternately praised and indicted in Ellis's account but Ellis himself. Employing the fruits of social scientific research, a hallmark of "modern scholarship," Ellis uses statistics to shame American Catholics into working harder for a very specific purpose. Referring to predictions of America's return to religion and morality, Ellis queries:

> to whom, one may ask, may the leaders of the coming generation turn with more rightful expectancy in their search for enlightenment and guidance in the realm of religion and morality than to the American Catholic intellectuals? For it is they who are in possession of the oldest, wisest, and most sublime tradition of learning that the world has ever known.[20]

Ellis, like so many other Catholic intellectuals, worried about squandering an intellectual inheritance through a failure to make the Catholic tradition a transformative force in American culture. Few other American intellectuals identified themselves as much with their past as Catholics. Most, in fact, continued to understand themselves as the self-reliant seekers on the road of progress moving toward a future of greater freedom from material limitations and the bogeymen of the past. Whether successes or failures, Catholic intellectuals travelled a road that enticed few secular intellectuals to become their companions.

My observations about Catholics' concern for the past should not be construed as a negative judgment against Catholics. Christopher Lasch proves helpful here in his distinction between nostalgia, which mediates the past as "outside of time, frozen in unchanging perfection," and memory, which, "draws hope and comfort from the past to enrich the present." Even more important, memory, unlike nostalgia, recognizes "our continuing indebtedness to a past the formative influence of which lives on in our patterns of speech, our gestures, our standards of honor, our expectations, our basic dispositions toward the world."[21] Lasch's comments evoke again questions concerning the epistemology of sacramental practices as formative in Catholic speech, gesture, and basic disposition to the world. This is not to exempt Catholics from fits of nostalgia but to highlight again the very different orientations of their intellectuals.

These differences are startlingly evident in considering Ellis's use of statistical studies in light of the conclusions of those studies themselves. In particular, the conclusions of Ellsworth Huntington and Leon F. Whitney in a 1927 *American Mercury* article, "Religion and 'Who's

Who,' " reiterate a gap between Ellis's understanding of religious identity and the intellectual and that of these authors.

The failure of the Roman Catholic church to produce a higher
relative number of leaders arises not only and perhaps not chiefly
from the fact that people of independent mind are likely to leave
the church, but from the fact that the church hangs on to its
adherents like grim death. Other denominations, especially those
that are intellectual rather than emotional (e.g., Unitarians who
have the highest representation of 1185 per 100,000), let the
weaker brothers and sisters drift away, and are thereby purged,
as it were. Not so the Catholics; they cling to even the poorest and
weakest. This may be good for the individual, but it lowers the
showing of the church as a whole.[22]

This scientific analysis then discusses the deleterious effects of celibacy since the best and brightest, even the most religious, do not sire
children. Sounding a bit like the promoters of eugenics and social
Darwinism, they conclude on the grim note that "the prospects for
their future improvement are slight because the best germ plasm among
them has been so terribly depleted."[23] Ellis makes no mention of a
depleted gene pool in his own use of the article. He concludes with a
challenge that bespeaks more confidence than uncertainty that Catholics who share in a rich intellectual heritage ought to be more effective
in their influence within American intellectual life. It is this hope in
the intellectual riches of the Catholic tradition rather than the agnostic's
intellectual heroics or Franchot's aestheticism or Giles's skepticism
or Phelan's *scientia* that serves as entry into the second part of this
essay.

The Roads Less Travelled

Here my intention is to indicate some possible locations of American Catholic intellectual traditions as well as to suggest some methodological strategies for analyzing these traditions. The traditions cluster around two relatively typical approaches employed by the
intellectual historian. The first set organizes itself around Catholics'
responses to various dimensions of their social situation in the United
States. The second identifies certain conceptual frameworks imbed-

ded in and formative of Catholic intellectual life in this country during the first half of this century.

Of all the possible candidates for an American Catholic intellectual tradition, none seems as plausible as one that incorporates the varied Catholic responses to their distinctive political context. Political, as I intend to use it here, has to do with the complex ordering of power and authority within a community and among communities. Obviously one could examine the articulations of Catholic perspectives on the separation of church and state and the free exercise of religion, focusing upon John Courtney Murray, who seems to constitute an entire intellectual tradition in and of himself. What if we reconceive John Courtney Murray's role as one who recapitulates the content of a much broader network of conversations? What if, in fact, we included all kinds of conversations that adapt or reject Republican and Democratic references to describe Catholics' ordering of power and authority, both internally and externally? My own reading of a variety of texts including sermons, public lectures, periodical articles, and books indicates that such a reconception may bring to light a very significant intellectual tradition that continues to shape American Catholic debates.

The postmodern methodologies, particularly those concerning discourse theory, prove immensely useful in such an analysis. Using Mary McClintock Fulkerson's introductory remarks in *Changing the Subject: Women's Discourses and Feminist Theology*, I will attempt to describe briefly how discourse theory might be applicable. First, discourse theory assumes language to be the interplay among complex systems of signifiers in which "words as signs are only able to mean by virtue of their relationship to other signs." Second and equally important, discourse theory rejects the reduction of all meaning to language and includes under discourse nonlinguistic signifiers. Appropriate examples of nonlinguistic signifiers in this case are religious practices, structures of authority, and enculturated norms of behavior. Fulkerson emphasizes the instability of meanings as diverse systems of signifiers interact. The discourses of Roman Catholic hierarchical polity, for example, interact with those of United States Republican and Democratic political theories and practices, and in the interaction, destabilize and transform each other.[24]

Fulkerson, of course, applies discourse analysis to indicate the instability in terms such as "woman," "women," and most especially "women's experience." Fulkerson claims that "By looking at the effects of multiple differential networks of meaning and their unpredictable effects, we are better able to appreciate the openness of signifying processes and to focus discourse analysis on situations of utterances."[25] By using "situation of utterances" Fulkerson is attempting to convey the complexity and therefore the instability of meanings associated with the texts or behavior produced as "effects of multiple differential networks of meaning." Like "women's experience," so the "American Catholic experience" has no single referent or meaning. Catholics in the United States simultaneously destabilize the networks of meanings related to both "Catholic" and "American" in forging networks of meaning between them. Turning from the well-trodden path that leads to Murray, we will now peruse five other sites where networks of meanings are located.

1. My own dissertation, "The Papacy in Mid-nineteenth Century American Catholic Imagination," considers the apologetic "utterances" of five American Catholics in their treatment of the papacy.[26] One discovers in these utterances the papacy as the champion of republicanism and savior of Western civilization, the pope himself as the man of the common people and for the common people, especially the poor, and the church under papal leadership as the single source for authentic liberty and true progress.

To dismiss these depictions of the papacy and the Roman Catholic church as rhetorical ploys or, even worse, as lies, ignores a crucial point. I would suggest that these "utterances" contribute to a discourse that constitutes a rather complex intellectual tradition. This tradition appears through those subjects who produce systems of meanings that communicate various configurations of the relationship between "Catholic" and "American." These signifiers in turn serve as interpretative resources for other "situations of utterance." For example, these five apologists use the forged networks of meanings between "American" and "Catholic" to defend the papacy's temporal powers as an extension of separation of church and state into the international context.[27] They also adapt America's operative philosophy, the commonsense realism of self-evident truths, to defend the declaration of papal infallibility.[28]

This discursive process seeks to answer a particularly U.S. Catholic question: how can we help America recognize that, in fact, it is really a Catholic nation? This question signifies a whole set of assumptions about the relation among the signifiers "American" and "Catholic." These assumptions inform a whole host of practices in the

United States Catholic community from education to the practices of voluntary agencies to the valorizing of medieval culture. Ellis indicates his own participation by linking the elevation of American Catholic intellectual life with the need among United States leaders for a religious and moral resource. Murray also abides within this discourse, reconfiguring certain sets of relationships signified by "American" and "Catholic" through the networks of meanings signified by "neo-Thomism" and "historical consciousness" to produce a self-consciously Catholic systematic defense of American political principles, particularly separation of church and state.

2. As Fulkerson points out, the dynamism of discourse arises from the instability of meanings, and certainly "American" and "Catholic" are among the most unstable. I have not even mentioned traditions like those of the Catholic Worker or the *Central-Verein* in which "American" and "Catholic" signify whole other sets of meanings. One might also consider the impact that "immigration" has had upon this discourse. What did the word "immigration" and the "immigrant" signify in the discourses concerning American Catholics? In *The Only and True Heaven*, Christopher Lasch asserts that "the fierce debate about immigration, one of the most important intellectual events of the progressive era, raised many of the same debates about the democratization of culture. . . ." He identifies three distinct positions on immigration: the exclusionist, the assimilationist, and the pluralist.[29] Catholics also participated in these debates with representatives in all three positions.

What dominated, however, was the assimilationist approach that sought to both Americanize and Catholicize the immigrants. This assimilation led in turn to a democratization of Catholic culture among the second and third generation of middle-class Catholics. This democratization is most evident in the various movements loosely identified with Catholic Action, including the Christian Family Movement, the Grail, even the Catholic Worker. The participants self-consciously articulated this democratization of socially engaged holiness and even demanded access to theological training previously the preserve of the clergy.

This discourse in all its complexity serves as an intellectual tradition or, perhaps more accurately, traditions, meaning networks of conversations and practices that have produced and continue to produce the multiple meanings of American Catholic. To understand its impact one only has to consider our normative use of the two party system, conservative/liberal, in our own discursive attempts to locate our Catholic contemporaries as well as our ancestors.

3. Catholics' engagement in the progressive era debates suggests another way of conceptualizing Catholic intellectual traditions in the United States. Another approach would be to identify Catholic exemplars within other broad intellectual movements such as the Enlightenment, Romanticism, the Social Gospel. Patrick Carey's *American Catholic Religious Thought* remains the best example of this approach.[30]

Let me offer but one example, with the dual purpose of demonstrating the possibilities in pursuing a single individual as well as introducing considerations of gender. Anna Hansen Dorsey, a self-educated author of light fiction and daughter of a Methodist navy chaplain, converted along with her husband, Lorenzo Dorsey, in the 1840s. Both found inspiration in the Oxford movement. Almost immediately after her conversion, Anna Dorsey began to write fiction highlighting the glories of Catholic faith. Her novels, many of which appeared in serial form in *Ave Maria*, resemble those extensively discussed in Anne Douglas's *The Feminization of American Culture*.[31]

Dorsey introduced *Ave Maria* readers to a variety of late nineteenth-century dilemmas in her fictionalized accounts. In "St. John's Eve," she presents a character who bears a remarkable resemblance to the agnostics of James Turner's account.[32] The unnamed character describes his international travels in search of the truth and presents his stoic acceptance of his inability to believe. He then wanders into a lush garden near a monastery where he experiences a series of conversions: first, a sort of John Stuart Mill's aesthetic awakening upon hearing the beautiful music of the monastic choir, and then a second, when he immerses himself in the natural beauty of the garden that surrounds him. The second conversion precipitates a life-threatening illness. Death is only averted through the care of a kindly monk who restores not only his physical health but also his spiritual well-being.

The monk proves a fascinating character whose practices of hospitality simultaneously manifest the care of his deceased mother and Mary, the Blessed Virgin. He transgresses gender-specific roles even as he upholds the Cult of True Womanhood. The monk, like any good mother, uses acts of kindness as well as a reasonable defense of faith to bring the lost son back to religious practice. Several other Dorsey stories depict women transgressing the rules operative in the Cult of True Womanhood in order to preserve spiritual values.

Dorsey's fiction has a place in discussions of the formations of middle-class culture, Catholic constructions of gender, and Catholic commentary on American intellectual and social life. Dorsey exposes her reader to a variety of issues, from the spirit-killing horrors of slavery to the possibility of unbelief. As important, Catholicism serves as more than set-dressing in these pieces where sacramental practices often become instrumental in the plot development. Here I would suggest is a Catholic conversational partner for Harriet Beecher Stowe and company.

4. Anna Hansen Dorsey's novel, *The Old Grey Rosary*, depicts the trials and tribulations of an elderly black woman, a former slave, and a struggling alcoholic. Dorsey presents the spirit-crushing impact of slavery on a person.[33] Without claiming too much for the novel, it strikes me as interesting because one finds so few sympathetic Catholic accounts of African Americans either prior to or after the Civil War. I will not rehearse here the troubling history of European American Catholics' defense of slavery; rather, I want to turn for a moment to African American Catholic challenges to such positions.

Cyprian Davis's *The History of Black Catholics in the United States* remains the central resource for identifying avenues of research in African American Catholic intellectual traditions.[34] In this text, Davis introduces his reader to a whole host of black Catholic lay leaders who seriously challenge complacency about a Catholic church too closely identified with American culture. Two notable spokesmen are Daniel Rudd from Cincinnati and Thomas Wyatt Turner of Washington, D.C. Both of these men challenged the racism manifest among American Catholics by appealing to a church that transcends national boundaries. In describing *Rerum Novarum* Rudd claims, "In its treatment of the rights of rich and poor it has not been equaled by any writer upon this subject, besides it comes with the authority of the teaching Church."[35] In 1919, Thomas Wyatt Turner, writing to Archbishop Giovanni Bonzano, the apostolic delegate, criticized Catholic University's refusal to admit blacks on the grounds that such a practice violated the very notion of catholicity.[36] Perhaps as we locate and study the "situations of utterance" of other African American Catholics, we will have also located an intellectual tradition rooted in the church's prophetic critique of social injustice and its refusal to be reduced to any one social configuration.

5. In this same vein, I want to briefly consider the Hispanic (Latino/Latina) community as another locale of American Catholic intellectual traditions. In ways which I view as quite distinct from African

Americans, Hispanics have been relegated to the margins. Consider for a moment how "Latin America" signifies "the Other" in the discourse of "America." In politics, the United States—a democracy; Latin America—dictatorships; in economics, the United States—a prosperous middle class; Latin America—a greedy aristocracy; in religion, the United States—Protestant; Latin America—Catholic; in intellectual endeavors, the United States—rational inquiry committed to human progress; Latin America—emotion and custom.

My point here is not to minimize the political and economic difficulties encountered by the majority of Latin Americans nor am I suggesting that Hispanics living within the U.S. borders identify themselves as Latin American. I am highlighting what has been operative in excluding Hispanics from various venues of power, both academic and ecclesial, within the Catholic community in the United States. While exclusionary practices are diminishing, due in large part to Hispanics' perseverance in hard-fought battles to gain recognition, stereotypes remain operative in too many cases. Still others mistake the work of Hispanic theologians as pertinent only to their communities.

Contemporary Hispanic theologians bring before us Hispanic cultures as bearers of rich and complex intellectual traditions that can serve as resources for the entire Catholic community. In discussing, for example, the networks of meaning that signify "personhood" within and among Hispanic cultures, Hispanic theologians provide clear alternatives to contemporary constructions of the individual as "autonomous self," a perspective shared by most Americans whether conservative or liberal.

As Roberto Goizueta has convincingly argued, "person" within Hispanic cultures has as its primary referent not "the autonomous self" but "community," primarily mediated through familial relationships that in turn mediate whole networks of cultural relationships.[37] Virgilio Elizondo introduces the term *mestizaje* to signify this network of cultural relationships that integrate the beliefs and practices of the Spanish and the indigenous peoples of Mexico in the Mexican-American community.[38] In Brazil or the Caribbean, West African culture offers an additional cultural resource along with Spanish and Indian.

Enculturated liturgical and devotional practices serve as determinative signifiers in the discourse of personhood. These practices trace their origins to the medieval church as much as to indigenous religions. Both prove to be sources of conflict with those U.S. Catholics well formed in Tridentine Catholicism.

Among the many devotional practices, those honoring *la Virgen de Guadalupe* play an especially important role in communicating the relational centered anthropology common throughout Hispanic cultures. Both Goizueta in his recent work *Caminemos con Jesus* and my colleague, Miguel Díaz, in his dissertation on Hispanic understandings of person, have demonstrated Guadalupe's contribution.[39] Hispanic cultures seem to exemplify what Christopher Lasch calls "real knowledge of the past . . . [which] requires a sense of the persistence of the past; the manifold ways in which it penetrates our lives."[40]

These Hispanic theologians, like the African American theologians previously mentioned, serve as resources for American Catholic traditions of critique of the failure of both American society and the Catholic church within that society. Yet their critiques come through their constructing specific networks of conversations and practices that provided their communities with alternative "Catholic" and "American" interpretive guides for raising particular questions and drawing particular conclusions concerning a whole host of issues.

I have now taken you to five very specific destinations in this journey on the back roads, and I want to conclude with possible ways to view the entire landscape that ordered American Catholic intellectual life during the first half of this century. This landscape organized itself around a single destination revealed in that opening section of the *Baltimore Catechism* in the answer to that question: "Why did God make us?" And of course the response is: "God made us to know, love, and serve him in this world and to be happy with him in the next."[41] That answer encapsulates a whole network of meanings and practices that permeated mid-twentieth-century Catholics' engagement in the intellectual life.

I invoke this response because it also captures what has made almost all Catholic intellectual work suspect when placed within the discourses of the "modern" and "postmodern." If the secular intellectuals stood alone facing the absurdity of their uncertain future, Catholic intellectuals stood in a crowd who shared a common destination. The crowd included not only their Catholic peers but all those marked with the sign of faith who had gone before them. In fact this crowd had a very specific identity, the Mystical Body of Christ. Operating within these complex networks of meanings which organized communal identity around this common telos, a wide variety of Catholics self-consciously sought to order their relationships to others and to God.

Although I am unable to develop this more fully, I will offer one brief example from the autobiography of Helen Caldwell Day's *Color, Ebony*. This African American convert was a founding member of an interracial house of hospitality that served the poor in Memphis, Tennessee from 1950 to 1956.

When the priest raised Our Lord, that we might adore Him in the Host, I would think that even while we gazed upon Him, we were part of His Mystical Body, members of Him and of each other. Then I could understand how He could say that the whole of the law lay in the commandments "Love God" and "Love your neighbor." They were really the same commandment, for neither is possible without the other. Love is the keynote of Christianity; with it, everything is possible, without it, nothing.

I could no longer justify hate nor prejudice against any person, for now I knew my neighbor was anyone whom I could love or serve or who could love or serve me. There's no one else left.[42]

Embedded in this narrative is a deep awareness of both "why God had made us" and the assistance of that crowd, the Mystical Body, through the epistemology of sacramental practice. This knowledge precipitates her self-conscious ordering of her relationship as an African American to the world and to God. Yet is this a sampling of mid-twentieth-century Catholic intellectual tradition? Or of mid-twentieth-century devotional literature? Or should we abandon such distinctions as leading us to the dead-end of the American tradition of "the rugged individualist intellectual"?

About a year ago, while driving the back roads from my little farm toward the city, I happened to catch an interview with Wendell Berry on our local National Public Radio affiliate, WYSO, Yellow Springs, Ohio. As I sort of listened, I also sort of thought about this talk. At one point in the interview, Berry made the comment, "No one knows the geography of our economy." Of course, he meant no one knows the origins of the foods we buy in the store. But what came immediately to my mind is how that statement summarizes our current understanding of American Catholic intellectual traditions. First of all, we have yet to produce an adequate map that locates region by region the various economies of American Catholic intellectual life. I have scouted out at least five specific sites of American Catholic intellectual traditions. Second of all, we also need to be more cognizant of the transnational geography that informs the economy of Catholicism and its impact on

American Catholic intellectual traditions. Third, we have to be Catholic skeptics in regard to the received geography of our intellectual economy that presents a landscape devoid of anyone but the autonomous secular intellectual who claims "no place" and therefore every place as his and occasionally her domain. Finally, we need to consider to what extent "the geography of our own economy" demands situating that landscape, in its every contour, as the locale that exists by virtue of its relationship with the creative, redemptive, and sustaining God.

Notes

[1] I have not travelled these roads alone and would like to thank those who served as guides as well as gracious companions. My thanks go especially to Patrick Carey, William Portier, Una Cadegan, Scott Appleby, Terrence Tilley, and Michael Baxter.

[2] For example, a classic treatment is *The Life of the Mind in America from the Revolution to the Civil War* (New York: Harcourt, Brace, and World, Inc., 1965). In John Higham and Paul K. Conken, eds., *New Directions in American Intellectual History* (Baltimore: Johns Hopkins University Press, 1979), Catholics are mentioned only in passing in a single essay. In Richard Hofstader, *Anti-intellectualism in American Life* (New York: Knopf, 1963), the index features a heading "Catholics" which includes the reference, "failure to develop an intellectual tradition," pp. 136-139. David A. Hollinger and Charles Capper, eds., *The American Intellectual Tradition: A Sourcebook*, 2 vols. (New York: Oxford University Press, 1993) offers no Catholic entries. (The most recent third edition will, however, feature a piece by John Courtney Murray in the second volume.)

[3] R. Scott Appleby, *Church and Age Unite!: The Modernist Impulse in American Catholicism* (Notre Dame, Ind.: University of Notre Dame Press, 1992).

[4] See William Halsey, *The Survival of American Innocence: Catholicism in an Age of Disillusionment, 1920-1940* (Notre Dame, Ind.: University of Notre Dame Press, 1980); Jay Dolan, *The American Catholic Experience* (Garden City, New York: Doubleday, 1985), pp. 384-454; Philip Gleason, *Contending with Modernity: Catholic Higher Education in the Twentieth Century* (New York: Oxford University Press, 1995); Philip Gleason, "American Catholicism and the Mythic Middle Ages," and "The Search for Unity and Its Sequel," in *Keeping the Faith: American Catholicism Past and Present* (Notre Dame, Ind.: University of Notre Dame Press, 1987), pp. 11-34 and 136-151.

[5] James Turner, *Without God, Without Creed: The Origins of Unbelief in America* (Baltimore: Johns Hopkins University Press, 1985).

[6] William A. Clebsch, *American Religious Thought: A History* (Chicago: University of Chicago Press, 1973).

[7] Turner, *Without God*, p. 209.

[8] Jenny Franchot, *Roads to Rome: The Antebellum Protestant Encounter with*

Catholicism (Berkeley: University of California Press, 1994).

[9] Paul Giles, *American Catholic Arts and Fictions: Culture, Ideology, Aesthetics* (New York: Cambridge University Press, 1992).

[10] Bolling's female companion, Kate, actually first uses the word to describe the neighborhood. Bolling then comments on her observation. Walker Percy, *The Moviegoer* (New York: Knopf, 1961), p. 63.

[11] Giles, p. 507.

[12] Ibid., p. 367.

[13] Ibid., p. 507.

[14] In response to Mrs. Broadstreet [McCarthy] declaring the Eucharist "a symbol and implied that it was a pretty good one. I then said in a shaky voice [intimidated by the company], 'Well, if it is a symbol to hell with it. This was all the defense I was capable of. . . . outside of a story, except [to say] that it is the center of existence for me; all the rest of life is expendable.' " Flannery O'Connor, *The Habit of Being: Letters*, with an introduction by Sally Fitzgerald (New York: Vintage Books, 1980, c. 1979), pp. 124-125.

[15] Turner, *Without God*, p. 243.

[16] National Catholic Alumni Federation, *Man and Modern Secularism: Essays on the Conflict of the Two Cultures* (New York: National Catholic Alumni Federation, 1940), p. 130.

[17] Quotes from John Tracy Ellis's essay, "American Catholics and the Intellectual Life" are taken from Frank L. Christ and Gerard K. Sherry, eds., *American Catholicism and the Intellectual Ideal* (New York: Appleton-Century-Crofts, 1961), p. 376.

[18] Ibid, p. 357.

[19] Ibid., p. 276.

[20] Ibid., pp. 377-378.

[21] Christopher Lasch, *The True and Only Heaven: Progress and Its Critics* (New York: Norton, 1991), p. 83.

[22] Quoted in Christ and Sherry, eds., *American Catholicism and the Intellectual Ideal*, p. 78.

[23] Ibid., p. 79.

[24] Mary McClintock Fulkerson, *Changing the Subject: Women's Discourses and Feminist Theology* (Minneapolis: Fortress Press, 1994). See especially pp. 61-116 (passim).

[25] Ibid., p. 78.

[26] Sandra Yocum Mize, "The Papacy in Mid-nineteenth Century American Catholic Imagination" (Marquette University, unpublished dissertation, 1987).

[27] Sandra Yocum Mize, "Defending Roman Loyalties and Republican Values: The 1848 Italian Revolution in American Catholic Apologetics," *Church History* 60 (December 1991): 480-492.

[28] Sandra Yocum Mize, "The Common-Sense Argument for Papal Infallibility," *Theological Studies* 57 (1996): 242-263.

[29] Lasch, p. 353

[30] Patrick Carey, ed., *American Catholic Religious Thought* (Mahwah, N.J.: Paulist Press, 1987).

[31]Ann Douglas, *The Feminization of American Culture* (New York: Knopf, 1977).

[32] "St. John's Eve," *Ave Maria* 2 (1867): 8-10, 22-25, 40-41, 57-59.

[33] Anna Dorsey, "The Old Grey Rosary," *Ave Maria* 4 (1868): 4-7; 22-25; 38-40; 56-60; 100-103; 153-157.

[34] Cyprian Davis, *The History of Black Catholics in the United States* (New York: Crossroads, 1990).

[35] Ibid., p. 166.

[36] Ibid., pp. 217-218.

[37] Roberto S. Goizueta, "U.S. Hispanic Theology and the Challenge of Pluralism" in Allan Figueroa Deck, S.J., ed., *Frontiers of Hispanic Theology in the United States* (Maryknoll, N.Y.: Orbis, 1992), pp. 1-22.

[38] Virgilio Elizondo, *Galilean Journey: The Mexican-American Promise* (Maryknoll, N.Y.: Orbis, 1983).

[39] Roberto S. Goizueta, *Caminemos con Jesus: Toward a Hispanic Theology of Accompaniment* (Maryknoll, N.Y.: Orbis, 1995) and Miguel Díaz, "A Study of 'Persons' in U.S. Hispanic Theologies, 1968-1996"[working title for dissertation under the direction of Notre Dame University, Theology Department].

[40] Lasch, *The True and Only Heaven*, p. 119.

[41] This response is actually a conflation of two questions: "Why did God make us? God made us to show forth His goodness and to share with us His everlasting happiness in heaven." "What must we do to gain the happiness of heaven? To gain the happiness of heaven we must know, love, and serve God in this world." These two questions appeared in *The Baltimore Catechism* prior to the 1950s. See, for example, *The New Confraternity Edition Revised Baltimore Catechism*, No. 3, with summarizations of doctrine and study helps by Rev. Francis J. Connell, C.SS.R., S.T.D. (New York: Benziger Brothers, Inc., 1949), pp. 5-6.

[42] Helen Caldwell Day, *Color Ebony* (New York: Sheed and Ward, 1951), p. 112.

The Back Roads:
Alternative Catholic Intellectual Traditions

Roberto S. Goizueta

I am grateful to Sandra for this fascinating and thought-provoking contribution to the contemporary debate about Catholic intellectual traditions in the United States. Her paper is both illuminating and challenging, bringing to light those places of Catholic intellectual ferment long relegated to the back roads of the United States' intellectual topography, while perceptively outlining how hitherto-obscured places, along the back roads, offer resources for reconfiguring that topography as we approach the twenty-first century.

In the first part of the paper, Professor Mize traces modern American presuppositions about the nature of "the intellectual," indicating how these presuppositions have functioned to marginalize Catholic intellectual traditions, indeed even to block their emergence. Once Catholicism is defined as mere obscurantism, or dogmatism, the terms "Catholic" and "intellectual" become presumptively contradictory categories. Even when an author is defined as a "Catholic intellectual," as in the case of Flannery O'Connor, the artificial disjunction continues to guide interpretations of the person's work: when O'Connor is writing as an intellectual, she is *ipso facto* not writing as a Catholic, and vice versa. This, one might add, is the more common form that modern anti-Catholic bias takes within the American Catholic intellectual community itself: we Catholic theologians will be allowed to retain our intellectual credentials so long as we remain at an appropriately critical remove from the everyday life of faith, that is, from the life of "overt pietism" (to use Sandra's phrase). Yet, as Professor Mize suggests, it is precisely this worshipping community which, by privileging non-linguistic modes of discourse, provides alternatives to the logocentric discourse of the academy.

The remainder of Professor Mize's paper develops the implications of this latter insight by, first, locating and, then, retrieving resources from within American Catholic intellectual traditions for challenging the reigning epistemologies and anthropologies which, both within and outside U.S. Catholicism, have relegated those traditions to the back roads. These intellectual resources, according to Professor Mize, emerge from the desire to formulate Catholic responses to the distinctive political context of the United States.

I find this a very helpful way of articulating what American Catholic intellectual traditions have in common. Indeed, this way of interpreting the traditions seems to underscore their distinctively American cast by highlighting their common, pragmatic concern with the possibility of living, worshipping, and thinking as Catholics in the political context of the United States.

It is here that I would like to "tease out" what, to me as a Catholic Latino, or Hispanic theologian, are some exciting questions and possibilities raised by Professor Mize. As she indicates, for example, American Catholic intellectual traditions have their own "back roads," along which one may find, among others, African-American and Latino Catholics. Indeed, as she points out, the very use of the terms "American" or "America" to refer exclusively to the United States itself represents an act of marginalization. (In Spanish, for example, we have the word "*estadounidense*," or "United Statesan" to refer to someone or something from the United States.) Indeed, the category "American" is often reserved, even more specifically, for the English-speaking population of the United States; everyone else belongs someplace else. Consequently, I appreciate very much Sandra's inclusion of Hispanic-American Catholic theologies as part of the American Catholic intellectual tradition. To suggest that U.S. Latino theology is a part of that tradition is to broaden and enrich our understanding of what constitutes the distinctively "American" context for Catholic theology.

When read "against the grain," then, the idea of an American Catholicism—in its true, inclusive sense—also suggests the possibility of locating American Catholic intellectual traditions and resources in previously unexplored places. There are, as she reminds us, multiple American Catholic intellectual traditions—or, at least, multiple "networks of conversations and practices" within which such traditions may emerge. In her paper, she refers to some of the ways in which U.S. Hispanic and African-American theologies elaborate critiques of American Catholic intellectual traditions from the margins or back roads of those very traditions.

Catholic Latino theologians, for instance, are wary of the American tradition of the autonomous intellectual as this has influenced not only the academy in general but American Catholic theologies in particular. We suspect that the modern science of theology is, to paraphrase Voltaire, neither science nor theology, as a result of which it is often disregarded by both the scientist and the believer. Catholic Latino theology retrieves the tradition of pre-Tridentine popular Catholicism, in its distinctively American, mestizo manifestation, as an important locus of American Catholic intellectual traditions over against attempts to either deny the very plausibility of popular religious practices in a post-Vatican II church or to interpret Catholic intellectual traditions within the horizon of the intellectual as autonomous individual and professional expert. For better or worse, the "overtly pious" is a part of American Catholicism once again—if, indeed, it had ever left. Moreover, Catholic Latino theologians are insisting that the "overtly pious" be taken seriously intellectually and, more specifically, theologically. Within a narrowly construed American Catholic intellectual tradition, the Catholic Latino theologian is too Latino, too foreign, to be American; within the tradition of the autonomous intellectual, the Catholic Latino theologian is too Catholic, too overtly pious, to be an intellectual. It should come as no surprise, then, that those American Catholics who, several generations ago, were themselves suspected of obscurantism, dogmatism, superstition, and idol-worship should today have similar suspicions of Latino Catholics.

Ultimately, as Sandra's paper suggests, the conflict is not between the American tradition of the autonomous intellectual and Catholic intellectual traditions, but between different—though overlapping—sources of authority. Indeed, there is really no such thing as an autonomous intellectual. The problem with the self-proclaimed autonomous intellectual is not so much that he or she rejects external, corporate authority; it is, rather, that he or she privileges a different authority, not the worshipping community but the modern professional academy which created the illusion of the autonomous intellectual in the first place and perpetuates that illusion, even if now, perhaps, in the (post)modern guise of the selfless self.

Insofar as Catholic Latino theologians insist on the priority of communal religious praxis as the locus of tradition and authority, we acknowledge the perdurability—within American Catholicism itself—of a Catholic theological tradition rooted in a worshipping community.

Here, the authority of tradition, as embodied in the liturgical life of a marginalized community, is experienced as a source of empowerment, liberation, and theological understanding not only for the community but for the individual as well, not only for the layperson but for the intellectual as well. Here, ecclesial tradition becomes a "dangerous memory" for the professional, autonomous intellectual. The past becomes a transformative force in the present.

Finally, to take seriously the plurality of American Catholic intellectual traditions, in their inclusive sense, is not only to retrieve resources of intellectual criticism but also to suggest new possibilities for dialogue among those traditions. Catholic responses to the "American" political context become increasingly complex, and collaboration in those responses increasingly necessary, as the term "American" itself becomes increasingly complex.

Consequently, the dialogue among American Catholic intellectual traditions calls U.S. Latino theologians to acknowledge not simply the differences among these traditions, by asserting the particularity and distinctiveness of our Hispanic-American context, but also to pursue the ways in which these differences may mediate a truly contextual "American" Catholicism to the larger church and society. In this way, Catholic Latino theologians could contribute both to dialogue among American Catholic intellectual traditions and to the elaboration of an American Catholic response to its particular sociopolitical context.

Catholic Latino theologians could play such a mediating role, for example, by establishing connections between our own praxis-based methodologies and North American traditions of pragmatism. I have already mentioned the pragmatic concern (even if not "pragmat*ism*") underlying the American Catholic desire to demonstrate the viability of Catholicism within the U.S. political landscape, in the broad sense described by Professor Mize. It seems to me, then, that the explicitly praxis-based theologies of U.S. Latinos could help mediate a critical, American Catholic retrieval of North American pragmatism—and this, without in any way denying the important differences between Latino or Catholic notions of praxis and pragmatist notions of human experience. (Indeed, it is curious—though understandable in the light of history—that Latin American and U.S. Latino theologians have so seldom sought intellectual interlocutors among North American pragmatists.) Through such intellectual mediation, however, the very Hispanic-American Catholics who, as Professor Mize observes, have been excluded from the "American" Catholic intellectual tradition, could, ironically, play an important role in the development of a truly contextual Catholic intellectual tradition in the United States. Precisely insofar as the inclusion of U.S. Hispanic Catholic theologies among American Catholic intellectual traditions provides opportunities for retrieving important aspects of the Catholic tradition, such as popular religious praxis, that inclusion also opens up new possibilities for building bridges between American Catholic intellectual traditions and other intellectual traditions in the United States.

Contemporary American Indian Religious Thinking and Its Relationship to the Christianity of Black Elk, Holy Man of the Oglala

Michael F. Steltenkamp

A growing disaffection has been felt by a number of American Indians toward people and ideas associated with institutional Christianity. Many think that this emotional chasm is not new, but has been longstanding. They assume that Indian people were victimized by Christian evangelization when certain Native religious practices were discouraged or forbidden. "White Man's Religion" was "shoved down the throats" of people who did not want to swallow it, but who did so, chokingly, in order to survive.

Criticizing all denominational presence among Native peoples without regard to the historical specifics of a given presence has become commonplace, and "Christian religion" is often seen as the ideological minion of a Euro-American imperialism which caused an Indian holocaust. Missionaries are regarded as co-conspirators with a government whose genocidal military policy eliminated many Native practices.[1] Indians, then, were forced to accept whatever material or spiritual salvation their conquerors offered.

Contrary to this popular perception, it will be shown that conversion to Christianity was a consensual decision often made by Indians because such action was primarily perceived as spiritually satisfying. Critics say that there was a "rice Christian" quality to the conversion phenomenon. However, it will be made clear that acceptance of biblical religion was an interior response to "the Supernatural" that helped people face the disappearance of traditional lifeways, and carry on with hope.

The major denominations have apologized publicly for errors committed in the past, but reconciliation is not popular with everybody. Some protest any kind of Christian outreach to Native America. They charge that irreconcilable differences exist between Native peoples and the biblical religion exported from Europe, with caricatured examples often cited as proof.[2] Neither condemning nor endorsing all Indian-and-missionary encounters, this essay addresses a widespread misperception held by both Indians and non-Indians that does not adequately reflect the experience of Native peoples or the missionaries who have been so long a part of their religious landscape.[3] This misperception is the product of an ideological milieu generations removed from the religious mentality of "ancestors" it is thought to represent. The experience of one such ancestor was recalled by an elderly Lakota who said that his father's "special helper" in religious ceremonies was a screech owl. When his father converted to Catholicism: "No more screech owl! He changed his practice."[4]

For many pre-reservation people, this type of experience was not exceptional. Over time, many embraced some type of Christian practice because the new way convinced them of its Supernatural authorship. New religious forms simply cast an appeal that the older ones were losing.[5] This was not true for everyone, of course, but many people's interior needs were satisfactorily addressed by new practices which seemed to work effectively within the altered world of early reservation life.

The Black Elk Image: Past and Present

The Lakota holy man Black Elk was not unlike the screech owl practitioner mentioned above. His experience can be a lens through which the religious quest of many will be observed. The famous medicine man was representative of a senior generation for whom some version of Christianity provided life-giving vision.[6]

Black Elk Speaks is perhaps the most widely read work dealing with Native America.[7] The book's poet-author masterfully sketched a portrait of the Plains life paradise that Native peoples inhabited before confronting American settlers and the civilization they brought. Readers cherish with Black Elk the simple joy of being human in an Eden that once was the North American continent, but the story concludes showing that Manifest Destiny exacted a murderous toll. The sad tale conjures up torn-apart tepees, extinguished campfires, slaughtered buffaloes, and massacred friends. Black Elk himself crystallized the different stereotypes associated with Indians of the frontier period—defeated warrior, saddened elder, wilderness ascetic, Native ecologist, and religious philosopher. His name became synonymous with the clean environment that vanished along with his people.

Fifteen years after the "life story," another Black Elk text appeared. Ever since, it has been consulted by heritage-minded Indians and interested others looking for information related to Plains Indian religion as it existed in times past.[8] Like its predecessor, *The Sacred Pipe* intimated that Black Elk's religion was wrenched from his life along with everything else he held dear. Readers were again entranced by the holy man's portrayal as nobly "monocultural." Intolerant others could be dismissed as "ethnocentric" (if not racist), but Black Elk won admiration for clinging to a dream of the way things were within an earlier, aboriginally pristine world. His monocultural portrayal has been lauded as representing legitimate resistance to the non-Indian ways which engulfed him (instead of being criticized as ethnocentric).

The man was, in fact, neither monocultural nor ethnocentric. Rather, he successfully adapted to changing times because of a multicultural perspective that few people knew he owned. Readers had passing knowledge of Black Elk's experience with Buffalo Bill in Europe, and occasional commentators called attention to universal themes congruent with the holy man's thought. However, on the popular level, Black Elk's appeal remained that of the noblest of "savages" (in the positive sense à la Rousseau)—immune to, and unaffected by, contact with anything non-Indian.

The Black Elk portrait was joined by "New Age" religion, and this union has contributed to a renewed interest in ethnic identity among Indian people. This renaissance includes some who sincerely seek to deepen their understanding of how "the Sacred" was traditionally perceived. There are also those who had been previously indifferent to religion, and those who had some kind of "falling out" with one of the mainline Christian denominations.

John Collier, the "New Deal" Commissioner of Indian Affairs, pointed to what many New Agers assiduously seek. Referring to Native cultures, he wrote: "They have . . . the lost ingredient."[9] Indians themselves turned to "tradition" in the hope of finding this "ingredient" that offered solace. The idyllic past and the hope it contained were perhaps accessible, some thought, in Black Elk's last literary utterance, *The Sacred Pipe*. By practicing the rites described, one might acquire the religious integrity that he once knew as a younger man.

Sam Gill challenged the idea of a "mother earth" spirituality that has been so broadly associated with Native America, but its popular appeal is still partly indebted to the primacy of Black Elk material. For example, *Mother Earth Spirituality* is a book that calls readers to an appreciation of the cosmos and an understanding of the Supernatural via traditional Lakota ritual.[10] The author angrily castigates Christian denominations that took root among his people, and tells of finding his Indian identity in the Black Elk books. It was the holy man, presumed to be someone who held out against the ravages of Christian influence, to whom he attributed his spiritual formation.[11]

Even more popular is another Lakota who won a large readership with his autobiography carrying the ambiguous title of *Black Elk*.[12] A university press turned down the text, but another was more entrepreneurial. Capitalizing on public misperceptions, it published his story. Perhaps to spur sales, it is suggested (erroneously) that the author is a modern-day embodiment of his namesake's spiritual legacy.[13]

After reading *The Sacred Pipe*, I sought to discover the power held within the ancient rites. I had been entranced by Neihardt's description of the holy man's worldview, and understood his "life-story" to be a diagnostic biography of Native America, or at least, a distillation of how all Indians regarded their history. In retrospect, this understanding was naive, but ignited within me a desire to find voices that could reveal "the Sacred" in terms more intimate than I had known. I wanted to find "the Supernatural" that seemed so close to primordial people such as Black Elk. It seemed providential that Joseph Epes Brown, author of *The Sacred Pipe*, was a visiting professor the year in which I began graduate studies. We spoke many times, and he bestowed his blessing on my quest by signing his book:

> To my good friend, and student, Mike,
> who is walking the Good Red Road,
> and who will help his students catch the Sacred Ball.

Such was the wind in my spiritual sail as I assumed a teaching position on the Pine Ridge reservation, Black Elk's home.

I shared the widespread opinion that Black Elk—and perhaps all truly native Natives—was committed solely to a pre-"Contact" theology. I accepted the popular thesis that pressure exerted by government agencies and Christian missionaries forced Indian people to abandon traditional religious practices. Indians might have accommodated many externals of Christianity, but within their hearts beat a desire to drum out anything associated with the intrusive religion.

As reported in *Black Elk: Holy Man of the Oglala*, I was surprised to learn that after the Wounded Knee massacre, Black Elk felt aimless, ill, and dissatisfied with what he was doing as a medicine man. I learned that he met Jesuit priests, was baptized a Catholic in 1904, on the feast of St. Nicholas (December 6), and was ever after known to fellow tribesmen as one who

> learned what the Bible meant,
> and that it was good. . . .
> He never talked about the old ways.
> All he talked about was the Bible and Christ.[14]

Through Neihardt and Brown, Black Elk's life-story was supposedly well-known—in all its nineteenth-century one-dimensionality. However, I interviewed the holy man's only surviving child and elderly friends, and discovered a man affectionately remembered as "Nick," the "faithful Catholic catechist." Because his work for the church was so important and time-consuming, he rarely spoke about ancient rites, buffalo hunts, and cavalry skirmishes. Thinking of Black Elk solely as a wistful warrior without weapons is, then, sorely askew.

I plied consultants with questions such as the following: Was Nick hostile toward "white people?" Did he wish these people would vanish? Was he sad that the old rites were not being practiced to the extent they once were? Did he think his people were religiously better off before Christianity and the missionaries came? I was surprised to learn that the answer to questions such as these was a simple, and emphatic, "no."

After learning the above (and more), I was disappointed to think that I was being denied access to "the lost ingredient" Black Elk might have possessed.[15] The holy man's daughter, Lucy Looks Twice, was quick to assuage my discouragement when she said that I already knew about the ancient mysteries that were most important to him! I learned that what he cherished was the doctrine and spirituality of what would today be described as a very typical Catholicism of the period, in contemporary parlance, a "pre-Vatican Council" theology and practice. The late-life discouragement that was implicit in Neihardt and Brown was not attributable to the emergence of Christian practices. Rather, whatever melancholy he had was due to the growing secularism he saw arising among his people. However, despite testimony from those who knew him, the holy man's earlier image is an enduring one that resists alteration.

Black Elk's pan-Indian stereotype is so firmly in place that when I speak of his work as a catechist, or when I show pictures of him being present at church assemblies of the period, someone in attendance might suggest that a kind of "Stockholm experience" took place. That is, along with his people, he was held hostage to alien ways, developed sympathy for his captors, and so hypnotically imitated the externals of their way of life: cutting his hair, wearing Western clothing, attending church services, and so on. Persons today who hold such an opinion should be aware that no one who knew Black Elk saw any evidence of psychological instability, nor did he ever communicate to anyone that he felt constrained.

Another type of challenge to Black Elk's Christian identity falls under the rubric of duplicity. Its gist is that he pretended to be one thing, a fervent Catholic, when deep inside, or in private, he was a diehard "traditionalist."[16] An example of this is an interpretation of Black Elk's praying the rosary.

Suggesting that the rosary beads masked a traditional Lakota prayer form, an Oglala woman has asked: "Who's to say Black Elk wasn't saying Lakota prayers to each bead?"[17] Persons wedded to the man's "traditionalist" image would be inclined to see this as a plausible explanation for his behavior. However, if anything was certain about Black Elk, it was his devotion *to the rosary* (as in "Hail Mary, full of grace . . . "). Contrary to what some might want to hear, this is not a debatable issue.

Apart from his daughter's testimony, I was told by his close friend John Lone Goose, his granddaughter Regina, and other Manderson residents that: 1) each said the rosary with him many times, 2) he said it by himself all the time, and 3) everyone in Manderson knew he said it all the time! If his praying of the rosary masked an older Lakota, beaded prayer form, no one who knew Black Elk was aware of his "con job" (or the older Lakota prayer form referred to).[18]

Shortly after the Wounded Knee occupation of 1973, a sign was torn off the meeting hall of St. Agnes Church in Manderson, which was Black Elk's reservation village. The sign indicated that the holy man was the church's first catechist, and that the meeting hall was dedicated to his memory. Hence, just as the hostage-syndrome argument attempts to explain away the holy man's involvement with Western ways, and just as the rosary is said to mask a traditional Lakota prayer, so the sign's destruction was an attempt to prevent a church's proclamation that the holy man was one of its fold.

Hilda Neihardt's claim that Black Elk's daughter abandoned Christianity makes it clear that some people (for whatever reason) strongly resist the holy man's association with anything other than traditional religion. An example of this is in the egregiously flawed *Encyclopedia of North American Indians*. Its entry on Black Elk says that "the role of staunch Catholic was forced upon him" and "he played it well to appease his oppressors."[19]

Revisionists need only look at Black Elk's opening utterances reported in *The Sacred Pipe*—the "canonical" nativistic text put together shortly before the holy man's death. Joseph Epes Brown intended to record traditional Lakota practices, but could not prevent the patriarch from stating several non-traditional religious tenets to which he subscribed. Namely:

> We have been told by the white men, or at least by those who are Christian, that God sent to men His son, who would restore order and peace upon the earth; and we have been told that Jesus the Christ was crucified, but that he shall come again at the Last Judgment, the end of this world or cycle. *This I understand and know that it is true* . . . [italics added].[20]

Black Elk could not speak to Brown about religious practice without also asserting his Christian faith. This was not surprising to anyone who knew him intimately because they knew that he took his Catholicism very seriously—right up to the end.[21] His theology included more than a pre-Contact inventory.

It is not easy to answer why efforts persist to remove this memory, but understanding why Black Elk and others converted and why they were able to be fervent in their Christian practice late in life is a more manageable task. In the torturous years that preceded the holy man's conversion, a yearning for new life stirred within the hearts of many Native peoples. Different forms of biblical religion became the means by which many found it.

Early Denominationalism: The Ghost Dance and Native American Church

While in Europe with Buffalo Bill's Wild West Show, Black Elk was exposed to the large world that existed outside his reservation home. He danced for Queen Victoria, fell in love, and visited European sites that are still popular tourist attractions. English, French, Italian and German people attended services at cathedrals, and this impressed the young Lakota. He was edified seeing them pay due respect to their Creator.

Letters sent from Europe reveal a growing respect for the religion he saw his hosts take to heart. Written when he was in his early twenties, one letter reports his fidelity "to the law" (his baptism) by "remembering God."[22] In another, he quotes 1 Cor. 13 and expresses a desire to see "where they killed Jesus."[23] Upon Black Elk's arrival home, the "Ghost Dance" religion was sweeping through the west. It was most popular among groups that were plagued by droughts, disease, and depression. Their blighted condition made them look for life wherever it could be found.[24] Black Elk joined this "revitalization movement" and subscribed to its decidedly Christian doctrine which told of a *"Wanikiye"* (Savior) who would restore all that had been lost.

On the Plains and elsewhere, people heard it said that God's son had taken pity on them, that he would raise the dead, restore the buffalo, and rid their turf of pioneers and cavalry. This made much sense to people like Black Elk who "knew" that years earlier non-Indians had actually killed God's son. No Indian would be so foolish to commit such an act. This time, God's son had chosen a wiser people, Indians, among whom to pitch his lodge!

A revelation that accompanied this "Christology" was that special "ghost shirts" should be worn, and these would protect people from bullets. This surely indicated great wisdom (if not Supernatural intervention) because many lives had been lost over the years due to bullets that easily pierced traditional buckskin clothing. Moreover, since the army had been called upon to stop the Ghost Dancers, white people must be fearful that the prophecies would come true. This was, at least, the thinking that prevailed.

Exposure to European Christianity had a formative impact on those who participated in this movement, but this exposure has been glossed over by most commentators. There also has been relatively little reflection on Ghost Dance "theology" and the "faith experience" it spawned among Native groups.[25] Instead, the religion's militant overtones and the infamous slaughter at Wounded Knee have absorbed people's attention. This focus has not helped explain why rosaries replaced screech owls, and why many Indians affiliated with mainline Christian denominations.

At the height of Ghost Dance activity, several versions of Christian catechesis were alive and well within Sioux country. Proselytizers were Native leaders whose visions gave hope to a starving and diseased population.[26] Denominational teachings, as well as individual interpretations of those teachings, gave idiosyncratic meanings to the Christian forms that were gaining new adherents. Everyone was familiar with the millennialist promise of salvation.

Mainstream Christian theological teaching did not, of course, affirm the teaching of how God would bring about a "new earth" for Ghost Dancers. Nonetheless, devotees formed what today would be called a denomination or "sect" of Christianity. Although distinctively Indian, it was not unlike other "Christian" groups that rose and fell throughout the centuries.

An example from Europe is not unlike its American cousin.[27] Just as the Sioux stopped working, raided supplies, danced into trance, and waited for their day of deliverance, so did the frenzied followers of Konrad Schmid's European flagellants of the fourteenth and fifteenth centuries. Just as the Sioux taught that the originator of the Ghost Dance was possibly the Savior, so did Schmid claim to be the God-Emperor Frederick II of Germany (1194-1250)—returned to rid the earth of evildoers and save the elect.[28]

"God" was made manifest to a Ghost Dancer through what might be called "invasive, foreign ideology" (i.e., biblical religion).[29] Ghost Dancers, however, would report their experience in different terms. They would regard biblical revelation as simply an example of the Supernatural's mysterious and unpredictable manifestation within their lives. They would say that this time God's mouthpiece was an Indian, Wovoka.

The Ghost Dance, then, was an appropriation of Christian doctrine by Indian people who longed for the "Second Coming" of God's son. Wounded Knee spelled the demise of Ghost Dancing, but it did not eradicate the hope harbored by many that God's son would come to save the people. Native theological reflection paralleled that of early Christian thinkers. Both groups eventually expected Christ's return at some date in the more distant future.

With little attention to the Christian theology it included, analyses of the Ghost Dance always dwell on the following historical facts: 1) the pitiful social conditions of reservation life contrasting with that of the pre-reservation period, 2) the people's desire for a return to better times, 3) the shooting of Sitting Bull by Indian police at the Standing Rock agency, 4) the sickly condition of Big Foot and his band of Minneconjou as they made their way to Wounded Knee, 5) reasons for fighting the Sioux harbored by Colonel Forsyth's Seventh Cavalry, 6) the botched surrender and subsequent slaughter of many women and children, and 7) Black Elk's tragic perspective à la Neihardt that his people's "dream" died in the snow at Wounded Knee. One such analysis is presented in a commercial video produced by Lakota people.[30]

Men and women are interviewed, and they reflect on that tragic moment of history. One interview is of a young man who reports an incident that he says occurred just before the bullets flew at Wounded Knee. He tells of a Catholic priest who did not use an interpreter (as was his custom), but instead administered in communal fashion "the last rites" to Big Foot's people. When the priest finished, a command was barked out by an officer, and the Seventh Cavalry commenced its murderous fire into the Sioux camp.

The video is lucid in telling of the tragedy, but its inclusion of a "last rites" episode never reported by Lakota survivors, priests, or army personnel only underscores the extent to which some are misinterpreting the missionary presence of yesteryear. A century of separation from the actual event has produced a revisionism that portrays: 1) an interpreter associated with a priest who, as a matter of historical fact, was fluent in Lakota, 2) the priest's canonically illicit and theologically groundless administration of a sacrament, and 3) the church's alliance with a Seventh Cavalry intent on murder. The video thus teaches inaccurate history, and ignores the Christian theology that dead ancestors accepted.[31]

A phenomenon of more recent times, the anti-Christian polemic contradicts what some say is their stated goal. Instead of honoring, they tarnish the memory of Ghost Dance "Christians" who were slain at Wounded Knee. That is, condemnation of Christianity is condemnation of what Black Elk's generation embraced.

Many of those who survived the Wounded Knee massacre did not relinquish a hope that Jesus would be their "savior." Ghost Dancing was doomed in 1891, but the religious thinking that made it popular was not. People still hungered for "good news" of God's son coming to earth, and many swelled the denominational ranks of Episcopalian "white coats," Presbyterian "short coats," and Catholic "black robes." Missionaries gradually enlisted Native priests, deacons, ministers and catechists who brought with them a lay-following who regarded biblical religion as a sign that "the Creator" had not abandoned them.

Biblical religion, whatever form it concretely took, inspired many Indians because it told of Old World tribes preserved through flood and famine. Biblical religion told of a Creator who saved people from their enemies, who led them through desert experiences, and who even gave his son to live among them. This son of God preached the Lakota tenet *mitak oyassin* (all are relatives), and promised new life to all who lived as he instructed.

George Sword spoke for many of Black Elk's era:

> When I believed the Oglala Wakan Tanka was right I served him with all my powers. . . . In the war with the white people I found their Wakan Tanka the Superior . . . and have served Wakan Tanka according to the white people's manner and with all my power. . . . I joined the church and am a deacon in it and shall be until I die. I have done all I was able to do to persuade my people to live according to the teachings of the Christian ministers.[32]

Sword and others "translated Christianity into the Dakota [sic] way of life" and interpreted it in terms of their previous religious experience.[33] Unlike the competing missionaries they encountered, people such as Black Elk and Sword did not cling to ethnocentric definitions of "the Supernatural." Their perspective was, rather, an expansive one. They were most attentive to an omnipresent and awesome fact of life—the immanence and mystery of *Wakan Tanka*.[34]

In their struggle for survival, the Lakota and other groups utilized whatever helped them succeed. Ethnicity did not draw boundaries in such matters because power came in the form of new weaponry that included not only guns and other material resources, but also new religious doctrine. Their cultural inventory expanded every time the people found something they considered advantageous.

Theologically, the Ghost Dance was a non-mainstream version of Christianity that joined Lakota tradition. Its Christian content was so apparent that one of the priests who visited Ghost Dancers at the peak of their activity was of the opinion it was "quite Catholic, and even edifying."[35] However, it was not the only Bible-based "denomination" that arose in that early period. Coming out of the Southwest, the ritual use of peyote spread onto the plains and drew adherents who considered it a specifically Native form of Christianity. Concurrent with the Ghost Dance period, but extant still, this "Native American Church" (its legal name) claimed 5 percent of the population at Pine Ridge in 1917.[36]

Criticized still for their consumption of peyote because it contains the hallucinogen mescaline, members of this "Church" profess their faith in "Jesus, light of the world." Church "services" bear little resemblance to other Christian denominations, but the people's use of biblical material could inspire the most ardent fundamentalist preacher.[37] In short, the Ghost Dance disillusion predisposed many to embrace more stable forms of Christian practice which, in some fashion, taught of God's son coming to save Indian people. The major denominations attracted most people, but the Native American Church, administered exclusively by Indian people, was another. Gradually, older practices moved into the background.

Besides providing spiritual direction, denominational representatives gave a modicum of material assistance to people who could not rely on the government's pledge to fulfill treaty obligations. This goodwill was established during a very difficult period, and is still remembered by reservation elders. By 1940, however, MacGregor noted a "trend" among the Lakota to act much like the local white population. People were moving "away from control by the Church" and from religious practice in general.[38]

Russell Means, New Age, and the New Traditionalism

The senior generation's religious outlook was forged in a wholly different milieu than the one in which younger people were being raised. By mid-century, for example, the socialization process of individuals like Russell Means, now a Lakota activist and actor, was far different from that of the ancestors. It is people like him, nonetheless, who today speak authoritatively on what constituted Native "traditions" from of old.[39]

Although Means projects the convincing image of a pre-reservation traditionalist whose religious convictions reflect those of mystic warriors from the past, his autobiography paints a different portrait. Raised in urban California, he moved with his wife and children to Cleveland, where he first attracted media attention. Struggling to make ends meet, he abandoned the inconspicuous life of a faceless accountant, and was inspired by activists Clyde Bellecourt and Dennis Banks to become "a full-time Indian" [his words] in 1970. Means adopted a style of dress that seemed authentically Indian, and assumed leadership within AIM, the American Indian Movement known for its takeover of Wounded Knee in 1973.

Since 1970, Means has been a visible presence in the forefront of issues affecting Native America. He and those associated with him made it fashionable for young Indian people to adopt wearing apparel and coiffure from times past which "reclaimed" the Native identity that Westernizing and "civilizing" forces had removed from their forebears. His image represented for many what "true Indian-ness" meant—despite objections to the contrary levied at him over time from Native people themselves.

When Means began his career as a social activist, he epitomized MacGregor's "trend" and was in a role that often included bitter denunciation of a Christian theology with which he was superficially familiar. Over time, he came to represent a coalition that spiritually united "Indigenous people" from around the world with "New Age" non-Indians, environmental activists, social justice advocates, and others whose religious thirst had not been quenched by participation within mainline denominations. The "movement" Means embodied actually extended beyond Native America since the reclamation of an idealized past, and the vision of a self-actualizing future, were not limited solely to Indian questers.

With the rise of environmental consciousness, denominational attempts to communicate the mystery of a Triune God competed with popular pantheism and often lost. Walking a sandy beach in summer, strolling through wondrous woods in autumn, and skiing soft slopes of majestic mountains in winter tutored more and more Americans in a new nature religion whose fresh feelings were so much easier to accept than the cerebral ennui of conventional catechetics. Those who once might have studied theology turned to courses in ecology. Ecologians began to flourish instead of theologians, and piety expressed itself in the yearly observance of Earth Day instead of weekly attendance at staid services in cavernous cathedrals. It seemed so much more "natural" to celebrate an all-powerful Creator's handiwork in nature, and to castigate a "Christian" culture that polluted environments so badly that were Indians to visit us from yesteryear, they would cry.

Many thought that their religious yearnings might be sated by plumbing the depths of Druid doctrine, sorting through confused thought by means of Confucian thought, or discovering how primal people lived within the Amazonian rainforest, Native North America, some Shangri-la realm near India, or Tibet, or any place but late twentieth-century America! Television shows portrayed the wilderness as a gentle haven for characters like "Grizzly Adams" and "Daniel Boone." Their celluloid lifestyles fueled viewer fantasies with the hope that non-Indians could find peace of mind and be one-with-nature in the same fashion as their Native friends.

A functional family might even be part of such an aspiration since real-life precedents did exist. Television showed that a family from the past could find bliss in a "Little House On The Prairie," and the example they set cast considerable appeal to asphalt-bound urbanites. The solace of suburban life simply did not match the promise of tranquility which was thought to exist on peaceful reservations or which was projected by John Boy's family at Walton Mountain.[40]

As vulnerable as anybody to late twentieth-century stress, anxiety, and disillusion, reservation and urban Indians were not immunized against the same dreamy sentiments that were entertained by their non-Indian neighbors. Together they harbored the hope of finding a lifestyle or religious practice that could ameliorate such strongly felt longings. A ready audience positively responded to Russell Means (and others) who called for "natural" peoples to cast off the yoke of institutional Christianity's varied forms. Already the "bible of the hippie movement," *Black Elk Speaks* was serving as the inspirational touchstone for activist Indians and other vision-seekers (like myself) who were spiritually restless.

Non-Indians were exploring religious alternatives, but the resurgence of Native "tradition" was heralded as a unique kind of spiritual retaliation. The claim put forth by some has been that this rebirth was "prophesied" by "elders" long ago (citations regularly come from Black Elk material).[41] Dwindling attendance at Christian churches within the Native world is cited as confirmation of the claim, and some think that institutional Christianity need no longer be tolerated within Indian country. Those who espouse this position say that "the ancestors," Black Elk being the archetype, would smile upon such an exorcism. However, this thinking is scripted by social forces completely unrelated to the religious disposition of any pre-reservation holy man.[42]

Autobiographical Evaluation of Trends on the Eve of the Millennium

Around the time Means was becoming a professional, anti-Christian Indian, institutional expressions of religion also were losing their lustre for me. This prompted my undertaking a "New Age" religious quest long before such questing became fashionably counter-cultural. For example, I participated in sweatlodge ceremonies twenty years ago, when relatively few people were involved in such activity.[43] Today, it is not uncommon for Indians, and a growing number of non-Indians, to participate in this ritual throughout the year.

In the last two decades, numerous people have quested for a vision of something Sacred that the Indian traditional world, however vaguely understood by Indians or non-Indians, was thought to contain. Religious journeys led these people into self-help, human-potential exercises and spiritual practices that appealed to them in a more personal way than the shopworn cliches of a church-going, Bible-reading, rosary-praying senior generation.[44] In this quest, Native Americans joined and were led by other native Americans who were not Indian. Together, they overtly set aside a reliance on biblical religion to find a spiritual strength they thought was possessed by their pre-Christian European or Indian forebears.

When Russell Means ventured into the world of Indian activism, I discovered the Black Elk material, and like so many others went in search of the living legacy bequeathed by the holy man. Fortuitous decisions and actions led me to the holy man's daughter and friends. From them I learned and wrote about the sixty years of Black Elk's life that were not addressed by Neihardt or Brown. Although the biography I produced generally has been regarded as "a real step forward in American Indian religious studies," remembrances of the holy man as a devout catechist do not cast the appeal of more fanciful, longstanding impressions.[45]

More mesmerizing than the life of a churchman is the image cultivated by Means. He stokes mythical history and conjures up a more romantic perception of the holy man when he writes:

In the first half of this century, Black Elk was led down the path blazed by Red Cloud, Crow Dog, Crazy Horse, Sitting Bull, and others of their generation.[46]

Being a product of the present, and removed as he was from the actual experience of Black Elk's time, Means cannot understand the holy man's identity "in the first half of this century" as being that of a Catholic catechist! Like others who are similarly ill-informed, Means could not know that Black Elk's reference to the "sacred tree of life" is the holy man's dream of one day seeing "the Christian life of all people."[47]

Despite this lack of knowledge, Means continues to be a master architect of opinion regarding what is, or is not, true Indianness. His broadstroke condemnations of white people and Christianity sound like racist rhetoric and religious bigotry, but he continues to be a marketable commodity. Film roles have been steady, and public appearances are numerous since promoters can always count on a good turnout.[48] Regrettably, the perspective he articulates is not unique.

Unlike Means, I contended with institutional religion since adolescence. It was also during this time that I first interacted with Indian people. In the course of seeking to learn their traditional wisdom, I saw that mention of the word "church" sometimes elicited an indifferent or negative response. This was not surprising because such a response was increasingly common in the non-Indian world as well.

Disengagement from denominational belonging had not been solely an Indian issue. However, since Christianity was associated with the culture that wreaked havoc on their ancestral ways, some Native people concluded its absence would alleviate many problems. Thus was begun an exodus from what some thought to be a failed experiment in biblical religion to the promised land of esoteric Native ritual. It has been thought that such ritual only needed a second chance to work its charm.

This line of thought is persuasive and wields considerable influence over many people. It was the same ideological stimulus that stirred within me nearly thirty years ago. Back then, I was sensitive to problems associated with religion, ethnicity, or caste, and sought to remedy my spiritual discomfort by acquiring a better definition of the mystically alluring Black Elk. I wanted to draw strength from the same Indian rituals that I assumed made him such an eminent religious figure.

To my great surprise and contrary to expectations, I learned that many from the holy man's generation were devout in their Christian practice. In telling me what they did, Black Elk's daughter and those who remember the holy man hoped that I would preserve this memory of "the elders," and that it would not be forgotten. In book form, the memory is at least on file, but the senior generation's Christian practice is still popularly perceived as never having existed, or never being heartfelt.

As a new century begins, the religious landscape of Native America sees Black Elk literature continuing to motivate Indians and non-Indians to seek a new religious identity by way of traditional Native practices. A corollary to this quest is that one abandons his or her institutional Christian involvement. On the eve of a new millennium, trends within the dominant society contribute to this "New Age" consciousness.

Prominent within this ideological scene is Russell Means. He expresses an extreme, but widespread, position that claims to represent the thinking of pre-reservation-era peoples. In oftentimes passionate terms, he states that the ancestors tried to resist Christian intrusion upon their lands, but contrary to this view is the historically well-documented acceptance of biblical ideas by the ancestors of Means himself! Earlier examples exist, but the easy acceptance of Christianity by Indian people led to what might be called Native "denominations"— the well-known, but theologically ignored Ghost Dance, and the Native American Church.

Many who shape opinion within the Indian world carry into the new millennium an understanding of what their ancestors believed that is contrary to what is empirically verifiable. If their influence prevails, the mainline denominations of today eventually might be subsumed under a syncretistic religion akin to what Handsome Lake started among the Iroquois two centuries ago.[49] On the other hand, it might come to pass that future vision-seekers look beyond the conventional "teachings," and discover what was said about the senior generation by Black Elk's daughter and friends.

Acquiring this new information, they might re-route their religious journey and find themselves re-evaluating their assumptions. Such is, at least, what happened in my case when I undertook the search. Contrary to expectations, such new information took me to the Jesuit priesthood, which is now part of my life.

Anecdotal experience aside, if Black Elk's dream materialized, the twenty-first century would see bloom "the Christian life of all people."

However, given the prevailing resistance to biblical religion within different parts of the Indian world, fulfillment of the holy man's dream will have to wait.

Notes

[1] Grant's famous "Peace Policy" was, in fact, administered by Protestant denominational leaders who, according to Catholic mission records, were not of one mind with their Catholic counterparts. Cf. Vine Deloria, Jr., *Red Earth, White Lies: Native Americans and the Myth of Scientific Fact* (New York: Scribner, 1995). A Lakota whose family has Christian roots in the early reservation period, Deloria now states that "Christianity has been the curse of all cultures into which it has intruded," p. 22.

[2] Russell Means, *Where White Men Fear to Tread* (New York: St. Martin's Press, 1995). Means says that "Marxism is as alien to my culture as capitalism and Christianity are."

[3] Generalizations regarding "all" Indian people and "all" historical events regarding them have shortcomings. This paper focuses on Black Elk because his paradigmatic experience does suggest that greater caution be exercised in speaking about Indian-missionary encounters.

[4] The word "Lakota" is now used by many (not all) western "Sioux" people when referring to themselves (the latter name bequeathed by their neighbors). Use of the term "Indian" remains an accepted self-designation and will be used interchangeably here with the word "Native."

[5] Regarding "religious liberty" being curtailed for Indian America, different groups experienced different forms of governmental censure or indifference.

[6] If an individual or group posits a salvific role for Jesus, then that individual or group is regarded here as "Christian." Also, "denomination" and "sect" are used synonymously so as to avoid a certain negative connotation associated with the latter.

[7] John G. Neihardt, *Black Elk Speaks: Being the Life Story of a Holy Man of the Oglala Sioux* (Lincoln: University of Nebraska Press, 1961). See also, Michael F. Steltenkamp, *Black Elk: Holy Man of the Oglala* (Norman: University of Oklahoma Press, 1993), pp. 177-178 n.5.

A theatrical production of Black Elk's life was the basis of "The Gospel According to Black Elk"—the title for a feature article in *American Theatre* magazine (December 1993). It stated that the playwright wove Neihardt's image of Black Elk into a figure that both Indian actors and audiences found very inspirational.

Julian Rice's *Black Elk's Story: Distinguishing Its Lakota Purpose* (Albuquerque: University of New Mexico Press, 1991) is a speculative work purporting to analyze traditional Lakota thought found within the Black Elk material.

[8] Joseph Epes Brown, *The Sacred Pipe: Black Elk's Account of the Seven Rites of the Oglala Sioux* (Norman: University of Oklahoma Press, 1953). Black Elk died August 17, 1950 (84 years old).

[9] John Collier, *Indians of the Americas* (New York: A Mentor Book, 1947), p. 7.

[10] Sam Gill, *Mother Earth: An American Story* (Chicago: University of Chicago Press, 1987). Ed McGaa, *Mother Earth Spirituality: Native American Paths to Healing Ourselves and Our World* (San Francisco: Harper San Francisco, 1990).

[11] The author uses the ceremonially bestowed name of "Eagle Man," and is well-known through speaking engagements and seminars held nationwide. Some who conduct "traditional Indian" religious ceremonies for non-Indians have been taken to task by other "traditionals" who decry "the exploitation of a sacred heritage for profit." There also exists among some activists a very vocal opposition to non-Indians teaching, or writing, or speaking about Indian culture or religion. The altruism of this concern is sometimes tempered when it is proposed that Indians only "be paid" to address the subject. Cf. also Fergus M. Bordewich's *Killing The White Man's Indian: Reinventing Native Americans at the End of the Twentieth Century* (New York: Doubleday, 1996). Religion figures into Bordewich's discussion of land claims (the intertwining of religion and politics, as will be shown with the Ghost Dance, is very difficult to disentangle). Black Elk's stereotype is used in the effort to get the Black Hills returned to the Sioux (the holy man presumably wanting this "sacred" land returned). Hence, it is politically important that the man's image be sustained in the sense of Black Elk-as-traditional, pre-reservation Lakota, and not in the sense of Nick Black Elk, Catholic catechist.

[12] William Lyon and Wallace Black Elk, *Black Elk: The Sacred Ways of a Lakota* (New York: Harper & Row, 1990).

[13] To make the masquerade even more credible for duped readers, the senior holy man is referred to by his first name and the author simply as "Black Elk." Contrary to the stereotype, this form of address is not employed by contemporary Lakota. Equating the thought of two men who share only a last name is as specious an assertion as anyone could make, but since the Black Elk image is so popular, it is not surprising that a publisher would try to profit through any association with the sainted patriarch.

Less well-known, but no less beholden to Black Elk material, is Iroquois Bill Elwell, Jr. In a cassette produced by Artistic Video and entitled "Native American Indian Sacred Purification Sweatlodge Ceremony," this "sweat leader" is shown explaining what might be termed a "theology" of the rite. Each phase of the ceremony is depicted as he conducts a session for non-Indian participants. His mispronounced Lakota vocabulary clearly is drawn from the Black Elk corpus. *Native American Indian Sacred Purification Sweatlodge Ceremony*, Artistic Video, P.O. Box 906, Miller Place, New York 11764.

[14] Steltenkamp, p. 54. Both Neihardt and Brown sought out Black Elk, and their visits were mediated and encouraged by Ben, the holy man's son (who served as interpreter).

[15] Some critics have suggested that my fieldwork intention was to learn of and write about Black Elk's Catholicism when, in fact, the opposite was my goal. The holy man's daughter, close relatives, and friends were the ones who insisted that his Christian practice is what he would have wanted me to report.

[16] Cf. Raymond J. DeMallie, *The Sixth Grandfather: Black Elk's Teachings Given to John G. Neihardt* (Lincoln: University of Nebraska Press, 1984). DeMallie points out that discussions of this topic usually dissolve "into political rhetoric rather than objective assessment," p. 80.

[17] Cf. Marianna Bartholomew, "The Search for Black Elk," *Our Sunday Visitor*, 29 May 1994, p. 10.

[18] From still another perspective, John Neihardt's daughter, Hilda, has done to Black Elk's daughter what John Neihardt did to Nick. In *Black Elk and Flaming Rainbow* (Lincoln: University of Nebraska Press, 1995), she suggests that Lucy regretted telling me about Black Elk's life as a catechist, p. 13. I am referred to as "an author" who "visited Lucy in 1973" (I was a teacher who regularly visited Lucy from 1973 until her death in 1978). Lucy is said to be a "pipe carrier" (a designation that gained currency in the 1980s that referred to Indians who practice "traditional ways") who abandoned her lifelong Catholicism.

In *Holy Man*, p. 168, I tell of Hilda Neihardt photographing Lucy holding a pipe (not Lucy's since she did not own one). Hilda's purpose was to show that the holy man's daughter carried on the tradition reported in *Black Elk Speaks*. According to Neihardt, Lucy's "conversion" to pipe-carrierdom resulted from reading *Black Elk Speaks* (something she says Lucy had not done until late in life)! Rather than evaluate this misinformation as a transparent advertisement for her father's book, Clyde Holler cited it as authoritative in his almost as faulty *Black Elk's Religion: The Sun Dance and Lakota Catholicism* (Syracuse: The University of Syracuse Press, 1995), p. 13.

Strangely enough, whatever appreciation Lucy held for the Lakota pipe tradition was partly attributable to me! On many occasions, we spoke about religious practices within Lakota and Catholic traditions. She was surprised that I regarded the pipe so highly (having never given it much attention herself). Because of my interest, she had her son make a pipe for me.

Hilda Neihardt never inquired as to what I knew of Lucy's disposition on various matters. I could have shown her the last letter I received from Lucy shortly before she died. In it, Lucy expressed a hope that my biography of her father would be a success (far from "regretting" our time together). She also said that she prayed her children would return to the sacraments (does that sound like someone who left the "fold?")!

Instead of contacting me (nowhere did she cite my book in her text), Hilda Neihardt simply wrote that Lucy quit her membership in a "white church." Sounding like Simpson defense attorney Johnnie Cochran when he said his task was to search for the truth, Neihardt rhetorically asks: "Isn't it always important that the truth be known?" (p. 119). Her question might not be as disingenuous as it sounds. She may be simply revealing a longstanding Neihardt-naivete regarding Lakota etiquette toward visitors (see note 21 below). She actually might think her description of Lucy's religious practice was accurate.

[19] Frederick E. Hoxie, ed., *Encyclopedia of North American Indians* (Houghton Mifflin Co., Boston and New York, 1996), p. 73. Since persons who portray Black Elk this way imply that he lacked integrity and was conniving in his duplicity (not an admirable image), I do not know why they think their "corrective" is flattering.

[20] Brown, p. xix. Black Elk makes an important qualification when he refers to those with whom the Sioux came into contact (those who settled and "tamed" the West). Namely, he distinguishes between "white men" who are Christian and those who are not! Addressing "how the West was won," commentators who should know better often lump soldiers, settlers, government officials, trappers, traders, and all missionaries into the category of "Christians." The pre- and early-reservation period was peppered with persons whose religious practice was not foremost in their mind.

[21] Julian Rice, p. xi, is of the opinion that *The Sacred Pipe* is "overtly Catholic." He and others cite acquaintances of Black Elk as saying the holy man never spoke about his work as a catechist (his silence on the matter then set forth as proof that he only had "old time religion" on his mind). However, it is common within Lakota circles for one not to volunteer information unless asked. Lucy, for example, was willing to be photographed holding a pipe and co-hosting a picnic for Hilda Neihardt and her entourage (quite out of character for Lucy). On this occasion, she was courteous to her guests, and did not refer to me as her "takoja" ("grandchild") who was putting together her father's biography. What she and I were doing conflicted with the stereotype that had attracted these people, so there was no need to identify me.

[22] Indian performers were required to "be of the same religious faith," and so were baptized into the Episcopal church. Cf. Raymond J. DeMallie, *The Sixth Grandfather*, p. 10.

[23] DeMallie, pp. 8-11, reports Neihardt saying that Black Elk informed him that his "spiritual power disappeared" while in Europe, and that this perhaps "led him to Christianity." Neihardt said that when Black Elk returned home "his power came back to him." If the holy man said this, or what he meant, will probably never be known.

[24] The classic work on this subject is James Mooney's *The Ghost-Dance Religion and the Sioux Outbreak of 1890*. Smithsonian Institution, Bureau of American Ethnology, Annual Report 14, pt. 2 (Washington, D.C., 1896). Cf. also Robert Utley's *The Last Days of the Sioux Nation* (New Haven: Yale University Press, 1963), Thomas W. Overholt's *Prophecy in Cross-Cultural Perspective* (Atlanta: Scholars Press, 1986), pp. 122-141, and *Channels of Prophecy: The Social Dynamics of Prophetic Activity* (Minneapolis: Fortress Press, 1989), pp. 27-50.

[25] Cf. DeMallie, p. 265. Black Elk told Neihardt that many people "believed in this Messiah business and were hoping . . . they would be through with the poverty." Holler speculates that it started because the Sun Dance had been banned. Since his interest and focus is on the Ghost Dance theme of restoring traditional culture (pp. 217-220), Holler is intent upon arguing that the holy man was a prisoner to the past. He disregards the central tenet (dear to Black Elk) concerning Christ's return (a vision which Black Elk had while dancing). DeMallie notes that one of Black Elk's Ghost Dance visions was filled with "imagery of the Transfiguration," ibid., p. 263n. Cf. also John Neihardt, p. 249.

[26] Forty percent of the Pine Ridge population was actively involved with dancing.

[27] Studies of religious movements elsewhere are: Bennetta Jules-Rosette, ed., *The New Religions of Africa* (Norwood, New Jersey: Ablex Publishing Corporation, 1979); Weston LaBarre, *The Ghost Dance: Origins of Religion* (New York: Dell Publishing Company, 1972); Vittorio Lanternari, *The Religions of the Oppressed: A Study of Modern Messianic Cults* (New York: Alfred A. Knopf, Inc., 1963); Peter Worsley, *The Trumpet Shall Sound: A Study of 'Cargo' Cults in Melanesia* (New York: Schocken Books, 1968).

[28] Wovoka, known also as Jack Wilson, was the Nevada Paiute who originated the Ghost Dance. Cf. Marvin Harris, *Cows, Pigs, Wars and Witches: The Riddles of Culture* (New York: Vantage Books, 1974), pp. 121 and 197.

These kinds of "socio-religious" phenomena are not ancient history. A century after the killing of Chief Big Foot and his Ghost Dancers at Wounded Knee, the Seventh Cavalry was replaced by ATF and FBI agents who confronted David Koresh's Adventists at Waco. Similarly, Ruby Ridge could have produced more fatalities, while the surrender of Montana Freemen is surprising for its lack of bloodshed.

A political agenda is either explicitly or implicitly part of the religious creed which these movements profess. In fact, the Ghost Dance's political content has always captured attention and distracted people from considering its religious ideology (Christianity) that lived on, in modified fashion, long after the Messiah's expected return in 1891.

[29] Perhaps because of its association with Western civilization, some activists have been avoiding use of the English word "God" and replacing it with "the Creator."

[30] "Wiping the Tears of Seven Generations," *The Native American Relations Series*, A Kifaru Production in association with Eagle Heart Productions, 1-800-322-1105 ext. 42, 1991.

[31] Utley, p. 215, reports that Fr. Craft was wounded after the fighting began, and that he crawled around the battlefield "giving first aid and administering last rites to the dying." Contrary to prevailing opinion, Craft stated that the Army did its best to prevent the carnage at Wounded Knee, and that many Indians were killed by their own people due to a murderous crossfire that erupted.

Adopted by chief Spotted Tail, Craft was a convert who stayed in the Jesuit order for six years before becoming a diocesan priest. Of Iroquois ancestry, he undertook missionary work among Indians and interacted with numerous historical figures of the late nineteenth century. The Army permitted him to mix with Big Foot's group, and he tried to soothe whatever tensions might exist. Curiously, his account of what occurred at Wounded Knee is more critical of Big Foot's people than it is of the Army. I am indebted to Thomas Foley for letting me read his unpublished manuscript *Hovering Eagle: The Life and Letters of Father Francis Craft, Sioux Missionary*.

[32] James R. Walker, "The Sun Dance and Other Ceremonies of the Oglala Division of the Teton Dakota," in American Museum of Natural History, *Anthropological Papers* 16, pt. 2, 1917, p. 159.

[33] Gordon MacGregor, *Warriors Without Weapons* (Chicago: University of Chicago Press, 1946), p. 102.

[34] The contemporary Indian rejection of anything associated with Christianity reflects a parochialism more reflective of early missionary attitudes than of traditional Native thought.

[35] Fr. Emil Perrig's diary (on file at Marquette University's Archives of Catholic Indian Missions) reported this conversation with Fr. Craft (who visited the dancers).

[36] Cf. Omar Stewart, *The Peyote Religion* (Norman: University of Oklahoma Press, 1987). See also Paul Steinmetz, *Pipe, Bible, and Peyote Among the Oglala Lakota* (Knoxville: University of Tennessee Press, 1990). Steinmetz discusses a group that calls itself the "Body of Christ," a Christian Pentecostal "denomination" among the Oglala not treated in this paper, but which is another example of the people's peculiar appropriation of Christianity.

[37] Christian snake-handlers within the Holy Ghost churches of Appalachia might perhaps be just as non-mainstream as Ghost Dancers were and Peyotists are. Even though some might consider these to be aberrant forms, they are still Christian.

[38] Gordon MacGregor, p. 103. Shortly before he died, Black Elk reprimanded younger members of his parish church for not attending to their religious responsibilities. Cf. Steltenkamp, p. 121.

[39] Tim Giago, founder and editor of the widely circulated newspaper *Indian Country Today*, has won considerable recognition for his outspoken positions that often echo those set forth by Means. Like Means, he has been criticized for promoting a version of Indian history that sacrifices fact (e.g., a regular target of his editorials is the Christian missionary presence).

[40] The popular show alluded to here is "The Waltons," while the concept of reservation life casting appeal was stated outright in the recording "Ball of Confusion" sung by the Temptations ("the only safe place to live is on an Indian reservation").

Besides the programs named in these paragraphs, television continued to exploit this motif, and two examples are worth noting. "Northern Exposure" depicted a down-to-earth group of Alaskan villagers for whom organized religion was non-existent. They derived spiritual strength from Native people and ordinary folk whose simplistic utterances were offered by script writers as profound insights. A similar production is entitled "Dr. Quinn: Medicine Woman." This wholly secularized, nineteenth-century feminist physician and friend of frontiersmen has a "faith life" that relies only upon the successful balancing of parenthood with profession.

[41] In referring to the anti-Christian element within Native populations, I have been careful to qualify what I say by noting that "*some*" Indians think this way. A tribal council member from an Oklahoma group told me the following: "My grandmother was keeper of our sacred bundle, so when people talk about being traditional, no one comes from a more traditional background than I do. But too many white people think they have to apologize to Indians for introducing Jesus to us. That's not right at all. We're glad we're Christians!" Not a Lakota, this person echoed the same kind of sentiments I heard when interviewing Black Elk's aged acquaintances and daughter.

⁴² Any group's social or religious activity (not just Indian) is not isolated from the larger social context within which it exists, e.g., dwindling church attendance also has occurred in the dominant population, or wearing long hair in the 1960s was first a trend among non-Indians and later was found fashionable (revived) within the Native world. In recent times, the phenomenon of body-piercing and tattooing has moved from the fringe of acceptability to being a rather common fashion statement (jewelry is poked through ears, noses, lips, navels, genitals, etc.). Curiously, the Sun Dance ceremony of Plains cultures has experienced a parallel resurgence. Its most notable feature is that participants have their bodies pierced (chests, arms, backs, etc.)—all within a solemn religious context (the scarification, tattoo-like, then proudly worn). Indian thought and activity certainly have their unique identity, but gain further approbation from forces outside the Native world.

⁴³ Cf. Michael F. Steltenkamp, *The Sacred Vision: Native American Religion and Its Practice Today* (Mahwah, N.J.: Paulist Press, 1982), pp. 38-46. The sweatlodge ritual is today a widely practiced religious ceremony that bears a superficial resemblance to a sauna experience. The ritual is conducted in different ways by different individuals and groups.

⁴⁴ Acting on the premise that groups need to identify culturally with the message being taught, Catholicism has struggled for some years to "*in*culturate" its theology and practice within Native America. The debatable presumption here is that liturgical forms of the Roman rite have been culturally relevant to the non-Indian Americans who catechize reservation communities, but not to Indians themselves. Hence the challenge is to find what ritual forms will be effective within Native contexts (some suggest a kind of Native American rite should be created). Because Roman doctrine and ritual have not been persuasive for many non-Indians (who have experimented with, or joined, alternative religions), inculturation appears not to be wholly the issue or solely an Indian concern. After all, in what way can the Mass or other sacraments ever be identified as culturally American? Given liturgical inculturation may flourish at some local levels, but perhaps never reach the point of institutionalization.

⁴⁵ *Kirkus Review*, June, 1993.

⁴⁶ Means, p. 543.

⁴⁷ Steltenkamp, *Holy Man*, p. 109. A good understanding of Black Elk's Lakota-Catholic religious perspective can be found in William L. Portier, "Dialogue Between Gospel and Culture: Historical Perspectives," *Current Issues in Catholic Higher Education* 16 (Winter 1996): 73-90.

⁴⁸ Despite always having an unpleasant word for anything associated with Christianity, Means does credit a Catholic nun, Sr. Adelaide, for steering him into a treatment center where he could address his longstanding problem with anger. Cf. Means, p. 524. A bookstore manager informed me that when Means appeared for a book signing: "He stood like a giant, even though he wasn't that tall. And he's so charismatic that it seemed traffic just stopped to let him cross the street."

⁴⁹ Cf. Anthony F. C. Wallace, *The Death and Rebirth of the Seneca* (New York: Knopf, 1969).

Notes on Catholic Americanism and Catholic Radicalism: Toward a Counter-Tradition of Catholic Social Ethics

Michael J. Baxter

For the past thirty years or so in the United States, Catholics working in the field of social ethics have been positioning themselves within what can be called a "Catholic Americanist tradition." The central assertion of this Americanist tradition is that there exists a fundamental harmony between Catholicism and the political arrangement of the United States of America.[1] This assertion has been advanced by both neo-liberals and neo-conservatives alike.[2] Indeed, it has been espoused by such a broad spectrum of theorists that it has become difficult to imagine an alternative to this Americanist tradition. The purpose of this paper is to bring into greater relief such an alternative tradition in Catholic social ethics, what I call the "Catholic radicalist tradition."[3]

This Catholic radicalist tradition is often presented as less than a *bona fide* intellectual tradition, as a loose set of provocative ideas put forth by Dorothy Day, Peter Maurin, and their associates in the Catholic Worker Movement. The proponents of Catholic radicalism have never really made their mark in the world of Catholic scholarship in the United States nor have they ever really tried. For the most part, their efforts have simply been directed elsewhere. Nevertheless, the Catholic radicalism articulated by Day, Maurin, and others represents a distinct and viable alternative tradition in the field of Catholic social ethics, one that is at least as compelling as the predominant Americanist tradition. The difference between the two traditions turns on different understandings of the nature of the *polis* in social ethics. Briefly put, in the Americanist tradition, the *polis* is identified with the modern state, in particular with the United States of America, and as a result, the state is seen as the primary mechanism for the implementation of justice. In the radicalist tradition, by contrast, the *polis* is identified with Christ and the church, and with smaller, practice-based communities whose forms of life are closely patterned after the body of Christ and the church.

This paper draws the contrast by focusing on these two traditions as they emerged in the 1920s and 1930s. The argument comes in three parts. The first part presents the dominant Americanist tradition in Catholic social ethics in the United States by describing several discursive features pertaining to the relationship between theology and philosophy, and how that relationship bore on Catholic political and economic theory. The second part describes the Catholic radicalist tradition in terms of these same discursive features, showing how it uses many of the same terms and categories as the Americanist tradition but construes them in a non-statist fashion, so that this radicalist tradition functions as a counter-tradition. In the third part, I suggest why this radicalist counter-tradition, which emerged during roughly the same period as this Americanist tradition, has not yet found a place in the discourse of Catholic social ethics, and why it is now so important for us to begin retrieving it and bringing it into greater relief. Though only a sketch of two traditions in Catholic social ethics as they developed in a particular period, this paper points to the complexity of Catholic social ethics in the United States, which consists of at least two (no doubt more) interrelated but distinct traditions.

The Americanist Tradition

The central assertion of the Americanist tradition—that there exists a fundamental harmony between Catholicism and political and economic order in the United States of America—was predicated on a division in the early twentieth century of Catholic scholarly discourse into three general areas of inquiry: (1) theology, (2) philosophy, and (3) all other disciplines in the natural sciences, social sciences, and humanities, including politics and economics. In this tripartite division, theology was effectively removed from the mainstream of academic inquiry, with the result that the disciplines of politics and economics were not shaped by substantive theological terms and categories. At best, theology entered these other disciplines only after passing through the discourse of philosophy, where all explicit references to the beliefs and practices of the church were translated into the much more general tenets of natural theology. This division, between theology on the one hand, and politics and economics on the other hand, enabled Catholics to posit a harmony between Catholicism and the United States. To understand how and why this was so, it is necessary to understand this separation between theology and philosophy.

Theology and Philosophy

The separation of theology and philosophy in Catholic scholarly discourse in the first half of the twentieth century was the product of both a theoretical paradigm and a set of institutional arrangements with a long history. In the spirit of Vico's adage that "the order of ideas must follow the order of institutions,"[4] this historical sketch begins with the institutional arrangements.

The institutional separation of theology and philosophy can be traced back to the *Ratio Studiorum* (1599), the Jesuit plan of studies that became the norm for all Jesuit schools in Europe and the Americas. A key feature of the *Ratio* was its three-tier structure: humanistic studies first, then philosophy, then theology. Taken as a whole, it was a highly integrated curriculum, but more often than not, students completed the first and second phases of study, humanities and philosophy, and then went elsewhere to pursue secular professional degrees and careers. The final phase, theology, thus came to function as an addendum to the curriculum, a course of study only for seminarians.[5] Due to the Jesuits' extensive influence in Catholic education, the separation between philosophy and theology became the norm for Catholic schools in North America, virtually all of which were founded by religious orders. Indeed, the separation became more pronounced because so many seminaries were set up as free-standing institutions. There were exceptions, of course, but the general pattern throughout the nineteenth and into the twentieth century was that Catholic colleges and seminaries in the United States developed into separate institutions.[6] Accordingly, the standard curriculum of Catholic colleges and universities in the first half of the twentieth century was centered around the study of philosophy, designed to provide students with a comprehensive, integrated intellectual vision and to place into proper perspective the other branches of study—the arts, the sciences, and the newly emerging social sciences. Theology had no place in this curriculum. It was taught in the seminaries, as part of a specialized course of study for future clerics.

Corresponding to and reinforcing this institutional division of labor between the Catholic colleges and seminaries was a theoretical paradigm that posited a sharp distinction between reason and revelation. This standard distinction of medieval theology became so exaggerated during the Enlightenment that philosophy came to function independently of theology, as an autonomous discourse based on reason alone. Attempting to hold the rationalistic character of philosophy in check, Vatican I (1870) described faith and reason as two mutually supporting avenues to truth.[7] Likewise, it was in order to promote a more integrated relation between revelation and reason that Leo XIII called for a return to the Christian philosophy of Thomas Aquinas. Both attempts failed, at least initially, because most early proponents of the Thomist revival, like their modernist rivals, worked out of post-Cartesian, post-Kantian epistemologies grounded in a reason uninformed by revelation.[8] As a result, despite attempts to integrate the two, theology and philosophy continued to function as separate discourses pertaining to separate spheres of knowledge: theology, as a discourse relegated to the domain of the seminary; philosophy, as the central academic discourse ordered all other branches of knowledge.[9]

The institutional arrangement and theoretical paradigm were in place in the early decades of the twentieth century and had enormous impact on the emergence and development of the Americanist tradition in Catholic social ethics. Precisely during this period, Catholic colleges and universities were themselves being transformed from little more than residential secondary schools into institutions of higher education in the modern sense. Departments were formed. Graduate programs were started. Professional societies were established. Academic standards were enforced. The vast reorganization of their curricula accommodated the newly emergent modes of academic knowledge, including the "disciplines" of political theory and economics. In this context, the arduous task of integrating these new disciplines into the traditional Catholic intellectual vision was given to philosophy, a philosophy, as we have seen, that was both institutionally and theoretically separated from theology. Granted, Neoscholastic philosophy was grounded in a number of tenets that were theological in nature, concerning the existence and nature of God, the human person, the soul, natural law, and so on; but this was "natural theology," a theology available to everyone on the basis of reason alone, and it did not address more substantive matters concerning the Trinity, the person and work of Christ, the sacraments, or mystical theology. The upshot was this: political and economic theory came to function as philosophical—not theological—modes of discourse.

Political Theory

Casting political theory in philosophical rather than theological terms had a definite advantage. After all, the United States is a religiously pluralistic nation, and its political discourse must be tailored accordingly. Only a political theory stripped of substantive theological content could gain currency in the discourse of the nation at large. The political theory of the Catholic Americanist tradition readily conformed to this protocol by positing a fixed plane of "nature" upon which political ideas and principles could be ascertained without reference to the beliefs and practices of the church.

The central philosophical claim here was that reality discloses a divine plan in the form of natural law. Because this natural law is also imprinted on the human mind, it is capable of grasping the law through direct intuition combined with the exercise of discursive reason. Natural law, therefore, beginning with the fundamental prescription to do good and avoid evil, provides a basis for deriving a series of particular determinations concerning the duties devolving upon people concerning marriage, family, property, work, leisure, worship, and so on.[10] This has special relevance for Catholic political theory because society should be organized in such a way that people are able to fulfill these duties, and the institution assigned the task of ensuring that this is the case is the state.

In traditional Catholic political theory, the state is a natural institution in several related senses. First, the state is the result of a natural human inclination toward political association.[11] Second, its structure and activity are ordered to the good as disclosed in natural law.[12] Third, its ends pertain to the natural as opposed to the supernatural realm of human life, that is to say, its ends are temporal rather than spiritual. But, because the temporal ends of the state are inextricably intermingled with the spiritual ends of the church, and because these spiritual ends have primacy over temporal ends, the state relies on and at times must defer to the pastoral guidance of the church. Politics cannot be theorized without reference to the life of the church and the workings of grace. This is why, even in the face of post-Reformation religious pluralism, official Catholic doctrine on church-state relations, as articulated in *Immortale dei* (1885), steadfastly held that the normative form of government is one in which Catholicism is the official religion of the state and that anything less is acceptable only as a compromise for the sake of public peace.

This traditional understanding of the state was appropriated by Catholic political theorists working in the Americanist tradition, with one crucial difference: the Americanist political theorists argued, in subtle and not so subtle ways, that the primary function of the state was to ensure religious freedom and that beyond this, the state was incompetent in matters of religion and must remain neutral. Critics of this Americanist position maintained that this shift of the state's protection of religion from a positive to a purely negative function would weaken the religious and moral strength of society. The Americanists countered that limiting the competence of the state to temporal affairs, as in the U.S. Constitution, would actually enable the church, as the true religion, to flourish in the spiritual order, and at the same time, allow the members of the church, as citizens, to disseminate their natural law morality throughout the temporal order without interference. The theoretical separation between natural law and the supernatural life of the church made this argument possible.

This theoretical separation gave rise to a host of dichotomies in Americanist discourse between the spiritual and the temporal, religion and morality, the sacred and the secular, and so on. These dichotomies enabled Catholic political theorists, on the one hand, to ground the authority of the state in God's will, as mediated through natural law, and yet, on the other hand, to avoid tying the activity of the state to any particular ecclesial body. The result was a peculiarly Americanist political vision, one that was grounded in an autonomous, reason-based "nature" and undergirded by an unspecified "God." It could hardly have been otherwise. After all, the only politics possible in a religiously pluralistic nation such as the United States would be a politics that appealed to everyone, a politics based on reason alone. In this sense, the rationalistic version of Neoscholastic philosophy, the dominant discourse of Catholic scholarship during the first half of the twentieth century, perfectly fit the agenda of the Americanist tradition. It also developed into a tradition that departed from official Catholic teaching on church-state relations. Indeed, Americanist political theorists simply dismissed the official teaching in one of two ways. One way was to affirm the doctrine as valid and logically compelling in theory, but then to declare it irrelevant to circumstances in the United States where the majority of citizens are not Catholic. This was the strategy undertaken by John Ryan in his widely circulated commentary on *Immortale dei*. The other way was simply to ignore it. Moorhouse F. X. Millar, S.J., co-author with Ryan of the leading textbook on church and state and an editor of *Thought*, used this strategy in scores of articles. Although he argued that the most sound theoretical basis for U.S. democracy is to be found in medieval Catholic political theory, never once (to my knowledge) did he seriously address the conflict between the First Amendment and official Catholic teaching on church and state.[13] Both ways were predicated on a "nature" decipherable by means of reason alone, which generated a peculiarly modern political discourse; politics was confined to a sphere free of substantive claims about revelation and the supernatural life of the church.

Economic Theory

This same Neoscholastic "nature"—autonomous, based on reason alone—shaped Americanist economic theory as it developed in the early twentieth century. In the traditional Catholic view, natural law calls for the use of the goods of creation in accord with the requirements of justice. Property may be held privately, but its use should be determined by the common good, even to the point that, as Aquinas argues, if one confiscates another's goods out of dire need, it should not be regarded as theft.[14] This vision of the goods of creation being used for the common good was articulated by Leo XIII in *Rerum novarum* (1891), with special attention to the problems of modern industrial production, as regards owners and workers, the just wage, time off for recreation and religious celebration, and so on. The vision was updated and re-stated by Pius XI in *Quadragesimo anno* (1931). In both encyclicals, the economic vision was embedded within a broader, overarching theological vision of humanity's supernatural end and the church's role in bringing humanity to that end. Thus, in *Rerum novarum*, Leo writes that the only way society can be cured of its ills is "by a return to Christian life and Christian institutions."[15] In *Quadragesimo anno*, Pius claims that "there can be no other remedy [for society's problems] than a frank and sincere return to the teaching of the Gospel," a teaching "which places God as the first and supreme end of all created activity, and regards all created goods as mere instruments under God, to be used only in so far as they help toward the attainment of our supreme end."[16]

This overarching theological vision is important in grasping the significance of the Americanist tradition. These Catholic economic theorists understood their task as extracting from this theological vision principles to be applied directly to legislative policy-making at state and federal levels. The most well-known of these theorists, John A. Ryan, used *Rerum novarum* as a basis for the Bishops' Program of 1919, a twelve-point policy-making program calling for, among other things, a national employment service, minimum wage, social insurance, and child labor laws.[17] Similarly, Ryan used *Quadragesimo anno* as a basis of support for the 1930s New Deal legislation.[18] His economic theory emphasized that the modern state should intervene in the economic sphere to mitigate the harsh realities of industrial capitalism. This state-centered, policy-making agenda compelled Ryan to ground his economic theory in natural law, based on reason alone. Thus, unlike the vision put forth by Leo XIII and Pius XI, Ryan's economic theory contained little reference to humanity's supernatural end or the role of the church in bringing humanity to that end.[19]

Generally speaking, Americanist economic theory, much in the same way as Americanist political theory, was shaped by a discourse stripped of substantive theological content. It had the same advantage, namely, currency in national discourse. In this sense, the Americanist tradition of Catholic social ethics was tailored to the exigencies of a religiously pluralistic society, and as such was conformed to the protocols of a modern liberal state, which preclude substantive grounding in the beliefs and practices of any specific ecclesial body. The discourse's theological content was limited to natural theology and thus remained on the level of vague generalities having to do with "religious values" and the "moral foundations of Christian civilization," which were assumed to be consonant with the aims and purposes of political and economic order in the United States. This Americanist tradition of political and economic theory, only briefly described, constitutes a dominant but not the only discourse within Catholic social ethics in the United States. The following section presents a significant counter-tradition, that of the Catholic radicalists.

The Catholic Radicalist Tradition

The Americanist tradition in Catholic social ethics is predicated on an institutional and theoretical separation between theology and philosophy, which inhibits any serious infusion of terms and categories into political and economic theory. The Catholic radicalist tradition, by contrast, promotes interaction between theology and politics and economics based on its claim that philosophical reason becomes too easily distorted when it is not elevated and corrected by the truths of revelation. This more theologically charged vision of politics and economics delivers a general critique of the modern state, and a particular one concerning the political and economic order prevalent in the United States. The nature of this critique can be grasped only in light of Catholic radicalism's alternative understanding of the relationship between theology and philosophy.

Theology and Philosophy

While the preponderance of Neoscholastics working in the decades after World War I accepted the separation between theology and philosophy, there was dissent. It came from an authoritative source, Etienne Gilson, a foremost medieval scholar of his day. Gilson took issue with those Thomists who held that appeals to revelation are foreign to genuine philosophical reflection. Against the Thomists working in a post-Cartesian epistemological paradigm, Gilson argued that Aquinas did not carry on philosophical speculation independent of theology. Rather, working as he did out of an Augustinian-Thomism, his philosophy was embedded in his theology and thus can rightly be called a "Christian philosophy." A true philosophy, he held, cannot be achieved without revelation acting as a support to reason.[20]

This refusal to grant full autonomy to the discourse of philosophy represents an early manifestation of the mid-twentieth-century revolt in Catholic theology against Neoscholasticism's two-tiered construal of nature and grace. Led in Europe by such theologians as de Lubac, Rahner, and von Balthasar, this movement rejected the concept of "pure nature" and focused instead on humanity in its concrete, historical condition, and thus recognized all persons and events as always already worked upon by divine grace.[21] The life of Christ and the church decisively shape the philosophical, rational, and natural within this intellectual vision.

Quite remarkably, this more integrated understanding of the relationship between theology and philosophy was put forth in the 1920s and 1930s by two of the most significant (though largely overlooked) representatives of the Catholic radicalist tradition in the United States. The first, Virgil Michel, a Benedictine from Collegeville, founded the liturgical movement in this country. Michel espoused an understanding of philosophy that was deeply shaped by liturgy and the sacramental life of the church. He states, for example, that "the liturgy is the traditional embodiment of the Christian philosophy of life."[22] He also argues against the theoretical habit of separating life into "the religious" and "the profane," as if the two were mutually independent. Such a separation, he notes, "has no foundation in fact." The phrase "in fact" emphasizes the historical, existential circumstances of the baptized Christian. Thus, Michel continues, "A baptized member of Christ is not a dual personality, one natural and the other supernatural; rather his human nature is supernaturalized, so that whatever he does . . . he must do all in Christ Jesus. Since, therefore, man's whole BEING is Christianized, all his actions should be Christ-like. Being governs operation."[23] As Michel sees it, then, only as we encounter and are transformed by Christ do we come to grasp and realize our true nature.

The second Catholic radicalist theorist, Paul Hanley Furfey, taught sociology at Catholic University from the mid 1920s into the 1960s. Furfey's social theory can only be described as resolutely theological, grounded in a trinitarian understanding of charity as "participation in the immanent life of God" and in the doctrine of "the mystical body of Christ." He called his social theory, "supernatural sociology."[24] Without being ordered to the supernatural, he insists, a natural law morality quickly degenerates into a minimalism that promotes conformity to the status quo. A supernatural morality, on the other hand, nourished by the life of the church, calls on Catholics to live heroic lives patterned after the example of Christ and the saints.

Dorothy Day, though less formal in her presentation, provides a similarly integrated understanding of the supernatural and the natural. These views can be found in the chapter, "Retreat," from her autobiography, *The Long Loneliness.* The theological reflections on the supernatural's relation to the natural come in her recollections of two priests, spiritual guides to Dorothy Day and other Catholic Workers. Roy Pacifique, a Josephite priest, upon visiting the House in New York, began talking about the love of God and apparently never stopped. "Father Roy talked to us of nature and the supernatural," Day recalls, with the accent on the supernatural, "supernaturalizing all our actions of every day."[25] This meant dying to the self through self-mortification, patterning one's life after the life of Christ, and trusting in God's providence in things large and small. The other priest, John J.

Hugo of Pittsburgh, who directed "the Retreat," also emphasized, as Day puts it, that "we have been raised to a supernatural level"; "we have been raised above ourselves by baptism, and the law of the supernatural life is love, a love which demands renunciation."[26] At one point in this chapter, Day writes that "in mortifying the natural, we must not injure the body or the soul. We are not to destroy but to transform it, as iron is transformed in the fire."[27] This cautionary note reflects the criticisms being leveled at the time against Roy and Hugo. Their supernaturalist perspective, like de Lubac's, was thought to denigrate nature, but in fact, within their perspective, nature has its own integrity and yet must be transformed. Day, in the chapter, "Retreat," shows a theological instinct that is fundamentally consonant with the leading emphases of the *nouvelle théologie*.

Political Theory

The Catholic radicalists' more integrated theology, along the lines of the *nouvelle théologie*, may seem to veer ominously toward "integrism." Following John Milbank's explanation, integrism refers to a viewpoint that insists "upon a clerical and hierarchic dominance over all the affairs of secular life, founded upon a 'totalizing' theology which presents a complete system. . . ."[28] In the realm of theory, integrism has been associated with the monarchist or restorationist thought of de Bonald and de Maistre;[29] in the realm of practice, with *L'Action Française* and Catholic corporatist movements in Europe and Latin America, which often exhibit fascist sympathies. The challenge for radicalist political theory is to show that an integral theology does not necessarily underwrite an integrist politics. The Catholic radicalist tradition accomplishes this by denying the crucial assumption of all integrist theory, the assumption that the primary political mechanism for the implementation of justice is the state.

With this denial comes crucial and insistent differentiation between the Aristotelian/Thomistic *polis* and the modern nation-state. In the Aristotelian/Thomistic *polis*, various activities—work, education, health care, leisure—are integrated into the overall life of the *polis* in such a way that it has a genuinely common life. In such a small-scale setting, government is capable of embodying the common good.[30] An attempt to recapture the small-scale character of the ancient *polis* can be seen in the Catholic Worker's espousal of a "localist politics."[31] Moreover, the localist politics of Catholic radicalism goes beyond houses of hospitality to encompass neighborhoods, villages, and provinces, any number of associations in which people relate to each other in a personal, dignified, face-to-face manner.[32] In the parlance of the Catholic Worker movement, this understanding of politics came to be known as "Christian anarchism," which constitutes, as Robert Ludlow explains, an advocacy of certain kinds of government, de-centralized, self-governing, participatory modes of government, and not, as many critics wrongly assumed, an opposition to government *per se*.[33] On the other hand, Christian anarchism does stand in basic opposition to that specific form of government embodied in the modern, bureaucratic state, and on this score, it departs sharply from the Americanist tradition.

The crucial difference centers on the characterization in Americanist political theory of the state as a "natural institution." Political theory in the Catholic radicalist tradition sees the nation-state—with its bureaucratic structures, defense of borders through military force, systems of surveillance, propagation of nationalist allegiance, and so on— as profoundly unnatural. In part, this perspective is derived from the Marxist claim that the nation-state is not and can never be an embodiment of the common good.[34] Indeed, from a Marxist perspective, the claim that the state is "natural" is a classic example of ideology, whereby a particular political and economic arrangement that benefits certain classes is given the status of natural, universal, eternal.[35] But in the Catholic radicalist tradition, the claim that the state is not "natural" stands on the basis of a christologically-shaped understanding of "nature," which comes into full view and takes proper form only in light of the supernatural.

Accordingly, Catholic radicalism's christologically shaped politics calls for selective engagement with the modern state. Some practices sponsored by the nation-state are unproblematic, such as obeying traffic laws, putting out the garbage, and using the postal service. Others are a matter of judgment, voting in elections, for example, or supporting certain political action groups. And others are to be resisted, such as paying federal taxes for war or abortion, and refusing conscription. In general, Catholic radicalism is much more careful and deliberate regarding the extent to which one cooperates with the state. At times, it engages in what Furfey called "the technique of non-participation."[36] This discernment requires regular, casuistic judgments about the kind of political activity in which one is involved. These judgments are made in light of the supernatural life, the only reliable guide to a full understanding of the good. The church, as the site of supernatural life and therefore of such discernment, serves as constitutive to the life of a genuine *polis*.

Economic Theory

As with political theory, economic theory in the Catholic radicalist tradition flows from a supernatural perspective, which gives shape to "natural" economic activity. Virgil Michel argued that the supernatural life of the Church provides the model for all natural, economic activity. In the Church, he claimed, through the *communio in sanctis*, the "intercommunication of holy things," each and every member has a share in the supernatural life of Christ.[37] Thus "we can speak of the common possession of supernatural goods by the fellowship of the members of Christ . . . we can say of the common treasury of merits of Christ and the saints, that what belongs to all belongs to each and what belongs to each belongs to all."[38] This all-for-one-and-one-for-all character of the Church's supernatural life is what shapes its natural life as well.

Concretely, the parish, at the center of which is the liturgy, becomes a center of genuine economic activity: the care of the needy and the poor, the practice of hospitality, the spiritual and corporal works of mercy, all of which are material manifestations of the economy of salvation.[39] Michel identified a host of other movements as embodiments of the supernatural life. The *Central-Verein*, a movement of German Catholics, delivered a sharp critique of modern industrialism and the welfare state and proffered instead a program of reform based on an organic social vision.[40] In the Antigonish movement, a cooperative in Nova Scotia, people banded together to solve their economic problems through study, adult education, and communal discussion, all under lay leadership and some clerical direction.[41] The National Catholic Rural Life Movement, a loose confederation of agrarian projects run by Catholics in the Midwest and West, resisted the economic trends toward industrialization and centralization and cultivated a life of faith in a farm setting.[42] Each of these movements represents an attempt to order economic production and consumption to the common good.

This economic ordering entails, in general, production geared to meet local needs. Markets, therefore, serve as a means of exchange for what is surplus to local needs, a means in which all who participate benefit. The people involved in production are given an opportunity to own the means of production, and also greater freedom in determining the shape of their labor and ownership, rather than having them shaped by the exigencies of large-scale, international markets.[43] The English distributists, G. K. Chesterton, Eric Gill, and Vincent McNabb, O.P., envisioned this kind of economics. All three receive honorable mention in *The Long Loneliness*.[44] Distributism's vision of a society of small productive units was not simply medieval nostalgia or a Luddite attempt to do away with machinery, as critics often charged. It was a call to transform modern industry for the sake of human flourishing.[45] People involved in industry would be marked by justice rather than its opposite, *pleonexia*, the desire to acquire more; and, in turn, would require theological virtues of faith, hope, and love. Only in light of the supernatural is the establishment of economic settings possible in which primacy is given not to profitability but to genuine human flourishing.

Given its emphasis on the supernatural life, combined with its emphasis on local, small-scale community, Catholic radicalism does not put forth a state-centered model of economic theory. Rather, the focus is on the life of the church. In this sense, just as in radicalist political theory the church serves as the *polis*, so too in radicalist economic theory it serves as the *oikos*, as a household wherein patterns of production and consumption are patterned after the economy of salvation.

Toward a Counter-Tradition

This far too brief discussion sketches out two traditions in Catholic social ethics in the United States, both Catholic, both drawing on traditional Catholic terms and categories, but each forming quite different construals of political and economic activity. One of these has obviously predominated in the world of Catholic scholarship in the United States: the Americanist tradition. It is not because it is so obviously more compelling, but for reasons already outlined. The Americanist tradition in Catholic social ethics emerged when United States Catholic scholarship was itself emerging and taking the form that has come to be associated with higher education in this country, with academic departments, graduate programs, scholarly journals, and professional associations. Catholic colleges and universities were obliged to enter what James Burns, C.S.C., a leading Catholic educator at the time, called "the new intellectual order of the nation."[46] Catholics were compelled to be a part of this order or face their schools' collapse. Catholic students sought an education and professional training as a means to advance up the socio-economic ladder, and if Catholic graduate schools refused to serve them, they would go elsewhere. This pressure to conform to the new standards in education was decisive.[47] In their conforming, these institutions served to legitimate the state emerging in the twentieth century as the embodiment of the aspirations of "America." The aspiration of Catholics to enter "the new intellectual order of the nation" correlates with the kinds of knowledge produced by the dominant Americanist tradition of Catholic social ethics.

This knowledge identified the social as embodied first and foremost in the nation. This scheme, in turn, relegated substantive theology to an area that is by definition not political, not economic, not social. Politics and economics are by definition not theology, or even significantly informed by theology. A distinctively Catholic theology has no place on the map of higher education's intellectual order. To include a distinctively Catholic theology would run counter to the protocols of a religiously pluralistic society, which demands that all knowledge discourses, including political and economic theory, be grounded in the life of the state, not the church. United States Catholic scholars grounded social ethics in a Neoscholastic understanding of the *natural*—and not the supernatural—ends of humanity. Substantive theological terms and categories, the discourses of christology, ecclesiology, soteriology, eschatology, and so on, are in effect relegated to a separate discursive field. To trace the emergence and development of the Americanist tradition in Catholic social ethics requires tracing the ways in which the institutional structures and theoretical paradigms of Catholic higher education conceal the possibility of the radicalist tradition in Catholic social ethics as a genuine intellectual enterprise. These intellectual and theoretical paradigms help to explain why Catholic radicalism never found a home in the academy in the United States.

One could argue that the situation has changed since Vatican II. With the disintegration of the so-called Neoscholastic synthesis and the emergence of *bona fide* theology departments, the discipline of theology is coming into its own. But theologians themselves undertook to transform their discipline into an academic one in the secular, objective, non-confessional sense, a transformation to ensure that theological inquiry has its place in the modern academy. The result has been a repeating, in post-conciliar fashion, of the pre-conciliar separation of theology from the other disciplines. The difference is that substantive theological terms and categories are no longer filtered through the discourse of philosophy where they become natural theology. After all, there has been no replacement of Neoscholastic philosophy. Rather, they are filtered through the discourse of Catholic social ethics, so that now, in this post-conciliar era, substantive theological terms and categories must conform to the agenda of what is usually called a "public" or (as I prefer to call it) "civil theology." It is in this context that the radicalist tradition in Catholic social ethics is judged, from a position within the Americanist tradition, to be too tightly linked to the beliefs and practices of a specific ecclesial body and thus in need of translation. In this way, theology continues to be sealed off from political and economic theory.

To change this situation, people working out of the radicalist tradition must historicize what appears to be the only normative Catholic social ethics appropriate for the United States' situation. This task is a necessary first step in presenting a genuine counter-tradition of Catholic social ethics. The counter-tradition can provide a political and economic theory that will assist the church in surviving the insidious and destructive pressures of contemporary capitalism and the modern state through the constructing and sustaining of practice-based forms of local participatory communities. In the early days of the Catholic Worker, Peter Maurin used to follow Dorothy Day around the apartment bombarding her with quotations from an incredibly eclectic collection of authors. One of those quotations was from Lenin: "There can be no revolution without a theory of a revolution."[48] As in the 1930s, it remains a necessity to generate "a theory of a revolution," a radicalist counter-tradition in Catholic social ethics.

Notes

[1] By way of clarification, I am not defining "Americanism" here in terms of the specific principles that were condemned by Leo XIII in *Testem benevolentiae* (1899). It can be argued, I believe, that over the course of the past century these two forms of Americanism have become intimately linked, inasmuch as Catholicism's embrace of U.S. political theory has led to a dissipation of Catholic theological discourse in ways that were adverted to by Leo XIII. But that argument is not being advanced here.

[2] Thus, the description "Americanist" pertains to the following variety of authors and books: John A. Coleman, *An American Strategic Theology* (New York:

Paulist, 1982); Charles Curran, *American Catholic Social Ethics* (Notre Dame: University of Notre Dame Press, 1982); Michael J. Himes and Kenneth R. Himes, O.F.M., *Fullness of Faith: The Public Significance of Theology* (New York: Paulist, 1993); David Hollenbach, *Justice, Peace, and Human Rights: American Catholic Social Ethics in a Pluralistic Context* (New York: Crossroad, 1988); Dennis P. McCann, *New Experiment in Democracy: The Challenge for American Catholicism* (Kansas City: Sheed & Ward, 1987); Richard John Neuhaus, *The Catholic Moment* (San Francisco: Harper & Row, 1987); George Weigel, *Tranquillitas ordinis* (New York: Oxford University Press, 1987), and *Catholicism and the Renewal of American Democracy* (New York: Paulist, 1989). It is important to note that the labels "neo-liberal" and "neo-conservative" are misleading in that they tend to distract attention away from the Americanist assumptions shared by both groups.

³ Elsewhere I have called this tradition "Evangelical Catholic," taking a cue from the typology laid out in David J. O'Brien's *Public Catholicism* (New York: Macmillan, 1989; reprint, Orbis Books, 1996). See Michael J. Baxter, C.S.C., "Writing History in a World Without Ends: An Evangelical Catholic Critique of Three Histories of Catholicism in the United States," *Pro Ecclesia* (Fall, 1996). But this label causes confusion for some readers because for them it implies an alliance with Christian neoconservativism or the so-called "Christian right." As will be clear by the end of this essay, the perspective I am advancing is far from anything that can be fairly characterized with these labels, so it seems best simply to avoid the word "evangelical" altogether. I use the word "radicalist" instead of "radical" in the hope of avoiding any self-serving, more-radical-than-thou overtones to my argument.

⁴ Giambattista Vico, *The New Science of Giambattista Vico*, 3rd ed., trans. Thomas Goddard Bergin and Max Harold Fisch (Ithaca: Cornell University Press, 1984), p. 78.

⁵ For a description of the *Ratio*, see John W. Donohue, S.J., *Jesuit Education: An Essay on the Foundations of Its Idea* (New York: Fordham University Press, 1963), pp. 32-62; and Philip Gleason, "American Higher Education: A Historical Perspective," in *The Shape of Catholic Higher Education*, ed. Robert Hassenger (Chicago: University of Chicago Press, 1967), pp. 15-33.

⁶ For a history of the development of seminaries in the United States, see Joseph M. White, *The Diocesan Seminary in the United States: A History from the 1780s to the Present* (Notre Dame: University of Notre Dame Press, 1989); and Christopher J. Kauffman, *Tradition and Transformation in Catholic Culture* (New York: Macmillan, 1988).

⁷ For an account of the concept of nature in the Decrees of Vatican I, see Hans Urs von Balthasar, *The Theology of Karl Barth*, trans. Edward T. Oakes, S.J. (San Francisco: Ignatius Press, 1992), pp. 302-325.

⁸ Alasdair MacIntyre, *Three Rival Versions of Moral Enquiry* (Notre Dame: University of Notre Dame Press, 1990), pp. 68-81.

⁹ For a general account of the impact of the Neoscholastic revival on Catholic higher education in the United States, see Philip Gleason, *Contending With Modernity: Catholic Higher Education in the Twentieth Century* (New York:

Oxford University Press, 1995), pp. 105-167. For the preeminence of philosophy in the standard curriculum, see especially pp. 136-142; for the marginal place of theology, see pp. 142-145.

[10] An excellent general description of Neoscholasticism can be found in Gleason, *Contending with Modernity*, pp. 114-123, from which the wording of my description is taken.

[11] Aristotle, *Politica*, I, 2, in *The Basic Works of Aristotle*, ed. and with an introduction by Richard McKeon (New York: Random House, 1941), p. 1114. Thomas Aquinas, On Kingship, 1, in *St. Thomas Aquinas on Politics and Ethics*, trans. and ed. Paul E. Sigmund (New York: Norton, 1988), pp. 14-15; ST I, 96, 4, in *Summa Theologiae*, Vol. 1 (New York: Benziger, 1947), pp. 488-89.

[12] Aristotle, *Politica*, I, 1 (*Basic Works*, p. 1127). Aquinas, *ST* I/II 92, 1 (*Summa Theologiae*, Vol. 1, pp. 1001-1002); *ST* 94, 2 (*Summa Theologiae*, Vol. 1, pp. 1009-1010).

[13] For a more extensive review of the work of Ryan and Millar, see Michael J. Baxter, C.S.C., "In Service to the Nation: A Critical Analysis of the Formation of the Americanist Tradition in Catholic Social Ethics," (Duke University: Unpublished dissertation, 1996), chapter four.

[14] Aristotle, *Politica*, II, 5 (*Basic Works*, pp. 1150-1151). Aquinas, *ST* II/II 66, 7 (*Summa Theologiae*, Vol. 2, pp. 1480-1481).

[15] *Rerum novarum*, n. 22.

[16] *Quadragesimo anno*, n. 136.

[17] "Bishops' Program of Social Reconstruction," in *Documents of American Catholic History*, ed. John Tracy Ellis (Milwaukee: Bruce Publishing Company, 1962), pp. 585-603. For an account of Ryan's work with the National Catholic War Council and the National Catholic Welfare Council (later renamed the Welfare Conference), see Joseph M. McShane, S.J., *"Sufficiently Radical": Catholicism, Progressivism, and the Bishops' Program of 1919* (Washington, D.C.: Catholic University Press, 1986).

[18] David J. O'Brien, *Public Catholicism*, pp. 169-177.

[19] The lack of theological content in Ryan's thought is noted by Charles Curran, *American Catholic Social Ethics* (Notre Dame: University of Notre Dame Press, 1982), pp. 85-86.

[20] Etienne Gilson, *Christianity and Philosophy* (New York: Sheed and Ward, 1939), pp. 82-102. For a summary of Gilson's position, see Ralph McInerny, *The Question of Christian Ethics* (Washington, D.C.: Catholic University Press, 1993), pp. 7-16.

[21] The phrasing here is from John Milbank, *Theology and Social Theory: Beyond Secular Reason* (Cambridge, Massachusetts: Blackwell, 1991), p. 206. My indebtedness to Milbank will be apparent by the end of this paper.

[22] Quoted in Paul B. Marx, O.S.B., *Virgil Michel and the Liturgical Movement* (Collegeville: Liturgical Press, 1957), p. 12.

[23] Ibid., p. 196.

[24] Paul Hanley Furfey, *Fire on the Earth* (New York: Macmillan, 1936), pp. 32, 51, 1-21 (passim).

[25] Dorothy Day, *The Long Loneliness* (New York: Harper and Row, 1963), pp. 246, 247.

[26] Ibid., p. 257.

[27] Ibid., pp. 256, 257.

[28] Milbank, *Theology and Social Theory*, p. 206.

[29] Ibid., pp. 54-61, 66-69.

[30] Thomas Pearson, "Kinesis Interview with Professor Alasdair MacIntyre," *Kinesis: Graduate Journal in Philosophy* 20, 3 (1994): 36.

[31] Robert Coles, *Dorothy Day: A Radical Devotion* (Reading, Massachusetts: Addison-Wesley, 1987), p. 107.

[32] Coles, *Dorothy Day*, p. 107.

[33] In Day, *Long Loneliness*, p. 268.

[34] Pearson, "Interview with MacIntyre," p. 36.

[35] Karl Marx and Frederick Engels, *Collected Works* (New York: International Publishers, 1976), vol. 5, Marx and Engels: pp. 1845-1847, 1859-1860. Ideology is a complex and much disputed notion; for an excellent account of its many uses, see Terry Eagleton, *Ideology* (New York: Verso, 1991).

[36] Furfey, *Fire on the Earth*, pp. 117-136.

[37] Virgil Michel, "Natural and Supernatural Society: II. Spiritual Communion of Goods," *Orate Fratres* 10, 7 (May 16, 1936): 293-94.

[38] Ibid., p. 296.

[39] Virgil Michel, "The Parish, Cell of the Christian Life," in *The Mystical Body and Social Justice* (Collegeville, Minnesota: St. John's Abbey, 1938), pp. 20-23.

[40] Marx, *Virgil Michel*, pp. 368-369. For a history of the movement surrounding the *Central-Verein*, see Philip Gleason, *The Conservative Reformers* (Notre Dame: University of Notre Dame Press, 1968); for Virgil Michel's connection with this movement, see especially pp. 190-191.

[41] Marx, *Virgil Michel*, pp. 371-372. For an account of the Antigonish movement, see Leo R. Ward, C.S.C., *Nova Scotia* (New York: Sheed & Ward, 1942).

[42] Marx, *Virgil Michel*, pp. 372-373.

[43] Alasdair MacIntyre, *Marxism and Christianity*, 2nd edition (U.K.: Duckworth, 1995), pp. xi-x.

[44] Day, *Long Loneliness*, p. 56.

[45] For an account of distributism as presented by Chesterton and his associates, see Dermot Quinn, "The Historical Foundations of Modern Distributism," *The Chesterton Review* 21 (November 1995): 451-471.

[46] James Burns, C.S.C., "A Constructive Policy for Catholic Higher Education," *Catholic Educational Review* 18 (October 1920): 467. For a review of Burns' proposal of this policy, see Gleason, *Contending with Modernity*, pp. 78-80.

[47] Ibid., pp. 34-38, 62, 69-72, 171-175.

[48] Day, *Long Loneliness*, p. 170.

Dorothy Day, An Ordinary American

James T. Fisher

Dorothy Day was not an Americanist; she was an American. Far from a simple declaration, this fact of her inheritance continues to vex those who would seek to understand her singular contribution to American Catholicism. Father Michael Baxter has discussed some of the ways in which the prophetic radical spirituality associated with Dorothy Day's Catholic Worker movement has differed from the accommodationist strategy of liberal Catholic "Americanists." Yet precisely because of Day's stature as a special kind of American figure, it is extremely difficult to compare Catholic radicalism in any meaningful way with the "Americanist" thought of individuals who lacked many of the cultural and personal resources at her disposal. Although Father Baxter's paper covers much broader terrain, I would like to treat a few of the ironies that continue to haunt students of the Catholic Worker movement.

When the anarchist Emma Goldman first heard Dorothy Day described as a Catholic radical she remarked, "That is a new one on me."[1] Sixty years later we cannot speak of this now-rich tradition without saluting the Catholic Worker movement and its roots in Dorothy Day's dramatic 1927 conversion to Catholicism. Biographers and other scholars have naturally highlighted her prior flirtations with communism as well as her flamboyant career as a Greenwich Village bohemian who purportedly loathed organized religion. Although Day was never of course a real communist, she did—as Sandra Yocum Mize has shown in a recent essay—draw upon her understanding of Marxist doctrine in composing *The Long Loneliness*, her 1952 autobiography.[2] Day's fascination with the "decadent" literary tradition associated with the Dutch-French novelist J. K. Huysmans probably constituted an even more important source, though it has been largely ignored by scholars, if not by creators of imaginative literature. In 1956 Day insisted that her friend, the novelist Caroline Gordon, excise a scene from *The Malefactors* in which a character drawn explicitly from Dorothy's life was described as having presided—prior to her conversion—at a black mass.[3]

There are even deeper roots of Day's conversion that have yet to be fully examined. If we broaden the category of "intellectual resources" to include the ideological assumptions that pervaded Dorothy Day's middle-class, middle-brow, middle-American upbringing, we may run a better chance at fully contextualizing her impact on American Catholicism. Day's Protestant Midwestern background has generally been treated either as a given, requiring little interpretation, or as so self-evidently stultifying that her decision to become a "rebel girl" of Greenwich Village was founded on good judgment and common sense. Her parents have been paid less attention than those of any figure of comparable magnitude in this century, perhaps due to a belief that in "dying to the old" self and "putting on the new," Dorothy was a kind of spiritual orphan, only to be "adopted" by Peter Maurin and in turn be-come herself the godmother to generations of Catholic radicals.

The neglect of her father by biographers and students of the Catholic Worker movement (myself included) is especially puzzling in light of Dorothy's enduring, immutable vocation as a journalist. John Day was a respected newspaperman and a distinguished horseracing writer who, in the type of promotional sideline common to journalists of his era, helped to found Hialeah race course near Miami. William Miller, whose unsympathetic account is the most detailed we have, depicted John Day as the quintessential late-Victorian American hollow man, a restless xenophobe who quoted Shakespeare and the Bible to spice up his articles for the *Saturday Evening Post*. In her "wholly autobiographical" novel, *The Eleventh Virgin*, Day described her parents' companionate marriage in a fashion that suggested they left little emotional room for their children.[4]

Any doubt that Dorothy fervently sought her father's approval—even after becoming a journalist for socialist publications—was dispelled by Day herself in a 1917 book review for *The Masses*. In the review, she confessed that John Day had destroyed the novel under consideration, but only after she had left it in his home.[5] One of the most volatile unexplored issues in her life is the role that her father's nativism—and the anti-Catholic literature she grew familiar with as a child—played in coloring her early understanding of the church and her sometimes dark mysticism. Less mystery surrounds the quite understandable professional rivalry between Dorothy and her father that probably masked a grudging mutual respect. "Dorothy, the oldest girl, is the nut of the family," the elder Day told a relative shortly before his death. "Now she's a Catholic crusader. She owns and runs a Catholic paper and skyhoots all over the country."[6]

Journalism was the Day family business and the resource from which she drew most deeply throughout her life. Despite his own precarious career in journalism, four of John Day's five children devoted their lives to newspaper work. Dorothy's older brother Donald Day was a foreign correspondent for the *Chicago Tribune*, while Sam Houston Day went to work at the *New York Journal American* in 1928, a powerful tabloid organ of the Hearst empire.[7]

The near total lack of information regarding Dorothy Day's relationship with Sam Houston Day represents the most significant lacuna in Catholic Worker scholarship. Between 1942 (when he became managing editor of the *Journal-American*) and 1961 Sam Day, known professionally as Houston Day, presided over one of the most widely read newspapers in the United States. Moreover, the *Journal-American* was clearly the most popular newspaper among Catholic readers in New York throughout the years Sam's sister Dorothy published her rather obscure penny-a-copy monthly from various locales in the city. The *Journal-American*'s stable of glamorous Catholic columnists—including Dorothy Kilgallen and Jack O'Brian—trumpeted a boldly "Americanist" integration of their faith with the urban, secular popular culture they helped define.[8]

Sam Houston Day did not have to convert to exert this great influence over a key segment of Catholic America. The promise of America exalted in the pages of his newspaper represented a shared understanding among writers and readers of all ethnic and religious persuasions. One of the paradoxes of "liberal" or Americanist Catholicism is that its spokespersons have often—perhaps unconsciously—re-problematized an issue that for many was already settled, if it had ever existed at all. Since, as Oscar Handlin explained in 1951, "the immigrants *were* American history," who was better situated to make that story their own than Catholic Americans?[9] Catholics were also fortuitously concentrated in cities, where a new mass culture was born and deeply influenced by their own tastes and values. This lower-case, non-theological "Americanism" was what Dorothy Day most objected to, for she envisioned Catholic radicalism not as a response to theological accommodations to the nation-state but as a counter-claim to a ubiquitous post-Protestant cultural order that could scarcely be named. It was not by accident that the inaugural issue of the *Catholic Worker* in 1933 was dedicated to the New York City police department—one of the great symbols of *practical* Catholic adaptation to the secular metropolis.

The heavily clerical champions of Catholic Americanism in the late nineteenth century and beyond often seemed to belabor what was a moot point for most of their constituents. They were much less able than a formerly Protestant woman to turn the most cherished of national myths—especially those involving the primacy of autonomous selfhood in American thought—to their own advantage. These Americanists often seemed too self-conscious, too intent on bold pronouncements that only seemed to heighten their sense of uncertainty. They were both Americans and Americanists and the more fervently they claimed to reconcile the two the less convincing they became. By the 1930s many of their heirs finally discovered the mystique they had long sought. The "liberal" tradition of American Catholicism was, after all, strongly allied with the Catholic Worker movement throughout most of its history, and many latter-day "Americanists" were at the very least "fellow-travelers" of Catholic radicalism. It is therefore somewhat misleading to poise the one tradition against the other.

My concern here has not been to highlight the incompleteness of Dorothy Day scholarship but to suggest that the deepest roots of Catholic Worker radicalism were much more "American" than those of the "Americanist" theorists against whom the Worker purportedly offered "a sign of contradiction." In addition to her deep grounding in all of the romantic remnants of what Sacvan Bercovitch called the "puritan origins of the American self," Dorothy Day brought to and through her conversion a tremendous capacity for regeneration-through-renunciation not immediately accessible to the first generation of "Americanist" clerics and politicians. With the passage of time, the stark differences in experience and worldview between a convert like Dorothy Day and Catholics of more conventional backgrounds would diminish. Middle-class intellectuals, in particular, could now condemn bourgeois culture with authority, so that a self-consciously

"Americanist" Catholicism would come to appear more anachronistic than controversial.

Notes

[1] Emma Goldman is quoted in David J. O'Brien, "The Pilgrimage of Dorothy Day," *Commonweal* 107 (December 19, 1980): 712.

[2] Sandra Yocum Mize, "Dorothy Day's *Apologia* for Faith After Marx," *Horizons* 22 (Fall, 1995): 198-213.

[3] Nancylee Novelle Jonza, *The Underground Stream: The Life and Art of Caroline Gordon* (Athens: University of Georgia, 1995), pp. 336-337.

[4] William D. Miller, *Dorothy Day: A Biography* (San Francisco: Harper & Row, 1982), pp. 1-2, 4-5, 309-312; Dorothy Day, *The Eleventh Virgin* (New York: Albert & Charles Boni, 1924).

[5] Dorothy Day, "Mary, Mary, Quite Contrary," *The Masses* 9 (August, 1917): 38.

[6] Miller, *Dorothy Day*, p. 311.

[7] Day's career as a journalist is treated in Nancy Roberts' fine study, *Dorothy Day and the Catholic Worker* (Albany, NY: State University of New York Press, 1984). Roberts does not deal extensively with the journalistic careers of Day's father and brothers.

[8] For a brief discussion of urban Catholicism and popular journalism see James T. Fisher, "Alternative Sources of Catholic Intellectual Vitality," *U.S. Catholic Historian* (Winter, 1995): 81-94.

[9] Oscar Handlin, *The Uprooted: The Epic Story of the Great Migrations that Made the American People* (New York: Grosset & Dunlap, 1951), p. 3.

The Politics of the Little Way:
Dorothy Day Reads Thérèse of Lisieux

Frederick Christian Bauerschmidt

Politics and Mysticism

In his book *Dialogue with the Other*, David Tracy puts forward the claim that "religious languages arrive in two basic forms: the rhetoric of the prophet and the rhetoric of the mystic."[1] This location of theological discourse between the poles of the mystical and the prophetic is one version of the call, heard largely from Roman Catholic theologians, for a "mystical-political" theology, which has as its general intention a desire to repoliticize the Christian faith without reducing it to "mere politics."[2] Again as David Tracy puts it,

> Without the prophetic core [of the Christian faith], the struggle for justice and freedom in the historical-political world can too soon be lost in mere privacy. Without the mystical insistence on love, the spiritual power of the righteous struggle for justice is always in danger of lapsing into mere self-righteousness and spiritual exhaustion.[3]

Or, as Edward Schillebeeckx puts it, "[Jesus] becomes either a politically neutral mystical figure who is alien to the world or a candidate of a political party (whether right- or left-wing) up for election."[4] To steer between these two poles without losing the distinctive value of either is the desire of those who employ the language of "political-mystical theology."

Good intentions aside, however, one might ask whether the distinction between prophetic and mystical rhetorics or, more simply, politics and mysticism, is in fact the best way to insure an inherently political character for theology without being reductive. In particular, I suspect that the antinomy of politics and mysticism conforms to another antinomy, one which has been used in modernity to underwrite a *realpolitik*: the antinomy between an ethic of responsibility and an ethic of ultimate ends. This particular articulation of the distinction is taken from Max Weber, who affirmed that these two ethical approaches "are not absolute contrasts but rather supplements,"[5] but also said that "we are placed into various life-spheres, each of which is governed by different laws."[6] The ethic of ends is needed to provide the ideal vision, while the ethic of responsibility makes sure that we do not confuse the ideal ultimate end with the pragmatic means necessary to approximate (though perhaps never reach) that ideal. To have, in Weber's terms, a true "vocation for politics," one must keep the ugly reality of necessary means segregated from the lofty vision of ultimate ends. Otherwise one runs the risk of irresponsibly putting into practice on a political level impossible ideals such as those embodied in the Sermon on the Mount. Politics is reduced to the "real world" technical manipulation of means, and, as Weber grants, "the decisive means for politics is violence."[7] Religion, on the other hand, provides the ideal. But a desire to see this ideal actualized leads to a quandary that issues in "the solution of the mystic's radical anti-political attitude, his quest for redemption with its acosmic benevolence and brotherhood. . . . It [i.e., mysticism] withdraws from the pragma of violence which no political action can escape."[8]

Weber's analysis might lead us to wonder whether even positing a distinction between "politics" and "mysticism" runs the risk of generating separate religious and political spaces (or "life-spheres"), precisely because the categories of "mysticism" and "politics" have been generated to sustain such separate spaces. To put this more directly, "politics and mysticism" should make Christians nervous because in modernity both of these terms have acquired persistent and antithetical overtones—politics and mysticism: public versus private, real versus ideal, social versus individual, violence versus peace. Thus while mysticism is rendered as the private ideal of individual peace, politics is the public reality of social violence. These two poles set up an anxious middle, a realm of compromise in which the "real" inevitably trumps the "ideal" in human social relations. In other words, putting the social character of Christianity in terms of a necessary oscillation between the poles of mysticism and politics ends up handing "real

world" politics over to the pragma of violence and leaving mysticism as a transcendent remainder which serves as a haven in a heartless world for the self and its ideals.[9]
This is not the only possibility. In something like Dorothy Day's appropriation of Thérèse of Lisieux's "Little Way," we see an alternative Christian practice which overcomes the antinomy of mysticism and politics through the positing of a politics of the Little Way. Thérèse and Dorothy Day seem an unlikely pair: one a nineteenth-century French Carmelite who became an icon of saccharine piety and the other the *doyenne* of Catholic radicalism in America. They seemed an unlikely pair to Dorothy Day herself. In her biography of Thérèse, Day notes that on her first reading of Thérèse's memoir, *The Story of a Soul*, she "found it colorless, monotonous, too small in fact for my attention." More to her liking were heroic saints such as Joan of Arc, typological prefigurations of leftist martyrs who lay down their lives for the proletariat.[10] In other words, on first reading, Thérèse was not "political" enough for Day. And yet Thérèse, the "Little Flower" who taught a "Little Way," the Carmelite nun who died of tuberculosis at age twenty-four, came to captivate Day. What was the appeal? How might we reconcile the enclosed, contemplative piety of a Carmelite with the social radicalism of Day and the Catholic Worker? Isn't the kind of bourgeois, inward-looking spirituality embodied in Thérèse something of a wholly different order than the spirit of anarchist pacifism that animates the Catholic Worker? Isn't Thérèse's spirituality precisely the kind of acosmic love that Weber identifies as a retreat from the political? In short, doesn't the pairing of Thérèse and Dorothy Day return us to the antinomy of mysticism and politics?
To understand Day's reading of Thérèse requires a transformation of our notions of both "mysticism" and of "politics"—a transformation that entails a willingness to acknowledge the risks involved in speaking of "the politics of the Little Way." There are "political" aspects to Thérèse's background and legacy which most of us would find unhelpful at best and pernicious at worst. On the one hand, one might speak of uncovering the politics of the Little Way in terms of the connection between Thérèse Martin's spirituality and the political allegiances of the extended Martin family, particularly her uncle Isidore and his promotion of the Assumptionist newspaper *La Croix*, which one writer has characterized as "virulently anti-modern, anti-republican, anti-Protestant, and anti-Semitic."[11] In this reading, Thérèse's Little

Way would reflect a world view that rejected modernity in favor of a romanticized Catholic past in which the church was the center of society, a past that now can only exist within the family enclave or the cloister walls, boundaries which serve to exclude the modern, the liberal, the Protestant, and the Jew. On the other hand, one might mean by "the politics of the Little Way" the techniques by which Thérèse was promoted as an icon of feminine sanctity: Jesus' passive plaything who remains eternally a child, the "victim" who revels in suffering and who has the good grace to die young of consumption. Presenting to women an ideal unattainable to anyone who progresses, either physically or psychically, beyond adolescence, the Little Flower's "Little Way of spiritual childhood" is in fact one more ploy by which women are infantilized and subjugated.[12]

In light of these aspects of Thérèse's background and reception, we might well suspect that the identification of the realm of "the mystical" as Thérèse's natural dwelling place is a bad faith gesture designed to procure for her a transhistorical space protected from both her historical circumstances and our historical queries. Rightly troubled by certain aspects of Thérèse's history, our identification of her as a "mystic" seeks to make her miraculously immune from the proto-fascist Catholic culture in which she was raised and the pernicious effects to which her image and story have subsequently been put. But any appropriation of Thérèse's Little Way that seeks to avoid the problematic antinomy of politics and mysticism must eschew "mysticism" as a protective category and acknowledge Thérèse's historical situatedness in all of its ambiguity.

While one might well be suspicious of the political uses to which the identification of Thérèse as a "mystic" might be put, it is clear that Thérèse herself does not fit easily into the modern category of "mystic."[13] She is on the whole uninterested in visions or mystical transports. At age ten she sees a statue of the Virgin Mary smiling at her while she lies sick, but this is of greater significance to others than it is to her; what strikes Thérèse is simply the beauty of the Virgin.[14] Near the end of her life she says that while she had "experienced transports of love" at age fourteen, "it wasn't a real flame that was burning me."[15] Her interest is not so much in "religious experience" (much beloved by modern theorists of mysticism) as in finding how being accidentally splashed with dirty dishwater by one of her fellow sisters, or listening to a sister who makes annoying noises in choir, or living under a neurotic and tyrannical prioress, or dying young, all fit into loving God and being loved by God. Thérèse's focus is resolutely on the mundane, the quotidian, the small. Her "spirituality" does not occupy a space apart from the details of everyday life. This means that Thérèse herself does not see her Little Way as something that floats, as it were, above the messy facts of history. Thus it cannot simply be absolved of any connection to either its context or its subsequent employment. However, the Little Way, like any other historical phenomenon, is "overdetermined" (i.e., determined by a multitude of factors),[16] and this complexity of determination makes for a certain looseness of fit between the phenomenon and its context and interpretation. It is the overdetermination of texts that makes possible novel interpretations; it is the overdetermination of practices that makes possible their fruitful employment in new situations. In the case of Thérèse and the Little Way, the fact that her autobiography, and the spiritual practice it reflected, grew out of the context of reactionary, bourgeois French Catholicism does not mean that it is reducible to that context. Many other factors were operative in the production of that text (not least of which being Thérèse's own agency), and reactionary Catholicism was itself a complex phenomenon (producing, among others, Peter Maurin, co-founder with Day of the Catholic Worker). Similarly, the frequent employment of Thérèse as a model of a perpetually adolescent feminine piety is not her *only* possible employment. Just as Thérèse draws selectively on the resources operative in her context, so too Day draws selectively on Thérèse, emphasizing some aspects and de-emphasizing others, so as to use her for particular purposes, which might well be at odds with other purposes to which she has been put. This is not an act of historical falsification, it is simply an aspect of that complex activity called "reading."

Thus what Dorothy Day offers is a particular "reading" of Thérèse's Little Way, which foregrounds its political possibilities and undermines the duality of "mysticism" and "politics." Day the "activist" reads Thérèse the "contemplative" in such a way as to produce something which is neither "mysticism" nor "politics" as these have been conventionally understood in modernity. Day reads Thérèse's Little Way not as a retreat from the modern world into interiority, but as charting a path for humanity through the wasteland of modernity to its supernatural destiny. In her reading, Day cultivates those aspects of

Thérèse which are particularly responsive to the concerns of late modernity.

Thérèse and Modernity

Pius X's oft-quoted approbation of Thérèse as "the greatest saint of modern times" might be read as just one more example of Pius' own virulent antimodernism: Thérèse is the greatest saint of modern times precisely because she so resolutely rejects all that is modern. The only proper form of Christian engagement with the modern world is retreat either into the monastery or into the pious family enclave. Yet, in another reading of Thérèse, one that Dorothy Day's appropriation of her opens up for us, she appears as one who creatively appropriates past traditions and practices, even the bourgeois and reactionary ones which largely constituted her milieu, to forge a new "way" for Christian faith in the setting of modernity.

As noted above, Thérèse Martin can neither be assimilated to the conservative French piety of her day, nor totally isolated from it. One might well be tempted, as Dorothy Day was, to dismiss Thérèse initially as a purveyor of bourgeois spirituality for the bourgeoisie. Her Little Way can appear to be the spiritual analog of the rage for collecting among the French middle class in the nineteenth century. Thérèse collects tiny virtues and sacrifices the way others collected tiny porcelain figurines. She serves her heavenly Father by being the ideal middle-class daughter; she serves Christ by being the ideal middle-class wife.[17] No doubt she appealed to some as a recognizable "type" for bourgeois Catholics who identified with her, and for the poor who yearned for the idealized middle-class family life in which she was nurtured. It also accounts for the disdain with which others held her.

For those who look beyond the trappings of Thérèse's bourgeois sensibilities, another temptation arises—to isolate her entirely from her bourgeois milieu, to make her spirituality wholly different from that of her family and the other Carmelites. Some feel a certain betrayal of Thérèse by her sister and fellow Carmelite Pauline who, after Thérèse's death, edited her memoirs, consistently toning down Thérèse's stronger phrases. Similarly, photos of Thérèse were retouched to give her face a gaunter, more ascetic appearance. The most popular images, the saccharine portraits painted by her sister Céline, also a Carmelite, depict a sweet-faced, pious maid holding a huge bundle of roses. Such a portrait hardly seems to square with the young woman who wrote of her "trial of faith" as a darkness that beckoned her: "Advance, advance; rejoice in death which will give you not what you hope for but a night still more profound, the night of nothingness" (213). Many readers of Thérèse discover her to be made of flintier material than her popular appropriation indicates, and feel that she is a victim of either misunderstanding or deliberate misrepresentation by her own religious community.[18]

Both the temptation to assimilate Thérèse to her milieu and the temptation to isolate her from it should be resisted. Thérèse herself asked Pauline to edit her manuscripts, and she had her own devotion to various pious images.[19] She very much expresses herself in the idiom of late nineteenth-century French piety. But this should not be taken to mean that her voice is simply an echo of that piety. As Simon Tugwell notes, between Thérèse and her family and fellow nuns "at least some element of disagreement and incomprehension cannot be denied."[20] In some cases, Thérèse finds conventional pious practices quite frustrating and useful only as a form of mortification. "[T]he recitation of the rosary is more difficult for me than the wearing of an instrument of penance" (242). More typically, Thérèse employs the conventional pieties of bourgeois French Catholic culture in unconventional ways. They provided her a vocabulary and syntax without which she could not speak, but in her speaking she gives them unexpected twists. When she takes up the language of "victimhood" so prevalent among her Carmelite sisters, Thérèse transforms it by offering herself, not as a "victim of divine justice," but as a "victim of divine mercy."[21]

In her reemployment of such conventions, Thérèse produces not a "spirituality"—a science of religious experience, but a true theology—a discourse on God. This theology attends to certain modern preoccupations. Bernard Bro has pointed out that Thérèse lived at roughly the same time as such quintessential modern thinkers as Rimbaud, Dostoyevsky, Nietzsche, Freud, and Marx. These figures announce the peculiar abyss of modernity; the void of human freedom coextends with the void left by the departure of God. Bro goes on to say that "the only way of appreciating Thérèse of Lisieux today is by adding her squarely to their company."[22] The Little Flower finds her place among the masters of suspicion; she, as much as they, confronts the abyss that strips away all prior securities. In this regard much might be said about Thérèse's theology; let it suffice here to mention two key points noted by Bro that focus on the way in which Thérèse's theology is unusually responsive to modern sensibilities.

Bro notes that unlike her Carmelite forbears Teresa of Avila and John of the Cross, Thérèse does not offer "degrees" of spiritual progress.[23] Michel de Certeau has argued that for a figure like John of the Cross, who still lived in a world that was hierarchically ordered, every movement was either an ascent or descent of the cosmic ladder, toward or away from God. However, with modernity's dismantling of the cosmic and spiritual hierarchy, any step forward, any motion, brings us neither closer to nor farther from our goal.[24] Eventually modernity replaces the ancient and medieval cosmic hierarchies with either a socioeconomic hierarchy or that odd, horizontal hierarchy that modernity calls "progress." Yet, Thérèse had imbibed deeply the anti-modern and ultimately antibourgeois sentiments of her family. Thérèse's family, with its extravagant religious fixation, its five daughters in the convent, and its odd and rather aimless father, must be seen as at least *unconventionally* bourgeois.[25] She was thus not inclined to seek to orient herself by reference to either worldly success or a faith in modern progress. Gathering fragments of the shattered spiritual hierarchy, Thérèse "wanders" through modernity with no goal but that kingdom revealed in the Cross. She possesses no security except faith without consolation. Thérèse wrote, "I have frequently noticed that Jesus doesn't want me to lay up provisions; he nourishes me at each moment with a totally new food; I find it within me without knowing how it is there" (165).

Her Little Way is not a "way of perfection," but, in Simon Tugwell's phrase, a way of *imperfection.* Her focus on her own littleness expresses not simply the saccharine piety of an eternally youngest child from a doting family, but it makes a radical statement about the impossibility in modernity of any "progress" up a ladder of perfection toward God. It is to recognize our "nothingness," "not [to] attribute to oneself the virtues that one practices, believing oneself capable of anything, but to recognize that God places this treasure in the hand of His little child to be used when necessary; but it remains always God's treasure."[26] She seeks a way to God that is "very straight, very short, and totally new." The Little Way is for her an "elevator," which is strikingly different from the stairs by which the strong climbed to perfection. The Little Way is in a sense not so much Thérèse's way to God as God's way to Thérèse, the way in which Jesus lifts her in his arms.[27] Thérèse is keenly aware that, in a world in which the spiritual hierarchy has been shattered, the only path is the *via crucis,* the path leading to the "death of love" revealed in the Cross. "To die of love is not to die in transports."[28] To die of love is to share in the poverty of the Cross.

Bro also notes that Thérèse's thought moves between the poles of desire and despair, the points of departure and breakdown characteristic of modern life.[29] Thérèse is conscious of herself as a woman of powerful desires. She tells of how she simultaneously desires contrasting vocations as warrior, priest, apostle, doctor, martyr. She comes to realize that love is the vocation that embraces them all.[30] In asking for this vocation, Thérèse is amazed at the abyss of her own infinite desire: "Jesus, I cannot fathom the depths of my request; I would be afraid to find myself overwhelmed under the weight of my bold desires" (196). Thérèse perhaps surpasses even Freud in seeing life as driven by a turbulent libido which has as much potential for destruction as for fulfillment. The abyss of desire, seen apart from Christ's own infinite "thirst" for the salvation of souls, is indistinguishable from nihilistic despair. Yet united to Christ's infinite desire, the abyss of Thérèse's desire becomes a participation in Christ's own love and is fulfilled even as it increases, by being drawn into the abyss of Christ's love: "it was this ardent thirst He was giving me as the most delightful drink of His love" (101).

For Thérèse, desire and despair are brought together most clearly in her "trial of faith," in which desire transforms despair into the purest form of hope. For the last year and a half of her life Thérèse was constantly beset by doubts, particularly about heaven. She had always felt absolutely sure in her belief in a heavenly homeland and had believed that those who denied heaven were deceiving themselves and denying their innermost feelings. But shortly after Easter in 1896, a few days after she coughed up blood for the first time, Thérèse writes that "[God] permitted my soul to be invaded by the thickest darkness, and the thought of heaven, up until then so sweet to me, be no longer anything but the cause of struggle and torment" (211). Rather than holding herself aloof from unbelief, Thérèse now finds herself one with unbelievers, and in the midst of her doubts she says "in her name and in the name of her brothers, '*Have pity on us, O Lord, for we are poor sinners!*' Oh! Lord, send us away justified" (212). Her trial of faith is taken up by Thérèse as her solidarity with the unbelief of the modern world, from which her family and her church had sought to protect her. As Barbara Corrado Pope writes, "Thérèse's ethics eschewed the noisy rancor of anti-modern militancy and thus reappropriated charity as the Christian's *modus vivendi* in an alien

world."[31] She joins her voice to the voices of the unbelievers to cry out
in trust in the God who is hidden from her: "Your love has gone before me, and it has grown with me, and now it is an abyss whose
depths I cannot fathom" (256).

Thus, the modern world of nihilistic doubt and despair forms the
backdrop against which Thérèse's theology is displayed. In this world,
the cosmic hierarchy has been laid low, along with it, the possibility of
knowing where to look to find God. God seems to have vanished from
the world; nature no longer reveals God's creative hand, but simply
matter without spirit. Thérèse feels this as keenly as Kafka or
Dostoyevsky. As Thérèse lies on her deathbed, looking at the sky
through the infirmary window, her sister Marie says, "You look up at
the heavens with so much love!" Thérèse simply smiles at her, but
later confides to Pauline: "Ah! she believed I was looking at the sky
and thinking of the real heavens! No, it was simply because I admire
the material heavens; the other is closed to me more and more." Yet
the opacity of the material heavens does not have the last word for
Thérèse. She adds, "Oh, certainly it's really through love that I'm looking at the sky; yes, it's through love for God, since everything that I
do, my actions, my looks, everything, since my Offering [i.e., her offering of herself as a victim of divine mercy], is done through love."[32]
Thérèse's Little Way is a response to the eclipse of God in modernity.
Thérèse now seeks God, no longer at the top of the great chain of
being, in the mundane details of everyday life, in the small sacrifices
entailed by living in a community of unexceptional human beings, in
the tiny struggles involved in finding one's way in the midst of doubts,
in the dying by degrees of consumption. It is a mistake to think that
the Little Way is a matter of adding up these little sacrifices so as to
equal a heroic life of martyrdom (the spiritual version of pinching
pennies), or piling them on top of each other so as to reach up to God.
Rather, through the sufferings of Christ on the Cross, *each one* of
those small sacrifices is a point of contact with the infinite love of
Christ which he takes up and offers to the Father in union with his own
sacrifice.

Dorothy Day Reads Thérèse

Thérèse's Little Way may be "modern," but is it "political"? Isn't
her focus on desire and despair a typically modern turn to the interior
and thus away from the social? Isn't her focus on the mundane an

evasion of the political? Even Dorothy Day cannot present Thérèse in a way that is conventionally "political." Her biography of the Little Flower, *Therese*, is in many ways unremarkable. It is not generally thought of as the most profound study of Thérèse nor as the best of Day's books. On the whole, it simply recounts Thérèse's life, paying perhaps an unusual degree of attention to Thérèse's family background and, in particular, her mother. Along the way, Day carefully notes events that reveal concern for the poor on the part of Thérèse or her family (e.g., 74-75), as well as making a few stabs at portraying Thérèse as "one of 'the people' " (83). Thérèse, Day points out, lived with the family of her wet nurse for the first year of her life in "a true peasant's hut, made of stone and mud with a thatched roof, with a manure pile in the yard next door" (37). She also mentions that Thérèse's mother "looked upon what she called the war machine with horror" (28), and that her father "would not have anything to do with dealings on the stock market" (138). Yet these few attempts to paint Thérèse's life in colors taken from the Catholic Worker palette seem forced and half-hearted. While working on the biography, Day acknowledged as much. After invoking Thérèse's Little Way in a column on the Catholic Worker making common cause with communists on some issues, Day adds:

> I'm not trying to say that the Little Flower would have gone out on picket lines and spoken on Communist platforms or embraced her Protestant neighbors, if there were any in the town of Alençon. She was a product of her environment, bourgeois, middle class, the daughter of skilled workers, comfortable, frugal people who lived apart from the world with their eyes on God.[33]

What makes Day's biography of Thérèse interesting is not that she successfully "radicalizes" Thérèse, but that she takes the time and effort to write about such a figure at all.

Day's most profound reading of Thérèse is not to be found in the biography, but in Day's own life, the way in which she interprets the Little Way against the background of her own radical, anarchist roots. Dorothy Day reads Thérèse's Little Way not as an evasion of the political but as an alternative politics. Writing in 1965, Day said:

> When a mother, a housewife, asks what she can do, one can only point to the way of St. Therese, that little way, so much misun-

derstood and so much despised. . . . And this goes for the priest too, wherever he is, whether he deals with the problems of war or with poverty. He may write or speak, but he needs to study the little way, which is all that is available to the poor, and the only alternative to the mass approach of the State. Missionaries throughout the world recognize the little way of cooperatives and credit unions, small industry, village commune, and cottage economy. And not only missionaries. Down in our own South, in the Delta regions among the striking farmers of Mississippi, this "little way" is being practiced and should be studied.[34]

The Little Way is "misunderstood" and "despised" as an alternative politics because of the modern identification of politics with, in Weber's words, "the leadership, or influencing of the leadership, of a *political* association, hence today, of a state."[35] In other words, in modernity, politics is statecraft. What makes the Little Way seem apolitical— even *anti*political—is its incompatibility with the *means* which Weber identifies as specific to the state: "the state is a relation of men dominating men, a relation supported by means of legitimate (i.e., considered to be legitimate) violence."[36] Yet what makes Thérèse's Little Way seem so irrelevant to politics is precisely what offers Dorothy Day a way of conceptualizing an alternative politics. Not bound to state power, the Little Way escapes the logic of violence by which state politics is ordered.

As an heir to the anarchist stream of the American radical tradition, Day was well aware that the state cannot be identified *tout court* with government, but is simply one particular mode of ordering social life, of pursuing the common good.[37] Attempting to influence the state is only one form of political action; seizing state power is only one kind of revolution. In Thérèse's Little Way, Day discerns another form of revolution, which "has all the power of the spirit of Christianity behind it. It is an explosive force that can transform our lives and the life of the world, once put into effect" (175). Day's life and the Catholic Worker movement as a whole offer many possibilities for reflection on the politics of the Little Way and how it is put into effect. The following two focus upon the politics of the powerless and suffering as the alternative to violence.

1. The Little Way and the Weapons of the Weak. Day stresses repeatedly in her invocations of the Little Way that it restores agency to those who are excluded from access to what normally counts as political power. She says in the preface to her biography of Thérèse that she "wrote to overcome the sense of futility in Catholics, men, women, and youths, married and single, who feel hopeless and useless, less than dust, ineffectual, wasted, powerless" (xii). For Day, the Little Way is an alternative to politics as statecraft because it does not presume that control is either the precondition or the goal of political action. As such, it is a mode of action which is realizable for the poorest of the poor. Thérèse is recorded saying near the end of her life, "What does it matter whether we're successful or not? What God asks of us is not to give up the struggle because of our weariness, not to become discouraged. . ."[38] The first political task of those who follow the Little Way is to overcome weariness and discouragement by surrendering control to Christ, the King who reigns from the Cross. Thérèse writes, "Jesus does not demand great actions from us but simply *surrender* and *gratitude*" (188). Yet once this surrender is made, action of a new sort becomes possible.

Day, like Thérèse, focuses on small, everyday actions as the key to the Little Way, and it is precisely the *littleness* of these actions that gives the Little Way its paradoxical effectiveness. Precisely because it eschews the need for control and operates on the level of the micropolitics of everyday life, the Little Way traces its path through the inevitable interstices that run through the apparently totalizing system of state power. Without displacing the state, which would simply lead to another state, the Little Way operates within it, making use of the opportunities the state unwittingly provides, without obeying its logic. Peter Maurin spoke of building a new society within the shell of the old. The Little Way, a series of tiny deviations—Day's aforementioned "little way of cooperatives and credit unions, small industry, village commune, and cottage economy"—are effected within the state apparatus. The smallness of these deviations exemplifies the new within the old, which allows them to escape the observation and repression of the dominant system.[39] At the same time these deviations cannot be planned for; they depend on surprising opportunities which come to us borne by time. They require both a practical wisdom and a surrender of the self and its desires to God. As Day writes, "We do the minute things that come to hand, we pray our prayers, and beg also for an increase of faith—and God will do the rest."[40]

   2. *Suffering rather than violence.* One of the most troubling points

of Thérèse's thought for contemporary readers is the emphasis she places on suffering, and in particular the *joy* which she finds in suffering. She is recorded as saying in her last months, "I have found happiness and joy on earth, but solely in suffering."[41] Similarly, some have seen in Dorothy Day's views on suffering an almost pathological fixation.[42] Day herself was aware that she was perceived in this way, noting "We have been called necrophiliacs, we have been accused of taking a morbid delight in the gutter and worshipping ash cans."[43] Yet both Thérèse and Day recognized that suffering was a reality which could not be evaded, and that promises of a painless utopia, a Kingdom of God without the Cross and personal sacrifice, were dangerous illusions. In fact, Day saw that one of the most pernicious aspects of the modern state was the way in which it used such promises to mask the violence of the constant warfare waged against the poor.[44]

The "personalism" of the Catholic Worker effected an unmasking of this hidden violence precisely because it entailed a willingness to take suffering upon oneself. Being a follower of Christ involves a solidarity with victims precisely because Christ himself was a victim. The necessity of bearing suffering can be seen most clearly in Day's pacifism. Unlike some versions of liberal pacifism, Day's commitment to nonviolence was rooted in the mystery of the redemptive value of suffering. She did not presume that nonviolence would necessarily reduce the amount of suffering in the world, but that suffering for the peace of Christ had a hidden redemptive value. One of the points she found most striking in Thérèse was her appropriation of Paul's enigmatic statement in Colossians 1:24: "I am now rejoicing in my sufferings for your sake, and in my flesh I am completing what is lacking in Christ's afflictions for the sake of his body, that is, the church." Day writes, "we must share in the sufferings of the world to lessen them, to show our love for our brothers" (175). In this suffering, this abandonment of self, the self's true freedom is found.

Day felt that the sheer scale of modernity's problems bred despair and moved many to succumb to the temptation of violence:

> So many in these days have taken violent steps to gain the things of this world—war to achieve peace; coercion to achieve freedom; striving to gain what slips through the fingers. We might as well give up on our great desires, at least our hopes of doing great things toward achieving them, right at the beginning. It is like the paradox of the Gospel, of giving up one's life in order to save it.[45]

A willingness to suffer, to give up one's life to find it, is a counter-logic to the logic of the state. Again, as Weber noted, "Today the relation between the state and violence is an especially intimate one."[46] The state uses its monopoly on legitimate violence to guarantee the security of its citizens, to protect them from suffering. The freedom of the Little Way is the freedom to suffer violence rather than inflict it. It is the cultivation of a certain kind of patience, an active waiting which joins in the groaning of all creation awaiting redemption. This patience requires a coldly realistic eye that recognizes suffering and yet does not succumb to the "realist" logic of the state and its recourse to violence.

Only by surrendering security and embracing suffering as the way of the Cross can an alternative politics be posited. Yet this suffering is not something willed for its own sake. Self-abandonment takes this form when it conforms to the love revealed in Christ's gift of himself on the Cross. Thérèse wrote near the end of her life she no longer desired suffering or death, but only love. "I possessed suffering and believed I had touched the shores of heaven, that the little flower would be gathered in the springtime of her life. Now, abandonment alone guides me. I have no other compass!" (178). Even suffering must be abandoned to divine providence. Dorothy Day too had no illusions that suffering itself was any sort of sure path to God. Only Christ is that. But in sharing the sufferings of the poor at a personal sacrifice, one encounters Christ: "Lord, when did we see you hungry?" Only in embracing Christ's way of the Cross can one resist the state's enticing promise of safety secured through violence.

Conclusion: Luminous Traces

As noted at the outset, laudable though the motives may be of those who argue for some version of a "mystical-political theology," one might well worry that the pairing of these terms grants too much to a conception of politics and religion that segregates them into different spheres. To frame the problematic in this way accedes too quickly to the conception of politics as statecraft, meaning the management of territory through the use or the threat of the use of violence. What Dorothy Day's reading of Thérèse offers is an alternative conception of politics, a politics of the Little Way in which the weak find their strength. Rather than the art of control, this politics is the art of surrender, the art of precariousness, the art of suffering in a world from which God seems so often eclipsed.

Difficult questions remain about the politics of the Little Way. In its surrender of control, does it become purely reactive? In its focus on suffering, does it pay insufficient attention to the alleviation of suffering? In its attention to the everyday, does it miss the reality of the large-scale structures of sin? These are serious questions, but at least two things might be said. First, these possible theoretical difficulties have been overcome in much of the actual practice of the Catholic Worker movement, which combines both a positive vision of a social order, not a state, and concrete social practices that seek to live out such a vision in which the suffering of the poor is alleviated. Second, we must ask ourselves whether such queries are not a form of evasion. We seek to evade the Little Way precisely because it is a politics which becomes the warp and woof of our very lives, leaving no space for a prepolitical, "mystical" self. We are perhaps much more comfortable with the antinomy of "mysticism and politics" precisely because it protects the private self from the violence it enacts in the public realm.

The Little Way is a path without such protections, in which the light before us is just enough to allow the next step forward in hope, knowing that we are following the path of Jesus who has gone before us. At the end of *The Story of a Soul* Thérèse writes: "Since Jesus has reascended into heaven, I can follow Him only in the traces he has left; but how luminous these traces are!" (258). Like Thérèse, like Dorothy Day, we live with the paradox of a Savior who has vanished, only to be mysteriously manifested. Eschewing the security of territory, the Little Way is the errant path charted through the world by God's pilgrim city, pursuing the luminous traces of Christ in the poor, the hungry, the homeless and the suffering. It violates our very notions of the political, based as they are on control and security, yet Dorothy Day devoted her life to the practice of this politics—the politics of the Cross.

Notes

[1] David Tracy, *Dialogue with the Other: The Inter-Religious Dialogue* (Grand Rapids, MI: William B. Eerdmans Publishing Company, 1990), p. 17.

[2] See, for example, Claude Geffré and Gustavo Gutiérrez, eds., *The Mystical and Political Dimensions of the Christian Faith, Concilium 96* (New York: Herder and Herder, 1974); Johannes B. Metz, *Followers of Christ: Perspectives on the Religious Life*, Thomas Linton, trans. (New York: Paulist Press, 1978); Edward

Schillebeeckx, *On Christian Faith: The Spiritual, Ethical, and Political Dimensions*, John Bowden, trans. (New York: Crossroad, 1987); and even Michael Novak's early work, *A Theology for Radical Politics* (New York: Herder and Herder, 1969). In listing these together, I do not mean to imply that they all fall equally under the critical comments I shall offer. The work of Metz, in particular, moves somewhat in the direction of what I wish to propose.

³ Tracy, *Dialogue with the Other*, p. 118.

⁴ Schillebeeckx, *On Christian Faith*, p. 3.

⁵ Max Weber, "Politics as a Vocation," in *From Max Weber: Essays in Sociology*, H. H. Gerth and C. Wright Mills, eds. and trans. (London: Routledge & Kegan Paul, 1948), p. 127.

⁶ Weber, "Politics as a Vocation," p. 123.

⁷ Ibid., p. 121.

⁸ Max Weber, "Religious Rejections of the World and Their Direction," in *From Max Weber*, p. 336.

⁹ Tracy's formulation "mystical-prophetic" is perhaps better in this regard because the prophetic is not clearly any more "realistic" than the mystical. However even this formulation is problematic, since it seems to degenerate into a version of Reinhold Niebuhr's love-justice dialectic, which is rooted in Weber's ends-means dichotomy. Also, the language of "mystical-prophetic" carries with it the baggage of Heiler's use of this distinction in his famous work *Das Gebet*. For a critique of Heiler on this point, see Rowan Williams, "The Prophetic and the Mystical: Heiler Revisited," *New Blackfriars*, vol. 64, no. 757 (July/August 1983): 330-347.

¹⁰ Dorothy Day, *Therese*, 2nd ed. (Springfield, IL: Templegate Publishers, 1979), p. viii. Subsequent references to this work will be in the text.

¹¹ Barbara Corrado Pope, "A Heroine Without Heroics: The Little Flower of Jesus and Her Times," *Church History* 57 (March 1988): 55-56.

¹² It is worth noting that Thérèse herself never used the precise phrase "the little way of spiritual childhood"; this was a phrase coined later to characterize her teaching. Still, it is difficult today to read Thérèse's descriptions of her status as Christ's "plaything" without hearing overtones of sadomasochism: "I told Him not to use me as a valuable toy children are content to look at but dare not touch, but to use me like a little ball of no value which he could throw on the ground, push with his foot, *pierce*, leave in a corner, or press to his heart if it pleased Him; in a word, I wanted to *amuse little Jesus*, to give Him pleasure; I wanted to give myself up to His *childish whims*." Thérèse of Lisieux, *The Story of a Soul: The Autobiography of St. Thérèse of Lisieux*, John Clarke, O.C.D., trans. (Washington, DC: Institute of Carmelite Studies, 1976), p. 136 (emphasis in original). Subsequent reference to *The Story of a Soul* will be made in the text.

¹³ In fact, few of those whom modern academics identify as "mystics" fit easily into that category, which is largely a construct of post-Kantian theology and philosophy. On this point, see Grace Jantzen's *Power, Gender and Christian Mysticism* (Cambridge: Cambridge University Press, 1995), esp. pp. 4-12, 304-321, 328-339.

[14] Indeed, though Thérèse describes her healing on this occasion as a miracle, it is not clear that she understood this to be any sort of extraordinary visionary experience. See *The Story of a Soul*, pp. 65-67.

[15] *St. Thérèse of Lisieux: Her Last Conversations*, trans. John Clark (Washington, DC: Institute of Carmelite Studies, 1977) p. 77 (July 7, no. 2).

[16] The term "overdetermination" is used by Freud to describe the multiple causes of a symptom and by Althusser in his work on Marx. For a brief discussion, see Raymond Williams, *Marxism and Literature* (Oxford: Oxford University Press, 1977), p. 88.

[17] Thérèse even looks to her cousin, Jeanne Guérin, who was married eight days after her profession, to see how a new bride should attend to her bridegroom, and goes so far as to compose a wedding invitation for her spiritual espousals. See *The Story of a Soul*, pp. 168-169.

[18] Thérèse herself said in the last months of her life, "God alone can understand me" (*Last Conversations*, p. 87 [July 11, no. 1]), which might be taken as egoism or a simple statement of fact.

[19] Thérèse notes her childhood fondness for pictures (*The Story of a Soul*, p. 71) and in her final days holy pictures were pinned to the curtains surrounding her bed. She had a particular devotion to a picture of the martyr Théophane Vénard, hugging and caressing it in her final days. See *Last Conversations*, p. 199.

[20] Simon Tugwell, *Ways of Imperfection* (Springfield, IL: Templegate, 1985), p. 219.

[21] See *The Story of a Soul*, pp. 180-181 and Thérèse's "Act of Oblation to Merciful Love" in ibid., pp. 276-277.

[22] Bernard Bro, O.P., *The Little Way: The Spirituality of Thérèse of Lisieux*, Alan Neame, trans. (London: Darton, Longman & Todd, 1979), p. 13.

[23] Bro, *The Little Way*, p. 39.

[24] Michel de Certeau, *The Mystic Fable: The Sixteenth and Seventeenth Centuries*, Michael B. Smith, trans. (Chicago: University of Chicago Press, 1994), p. 289.

[25] Patricia O'Connor notes that the religious perspective of Thérèse's family was "sharply at odds with the bourgeois ethic all around the Martins. . . . What set them apart from many other Christian families is that the Martins took this idea of offering a life to God not as an outmoded residue of the Medieval Church, but quite literally" (*In Search of Thérèse* [Wilmington, DE: Michael Glazier Inc., 1987], p. 72).

[26] *Last Conversations*, pp. 138-139 (August 6, no. 8).

[27] *The Story of a Soul*, pp. 207-208. Cf. her letter of July 18, 1897 to Maurice Barthélemy-Bellière in Thérèse of Lisieux, *General Correspondence, Vol. II: 1890-1897*, John Clarke, O.C.D., trans. (Washington DC: Institute of Carmelite Studies, 1988), pp. 1152-1153.

[28] *Last Conversations*, p. 73 (July 4, no. 2).

[29] Bro, *The Little Way*, pp. 39-40.

[30] *The Story of a Soul*, pp. 192-194.

[31] Pope, "A Heroine without Heroics," p. 59.

[32] *Last Conversations*, p. 141 (August 8, no. 2).

[33] *Catholic Worker*, April 1952. Reprinted in Dorothy Day, *By Little and By Little: The Selected Writings of Dorothy Day*, Robert Ellsberg, ed. (New York: Alfred A. Knopf, 1983; reprinted as *Dorothy Day: Selected Writings* [Maryknoll, NY: Orbis Books, 1992]), p. 274.

[34] *The Catholic Worker*, December 1965. Reprinted in Dorothy Day, *On Pilgrimage: The Sixties* (New York: Curtis Books, 1972), p. 258.

[35] Weber, "Politics as a Vocation," p. 77.

[36] Ibid., p. 78.

[37] See her lengthy quotations from Robert Ludlow on this point in Dorothy Day, *The Long Loneliness* (New York: Harper and Row, 1952), p. 268.

[38] *Last Conversations*, p. 36 (April 6, no. 2).

[39] See Michel de Certeau, *The Practice of Everyday Life*, Steven Rendall, trans. (Berkeley: University of California Press, 1984), esp. pp. 29-42.

[40] *The Catholic Worker*, September 1957, reprinted in *By Little and By Little*, p. 285.

[41] *Last Conversations*, p. 123 (July 31, no. 13).

[42] See in particular James Terence Fisher, *The Catholic Counterculture in America, 1933-1962* (Chapel Hill, NC: The University of North Carolina Press, 1989).

[43] *The Catholic Worker*, April 1968, reprinted in *A Penny a Copy: Readings from* The Catholic Worker, Thomas C. Cornell et al., eds. (Maryknoll, NY: Orbis Book, 1995), p. 172.

[44] See *The Catholic Worker*, February 1942. Reprinted in *By Little and By Little*, p. 264.

[45] Dorothy Day, in *Liberation* (September 1957), reprinted in *By Little and By Little*, p. 280.

[46] "Politics as a Vocation," p. 78.

Theologies of Work in the U.S. Grail:
The Founder's Vision[1]

Patricia Mary DeFerrari

Introduction to the U.S. Grail

The U.S. Grail is part of an international movement of women who support each other in their search for God and in working toward transformation of the world into a place of justice, peace and love.[2] The U.S. Grail has centers at Cornwall-on-Hudson, New York; Loveland, Ohio; and San Jose, California. Grail centers offer educational programs on concerns of women, social justice, care for the planet, personal growth, and spirituality. The Grail also sponsors other activities in cities throughout the country, including San Francisco, Chicago, Boston, Cincinnati, Philadelphia and Milwaukee, among others. There are currently about 250 members in the U.S. Grail.

The International Grail Movement began in the Netherlands on November 1, 1921, when five women started a new life together in a large country house in a suburb of The Hague. Their aim was to work out a way of life and training for a community of lay women dedicated to serving God and God's kingdom in the world. Their ultimate goal was to convert the world to God. They intended to use the means and possibilities the world offered in order to usher in a new era in Christian history. The community they formed, the Society of the Women of Nazareth, would become the core group of the Grail Movement.[3]

The vision for this community began with Jacques van Ginneken, a Jesuit priest and scholar. During his novitiate, van Ginneken was introduced to the question, "Why is the world not yet converted?" Van Ginneken took this question to heart and devoted his whole life to it.[4]

He believed that what was needed to convert the world was a spiritual movement, a movement of people who would give themselves fervently to God in the midst of the world. This movement ought to be centered around a fiery kernel of people, whose radiant love would permeate the members of the movement and through them enkindle the world with a fiery love of God.[5] Van Ginneken aims for this love of God when he speaks of converting the world. While he dedicated his life to attaining a world ruled by Christian principles, he did not intend that all people should convert to Catholicism.[6]

Van Ginneken's experiences, studies, insights, and prayer also convinced him that a new expression of women's apostolate in the church was needed to realize God's purposes in this period of history.[7] The result of this vision and commitment was the founding of the Society of the Women of Nazareth. By the mid-1930s, the Grail had spread to other countries, including Germany, England, and Australia. Lydwine van Kersbergen and Joan Overboss, who brought the Grail to the United States in 1940, came in 1944 to Loveland, Ohio to found Grailville, which became the primary center for the national movement.[8]

Fundamentals of Jacques Van Ginneken's Spirituality

In August 1932, van Ginneken gave a series of thirty-two talks at a retreat for Grail leaders held at the Tiltenberg, the training center for the International Grail. He based these talks on the Spiritual Exercises of Ignatius of Loyola. Less than a month later, van Ginneken presented a ten-day course of thirty-two lectures on the apostolate of women, which he based on his own extensive studies of history, ethnology, psychology and contemporary culture. These two series of lectures provide a primary source for the commitments and principles that shaped van Ginneken's vision for women in the conversion of the world.[9]

In these talks, van Ginneken urges Grail leaders to strive toward a total inward giving of themselves to God in the concrete responsibilities of life.[10] Giving oneself completely to God involves answering the purpose for which God created the individual. Every person has a special service to render.[11] Nonetheless, neither deeds nor words will win the world to Christ, but radiant love will influence the world, enkindle it with love of God, and bring about its conversion.[12]

Van Ginneken identifies two practices as fundamental to a life dedicated to God: "the obedient cross" and "love of all mankind for God's sake."[13] "The obedient cross" refers to a practice of obedience that includes mortification or self-denial. Obedience is always ultimately directed toward God, although often obedience to God requires obedience to one's leaders, God's representatives on earth.[14] Van Ginneken encourages his listeners to be faithful to the demands of their leaders and to take up any and all tasks asked of them. Such obedience may require self-mortification, that is, a dying to one's own desires, but it leads to great blessings.[15] Obedience, however, should not be a passive acceptance of orders. Obedience requires use of one's intelligence and initiative, especially when working in the Grail centers. Obedience is efficient only when initiative is allowed to develop with it. When a command is given, the individual should be allowed to make decisions regarding the details of implementation.

> If you prompt them word by word under obedience what to say, and you demand that they carry it out exactly like that, you kill every human initiative. Jesus did not obey like that, neither did He will that women should be made to obey like that.[16]

To take the initiative daily in obedience to the cross requires self-denial and self-sacrifice.

Van Ginneken provides several reasons for practicing mortification. Such practice proves to be an excellent tool in gaining mastery of the soul over the body. The body, not seen as the soul's enemy, is its servant. A strong apostle needs both sound mind and sound body under the spirit's direction.

> The body should possess a sound mind, and the body should be kept in control and should not revolt against the spirit. However, we are not pure angels. Be sure your body remains capable of serving the spirit. The body should be allowed to live and work.[17]

Van Ginneken suggests that his listeners collect an anthology of extreme penances that are not unhealthy. He notes that such a list will necessarily vary from individual to individual.[18]

Mortification also aids in developing talents. A person cannot develop skills or discover new talents without hard work accompanied by a certain amount of unpleasantness. At the very least, development requires that a person go against natural preferences for the easy and familiar. A person unwilling to mortify herself will never develop all the beauty God has given her[19] because "The cross is the principle of growth in the spiritual life."[20] Van Ginneken elaborates on this point in a retreat talk on suffering. He argues that suffering makes us great and allows us to reach our full potential, to "let our powers reach their 100%." Apostles must remember the power of suffering when the burdens of life and work press upon them.[21]

Furthermore, the example of mortification inspires vocations, presumably religious ones. Van Ginneken's own experience verifies this. He admits that as a teenager he was drawn to his vocation by the example of people "who went against their own inclinations and became happy through it."[22] Grail women must not fear mortification; their sacrifices of love "will reach the aim. The world loves to see those who give themselves, and every woman's heart will be jealous of you and you will win them for Christ."[23]

A fundamental function of mortification is penance, atoning for sins, and correcting faults. Intelligent penance has an "element of reversal" to it. In other words, it is directed against the sin committed or the fault perceived. Thus, a penance for vanity would be quite different from one for carelessness. Wearing dark clothes and a veil might help overcome vanity but would do nothing for carelessness.[24]

Although van Ginneken urges penitential practices that respect each member's individuality, the purpose is never simply individual sanctification. On one level, the practice itself is communal in that members assist each other and help each other in mortification. But the practice of penance also builds solidarity on a much deeper level. As van Ginneken sees it, penance is effective only because the individual's efforts are united with the sacrifices offered by Jesus. Sacrifice incorporates a person into the Mystical Body of Christ. This incorporation allows a person through her penitential practice to atone for another's sin. Such vicarious suffering especially pleases God because the person becomes more like Jesus.[25] Van Ginneken consistently links mortification with loving service to one another. "Only then the womanly form of penance will triumph in your training house when that penance results in service to one another."[26] *Love* is "subjecting oneself to another and doing good for that person."[27] In short, the first fundamental in van Ginneken's spirituality, "the obedient cross," serves the second fundamental, "love of all mankind for God's sake."

The Place of Work in Van Ginneken's Spirituality

Work is a crucial element in van Ginneken's spirituality for several reasons. First of all, work allows people to become what they were created to be while rendering the service they owe to God. Work provides a concrete way of obeying God's will, which, in turn, will fill a person with God, making that person happy and radiant. In this context, all forms of work are honored whether manual, intellectual, or artistic. Van Ginneken emphasizes the kind of work does not matter as long as the work is God's will for the individual. Servants, factory workers, and professors equally please God when they do God's will.[28]

Work is also a form of mortification in that it often requires self-denial and self-sacrifice.[29] As such, work develops personal talents, builds solidarity, and increases compassion. "If you do not do your work, you steal from God and from your leaders. You render your gifts useless."[30] Throughout his retreat talks, van Ginneken emphasizes the importance of working conscientiously.

> Those who do their duty in all simplicity, even when it comes hard and costs at times trouble and well nigh superhuman effort . . . those who live silently on in the happy consciousness of living for God . . . all of those are filled with a deep peace which brings them happiness and radiates out to others.[31]

Van Ginneken urges Grail women to work intelligently and to sacrifice all to accomplish their given tasks. Taking full responsibility requires thorough and systematic plans to accomplish their work assignment, whether cooking, scrubbing, keeping accounts, or choreographing dances. Just as the wise virgins in the gospel parable carried extra oil for their lamps, so Grail women must foresee difficulties and prepare for them. Such intelligent work requires self-knowledge and rigorous honesty. If an individual knows she cannot manage the task given her, she must immediately inform her supervisors. "You must not promise to look after something and then not accomplish it."[32]

Van Ginneken addresses the question of work not only in the individual's life but also in the life of the Grail community. The Grail movement is first of all a spiritual movement, "seeking the far-removed, great good of the world's conversion."[33] All Grail work must be examined in light of this goal. All Grail houses must judge whether they are truly striving after this great good. As van Ginneken repeatedly reminds his listeners, this goal can only be attained through radical self-surrender, a surrender made daily. "The apostolate for each one of you is your daily plodding in a tough job here and an unpleasant job there and a busy job another time."[34] The conversion of the world happens in the struggle of everyday life. Doing good not only develops the Grail's work but also influences others' work, because people will imitate the Grail. Their accomplishments may not have the Grail name attached to it, but the Grail will have enkindled in those people the desire to do good work.[35]

Van Ginneken sees prayer as the foundation of the Grail's work. He warns of the danger of neglecting prayer and meditation. "I know that you are busy and think: I can forego my hour of prayer, the work comes first. That is faulty logic. Prayer comes first."[36] Prayer is both a great gift and an injunction from Jesus, who taught his followers to pray always. Yet true prayer must include both penance and deeds. Prayer is nothing unless it arrives at daily mortification and the practice of charity.[37] Praying always means, at the same time, working, so that work is prayer.[38] Furthermore, praying as well as working is a communal activity.

> You should not say: I must have a prayer hour, but you should be willing to give another person a prayer hour as well. And you should understand that it is the same whether *you* get one or she. In other words, we work in a movement . . . you must make one another holy.[39]

As a movement, the Grail seeks more than the sanctification of its own members; it seeks the sanctification of the world. The Grail strives to be "a sacrificial community for the conversion of the world by revolutionary methods."[40]

While van Ginneken repeatedly reminds his listeners of the importance of their work, he also notes that neither human deeds nor accomplishments effect conversion but God's grace does. Similarly, eloquent words and marvelous accomplishments will not attract people as much as a radiant spirit will.[41] Rather than transforming the world through their work, the Grail's work will transform them into loving individuals and a loving, united community. This transformation will ignite the transformation of the world. Van Ginneken thus places a tremendous amount of trust in the transformative power of faith-filled work.

Assessing Van Ginneken's Vision of Work

One clear limitation to van Ginneken's vision of work is his reliance on a dual anthropology. His complementary view of women and men assigns each a rather stereotypical set of positive and negative qualities, strengths and weaknesses. In a retreat talk on the differences between men and women, van Ginneken characterized women as gentle, that is, sweet, compliant, soft-hearted, meek, sensitive, warm-hearted, friendly, thoughtful, patient, affectionate, and, above all, loving.[42] In contrast, men were described as strong, that is, rigorous, self-reliant, persevering, dignified, prudent, and wise, possessing equanimity, determination, judgment, talent for leadership, willpower, self-respect, courage and energetic daring.[43] In another lecture, van Ginneken maintained that men are naturally analytical in their thinking, while women are intuitive.[44] When speaking about asceticism, he suggested that fasting is proper penance for men because tongue and taste pose the greatest temptation to them, while the primary feminine fault is vanity.[45]

Although van Ginneken was rather conventional in the way he divides qualities between men and women, he did not see these differences as sharp or rigid distinctions. Indeed, the ideal person develops both womanly and manly qualities, just as Jesus did.[46] Van Ginneken's respect for women is genuine. He founded the Society of the Women of Nazareth because of his profound faith in women's vision and his conviction that the conversion of the world depended upon the influence of women, an influence which could be realized only through a movement of women led by women. Accordingly, he encouraged the women to organize themselves in such a way as to be independent of the control of local priests or of Roman congregations. They were to be a lay organization associated with the local bishops. He advised them to avoid having priest directors; it would be better to give themselves retreats. If they did invite priests to come, they should choose from different orders each year.[47] Women of the Grail Movement were to be public leaders both in church and in society.[48] This tremendous faith in women as self-directive has proven to be a powerful factor in the evolution of the International Grail Movement, particularly so in the U.S. Grail Movement.

Another limitation of van Ginneken's vision of work lay in his restricted treatment of the socio-political dimensions of work. Although van Ginneken recognized that all workers, including and sometimes especially women, were often forced to labor under very unsatisfactory conditions, he did not question the social and political structures governing the workplace, particularly the factory. Work among the factory girls of Haarlem was one of the Women of Nazareth's first projects. In the last lecture of his "Course on Woman," Van Ginneken discussed the Grail's social program for working girls. He believed that the Grail's goals in this work ought to include both protection of human rights and spiritual conversion. In referring to human rights, he meant protection from sexual harassment and abuse; he did not mean shorter working hours or higher wages. The Grail's goal should not be to restrict the amount of work girls do, but to teach them to carry their crosses joyfully. Van Ginneken opposed Catholic labor unions. He characterized them as masculine organizations and "enemies of the dawning matriarchate." He saw their goal of raising all workers' wages, including women's, as ultimately detrimental to women. Van Ginneken recognized that factories hired women precisely because they were willing to work for less than men. Consequently, by van Ginneken's calculations, the rate of employment among women was higher than that of men. If women demanded the same wages as men, van Ginneken believed they would not be hired at all. Women would then lose their economic edge in society and with it their basis for influencing culture, which should be the Grail's ultimate goal. Van Ginneken also criticized the unions for focusing on the issue of an eight-hour day, when the real task was to develop a Christian culture.[49]

In a conference devoted to analyzing conditions of the modern world, van Ginneken criticized both capitalism and communism. After discussing each economic system in detail, he noted their common characteristics: divinization of technique, victory of matter, high tension in people, and either bitter or calculated heroism. Van Ginneken condemned both capitalism and communism and promoted Catholicism as a third force alongside these economic systems. He saw the effective strength of Catholicism in women who were capable of the extreme love and self-sacrifice needed to counterbalance the greed and materialism of capitalism and communism. At the same time, he proposed that the Grail ought to become "a world firm with power and capital."[50] Here van Ginneken's analysis lacks consistency and clarity.

Despite the limits of his social analysis, van Ginneken's tremendous faith in women's vision and commitment empowered Grail members to engage wholeheartedly in their work in such a way that it became transformative of them and of those whose lives they touched. The concluding section of this paper will discuss the basic elements of a theology of work evident in the first decades of the U.S. Grail Movement. It will then sketch some of the factors that raised new questions for the Grail and pushed Grail women to new understanding and practice in later decades.

Continuing Influence and Development of Van Ginneken's Vision in the U.S. Grail

Work has been a foundational element in the thought and practice of the U.S. Grail from its beginning in 1940. Virtually every piece of literature published by or about the U.S. Grail in the 1940s and 1950s includes mention of work.[51] Women who were present at Grailville during those years all note the centrality of work in their daily life. Work was part of their individual and communal prayer life and the basis for intellectual and creative development.

Common themes in all of these publications reflect a continuation of the values espoused by van Ginneken. First of all, work contributes to and is a part of the dignity of human beings. Work allows people to develop their talents and their personality. Work is worship; it begins in prayer and is accomplished for the glory of God. Women of the American Grail especially respected the sacramentality of work. Participation in work reveals something of the hidden nature of God and of human beings. Work is primarily for service; it is a service of love. Kahlil Gibran's phrase, "Work is love made visible," seemed to be the motto of life at Grailville during the first two decades of their existence.[52]

Work was significant to the women of the Grail as a fundamental element in their larger project of building a sound Christian culture, a project embraced by van Ginneken in his vision for the International Grail. The U.S. Grail also came under the influence of the National Catholic Rural Life Movement, of which it was a part, as well as that era's wider back-to-the-land movement. Consequently, American Grail women promoted agriculture as the first of the arts and the basis of culture, and wrote about the nobility of rural work. In contrast to van Ginneken, they criticized the conditions of factory labor and the use of modern machinery. Whereas the priest saw the development of modern machinery as liberating for women, Josephine Drabek warned that too much emphasis on efficient, labor-saving machines for the housewife ignored the reality of how much manual labor is a part of housekeeping and failed to respect its influence on the life of mind and spirit.[53]

Grail women's commitment to building a Christian culture kept them attuned to social and institutional questions of work on the national and international levels as well as the local one. Their apostolate had multiple goals: to evangelize individuals and to change existing institutions or create new ones based on Christian principles. Two important principles guided the economic dimension of their apostolate. Economy must serve human needs and be organized in such a way as to promote human responsibility. Grail programs developed in light of women's participation in the economy not only as industrial workers but also, and perhaps more significantly, as consumers and home producers.[54]

During the 1950s, the Grail began establishing centers in cities throughout the country. The Gateway Center in Detroit was especially concerned with meeting the needs of working women. Out of their efforts the Grail Council on Service Careers was established. A "service career" refers to work a woman performs as a service of love and thus contributes to the Grail's apostolate. Examples of careers which support meaningful concerns include nursing, teaching, social work, and secretarial work. In their statement of purpose, the Council identified two primary goals: to direct more students toward service careers and to educate women in maintaining positive attitudes toward their service career roles.[55]

To fulfill these goals, the Council developed workshops and seminars particularly for working women. The Detroit team's first program began by asking, "Is there a need for such a program?" Program participants then posed the following questions.

What is the present situation of working women? Are they on the whole making a positive contribution to the community through their work? Are they in jobs geared to service? Are they exercising an influence as women? Are they developing their own potentialities as persons, as women, as Christians? Do they have a positive attitude towards their role as single working women? Is their role generally recognized by society, by Catholics?[56]

The discussion in response to these questions relied upon a public opinion survey prepared by the Gateway and a series of articles on the topics from various secular and Catholic journals. The second part of the program laid out three elements of a possible solution. First, the working woman must have a positive concept of her role. Second, she needs communication on a deep level. And, finally, she needs status. She needs to be recognized by church and society. In later programs, these elements developed into topics such as the meaning of work, qualities women bring to their work as women, building community through work, women's work and the international scene, and the supernatural sources of work in love.[57]

In the 1960s and 1970s, Grail women became a part of the feminist movement in this country. They became more critical of the power structures in society and church and of the assumptions underlying the roles traditionally assigned to women in society and church.[58] Grail women questioned their own organizational and decision-making structures, eventually moving from a centralized, hierarchical structure to a more decentralized structure which allows all members to participate in and share responsibility for the decision-making process.[59]

During this same period, Grail women continued their work in areas not previously mentioned in this paper. They actively sought to promote interracial justice, civil rights for all, community development, and increased ecumenical cooperation among Christian churches. Through their center in San Jose, California, the Grail also became associated with the United Farm Workers. Collaboration with Latin American Grail sisters introduced the U.S. Grail to liberationist goals; Paulo Freire gave workshops at Grailville in 1969 and 1973. All of these programs, activities, and affiliations had tremendous influence on how Grail women dealt with issues of women and work.[60]

Women of the U.S. Grail have continued to face the challenges that their work and world in the 1980s and 1990s pose for them. Concern for economic and social justice in the context of increasing globalization and ecological degradation shapes and motivates most Grail programs today. The Grail in San Jose, California is in the process of developing and building the San Jose Grail Housing Community, which will provide thirty-five units of affordable, for-sale housing, a women's/community center, and a child development center.[61] Grail teams in the Bronx, Cornwall-on-Hudson, and San Jose have sponsored north/south exchanges which bring together Hispanic and Anglo women. The New York teams are currently preparing for a Women of the Americas gathering at Grailville in 1998.[62] Global Village programs for teenage women have been held annually at Grailville for several years. Since the late 1980s, the Grail has also renewed and deepened its commitment to caring for the earth. Grailville and Cornwall-on-Hudson offer programs on permaculture (sustainable agriculture), solar greenhousing, organic gardening, composting, recycling, and many other environmental programs.[63]

From its beginning, the Grail has been a spiritual movement to empower women for the transformation of the world. Grail women's self-understanding and their work has been rooted in their religious search. At the same time, they have undertaken work in a world they see alive with the Spirit of God, so that their experience of work has been itself a source of spiritual growth. Even the preceding, very brief sketch of the work of the U.S. Grail gives an indication of how this interaction between understanding and practice has been a vital force in its history.

Notes

[1] This paper is essentially an introduction to a larger work in progress, namely, the author's dissertation (Ph.D.), *Theologies of Work in The U.S. Grail, 1940-1995*, The Catholic University of America.

[2] "The Grail," brochure (Loveland, Ohio: Grailville, n.d).

[3] Eleanor Walker, "A Short History of the Grail," *Grail Review* 5:4 (1963): 1. For a more detailed account see Rachel Donders, "Beginnings," in *History of the International Grail, 1921-1979* (Loveland, OH: Grailville, 1984), pp. 1-8.

[4] Lydwine van Kersbergen, "Rev. James van Ginneken, S.J., Founder of the Ladies of the Grail," n.d., p. 1. The U.S. Grail Movement Archives, first collection, box 83, file 63. Hereafter cited as GA I: 83, 63.

[5] Donders, *History of the International Grail*, pp. 2-3. Donders cites a conference given by van Ginneken in 1918. Van Ginneken speaks about a fiery kernel of people enkindling the world with love of God in several places throughout his retreat talks and his "Course on Woman in the Apostolate," see note #9.

[6] Van Kersbergen, "Rev. James van Ginneken, S.J.," p. 21. Catherine Leahy made this same point in an interview with the author on June 15, 1996.

[7] Walker, "A Short History of the Grail," p. 1. Van Kersbergen and Donders also refer to this. For a more detailed account of van Ginneken's view of women, see

Marjory Krijnen, "Professor van Ginneken, S.J. and His Time," *Grail Review* 7:2 (1965): 4-15. Van Ginneken's "Course on Woman in the Apostolate" is a primary source for this material (see note #9).

[8] For a brief history of the Grail in the United States, see Joyce Dietrick, Janet Kalven, Peg Linnehan, and Dorothy Rasenberger, "The United States of America," in *History of the Grail: Individual Countries*, ed. Mary Gindhart (Loveland, OH: Grailville, 1984), pp. 78-86.

[9] Rachel Donders, *History of the International Grail*, p. 14. GA II: 21, p. 8. Lydwine van Kersbergen and Joan Overboss brought Dutch transcriptions of these lectures to the United States. They were translated into English by an anonymous Grail member in 1942, GA I: 1, pp. 1-20. Hereafter, talks given at the retreat will first be cited by title, followed by number and page, e.g. "The Holy Spirit and the Feminine Apostolate," R31, p. 1 for the first page of the thirty-first retreat talk. Lectures from the "Course on Woman in the Apostolate" will be cited as, e.g., "*Mère* Anne Javouhay," C16, p. 1. Subsequent citations will give only the lecture number and page.

[10] "Multiple Formation of Nuclei," C23, p. 1.

[11] Untitled, R2, pp. 2 & 4; "Sin," R6, p. 1; "About Personal Sins," R8, especially p. 2. Van Ginneken frequently encouraged Grail members to pray and reflect on John Henry Newman's prayer, "Lord, let me grow to be that for which you have destined me."

[12] "Love is Humility," R19, p. 4; also "Christ's Plan for Us," R15, p. 3; "Jesus's Methods of Apostolate," R18, p. 4. This theme is also found throughout his "Course on Woman."

[13] "The Last Judgment," R11, p. 1.

[14] R11, p. 2.

[15] Van Ginneken gives the example of the Women of Nazareth's experience with Aengenent's demand that they give up their own projects to undertake care for the girls of the diocese of Haarlem. At first, it seemed as though they were giving up their dreams, but in the end they were blessed with a much more prosperous movement through which they could work for their original goals. Walker and Donders both describe this episode in their histories of the Grail, as does van Ginneken in C20, "The Attitude of the Pope Towards the Apostolate of the Lay People," pp. 5-7.

[16] "The First Missionary Sisters in the 17th Century: *Les Femmes Savantes et Précieuses*," C15, p. 7. Here van Ginneken is commenting on the *Klopjes*, a seventeenth-century religious order of women founded by Dutch Jesuits. The *Klopjes* took vows of celibacy and of obedience to a priest, Jesuit or Franciscan, who would determine the nature of their work. The women had no say in what they would do. Van Ginneken declares that their treatment "really calls to heaven for vengeance" (C15, 6).

[17] "The Hermits in Egypt," C9, pp. 4-5.

[18] C9, p. 5.

[19] Van Ginneken elaborates on this point by telling the story of a young boy who refused to eat fish. When he grew up, he learned to use his intelligence, and he

began to see that he must mortify himself. He ate fish, first with repugnance, and later with relish. "If this child had never begun to overcome his aversion in this point, this part of his taste would never have been developed." Thus, mortification allows one not only to use but to develop talents" ("The Cross," R5, p. 2). Alden Brown provides a synopsis of van Ginneken's understanding of self-mortification in his book, *The Grail Movement and American Catholicism, 1940-1975* (Notre Dame, IN: University of Notre Dame Press, 1989), pp. 15-16.

[20] R5, p. 2.

[21] "Suffering," R22, pp. 5-6.

[22] R5, p. 4. Van Ginneken also thanks his mother for teaching him to mortify himself. "I still remember that once—my father had just died—I wanted to have a big piece of chocolate, and I could have had it, too. But Mother said, 'My boy, your father has just died and now you must do a mortification for your father. I shall put that piece of chocolate in the cupboard here; you can easily get at it. You may take it, but I advise you to leave it lying there for another two hours.' And, of course, I left it, and my mother knew very well that I would, even if I had to leave it from two o'clock until seven" (R5, p. 4). An important point of this story is that van Ginneken was taught to do mortifications for someone else, in this case his father, and not just his own sanctification.

[23] "Strictest Spirituality and Most Free Woman of the World," C22, p. 11.

[24] C9, p. 6.

[25] "Penance-Atonement," R9, p. 3.

[26] "Death," C10, p. 1.

[27] "Love is Humility," R19, p. 1.

[28] "A Higher Culture with *'Kadetten'* and *'Jonge Garde'*—Universities in the Missions," C31, 6. Van Ginneken highlights this point in a retreat talk, "Jesus did manual labor for fifteen years of his hidden life. During those years he was simply nothing more than a subordinate. What we do makes no difference, if only we do God's will" ("The Hidden Life of Jesus," R17, p. 4).

[29] Van Ginneken points to Thomas Edison as an example. After years of hard work, some of it "wasted," some of it experimental, Edison succeeded in creating artificial light. He gave his whole life over to this endeavor. Van Ginneken notes, "to stick with a problem and solve it after years of work is mortification" ("The Most Extreme 'Religion' Should Be Practiced in the Widest Possible Sphere by Means of 'The Circles of Action,' " C24, p. 14).

[30] "About Personal Sins," R8, p. 2.

[31] R2, p. 5.

[32] "The Fatal Results of Daily Sins," R7, p. 6. Van Ginneken continues his discussion of the need for self-knowledge in R8.

[33] "Meditation on Heaven and Hell, Which is a Meditation on the Love of God," C12, p. 1. Van Ginneken notes that this goal distinguishes the Grail movement from all other associations for girls and young women.

[34] "Strictest Spirituality and the Most Free Woman of the World," C22, p. 7.

[35] "From Missionary Orders to Lay Organizations: Results of the Success of *Mère* Javouhay," C17, p. 1 and C22, p. 12.

[36] R8, p. 2.

[37] "The Béguines, The Sisters of the Common Life, and Anna Bijens," C13, pp. 6-7 and 13.

[38] C13, p. 13.

[39] C13, p. 8.

[40] "St. Bernard's Devotion to Our Lady as a Personification of Divine Grace" and "St. Joan of Arc," C12, and C17, p. 9.

[41] Van Ginneken makes this point in several places throughout his conferences. One such example can be found in his seventeenth retreat talk in which he emphasizes the importance of doing God's will. "If you give a performance with 10,000 Grail members and run it smoothly in every detail, don't think that you turn the world upside down. Only when the heavenly Father gives you the charm, that is, the grace to influence the listeners is your demonstration a success" (R17, p. 4).

[42] "Contact with the World of Young Women Carried as Far as Possible," R25, p. 1.

[43] R25, p. 1.

[44] "Women and the Fathers of the Church," C8, p. 8.

[45] C9, p. 6.

[46] "The Masculine and Feminine Character," R25, p. 2.

[47] "Mary Ward's Effort, Which Failed, and the '*Klopjes*,' " C14, pp. 9-10 and 17; C20, 1-4. Van Ginneken remarks, "Our Lord did not institute priesthood in order to give the priests authority over everything" ("*Mère* Anne Javouhay," C16, p. 12).

[48] This goal is implied throughout the retreat talks and the Course on Woman, in which van Ginneken addresses the formation of women as spiritual and social leaders. At one point, van Ginneken notes, "We must stop considering man as the only force in public life" (C24, p. 24).

[49] "Dawning Matriarchate: Social Programme of the Working Girls," C32, p. 2.

[50] Ibid., p. 23.

[51] Particularly significant articles on work include Adé Bethune's talk on work given at the "Vineyard" course in 1942 (GA I: A10, p.1), Josephine Drabek's *Hymn to Work* published in 1946 (GA I: 19, p. 11), *Land and Life for Woman*, a series of talks given on Woman's Day of the National Convention of the National Catholic Rural Life Conference in 1946 (GA I: pp. 10, 15), and a series of talks on work given by William Schickel in 1952 and 1953 (GA I: pp. 85, 28). Grace Elizabeth Gallagher wrote an article for *The Wanderer* ("New Horizons for Young Women," 11/25/43) in which she describes her daily experiences of work while participating in a Grail course during the summer of 1943. Her reflections indicate the centrality of physical labor to the spiritual and intellectual development of course partici-pants.

[52] Josephine Drabek popularized this phrase in her book, *Hymn to Work*. The words were also painted in large letters on the wall of the bakery at Grailville.

[53] See van Ginneken, C24 and Drabek, Introduction to *Hymn to Work*, p. 7 and "Nobility of Rural Work," pp. 10-13 in *Land and Life for Woman*.

[54] Janet Kalven, "Issues Between Father John Fitzsimons et al. and Us,"

typewritten notes, 3/9/47, p. 1. GA I: 8, p. 2.

[55] "Council on Service-Career," flyer, n.d. GA I: 26, p. 8.

[56] Flyer, Grail Council on Service Careers, Detroit, Michigan, Summer, 1957. GA I: 26, p. 9.

[57] Ibid.

[58] For a discussion of the development of feminist consciousness in the Grail, see Janet Kalven, "Women Breaking Boundaries: The Grail and Feminism," *Journal of Feminist Studies in Religion*, Vol. 5, No. 1 (Spring 1989): 119-141.

[59] Janet Kalven, "Grailville in the Seventies and Eighties: Structural Changes and Feminist Consciousness," *U.S. Catholic Historian*, Vol. 11, No. 4 (Fall 1993): 45-47. Alden Brown also chronicles this shift in structure in his book, *The Grail Movement and American Catholicism*, chapters 8 and 9.

[60] A sampling of Grailville programs during this period may give the reader a sense of the ways in which Grail women were educating themselves, broadening their vision and commitments. Workshops and seminars included the following: Josef Goldbrunner, "The Person and the Community" (1961), Walter Ong, "The Humanities in a Nuclear Age" (1962), "Which Way for Women?" (1966), Benjamin Payton, "Metropolitics and the Socio-economic Challenge of Urbanization," (1966), Halloway C. Sells, "Negro History" (1968), "Crisis and Hope: Toward Theological Understanding in Today's World" (1969), "Gospel and Liberation Week" (1972), "Mobilizing Womanpower: The Alinsky Approach" (1973), "Women's Life Styles across the Generations" with Mary Daly (1973), "A Gathering for Simple Living—Global Justice" (1977), and "Feminism, Socialism and Christianity" with Rosemary Ruether (1978). A few of the longer-term programs for women included a Low Income Women's project, the Women's Project, weekend programs for women in ministry, the Semester at Grailville, the Seminary Quarter at Grailville, and the formation of a Professional Women's Group for Grail members.

[61] Further information is available from San Jose Grail Development Corporation, P.O. Box 611466, San Jose, CA 95161. (408) 258-3673.

[62] Further information is available from Grail Center Cornwall-on-Hudson, P.O. Box 475, Cornwall-on-Hudson, NY 12520-0475. (914) 534-2031.

[63] For further information, contact Grailville Conference and Education Center, 932 O'Bannonville Road, Loveland, OH 45140-9710. (513) 683-2340.

Part II

AESTHETICS

Sinners, Judges, and Cavalrymen: John Ford and Popular American Catholicism

Anthony B. Smith

Two recent books on American Catholic cultural expression, Paul Giles, *American Catholic Arts and Fictions* and Lee Lourdeaux, *Italian and Irish Filmmakers*, have opened a new appreciation of the Catholic art of film director John Ford.[1] Both Giles and Lourdeaux have taken advantage of David Tracy's work on the Catholic analogical imagination and challenged simplistic readings of Catholicism that reduce it to visible symbols of crosses, rosary beads, and priests in Roman collars.[2] Giles insightfully points to the "ontological burlesque" within Ford's films—a gesture, grounded in a Catholic understanding that we are all equal in the eyes of God, that delights in subverting social hierarchies and mocks the pretensions of elitist sensibilities.[3] Lourdeaux situates Ford in a tradition of ethnic Catholic filmmakers. He also extends Tracy's ideas by using Richard McBrien's argument that the three characteristics of Catholicism are sacramentality, mediation, and communion.[4] His suggestion of four "landscapes: Irish America, Ireland, foreign lands, and the wild West" helps illuminate the particularly Irish expression of Catholicism in Ford's work.[5]

Previous studies of Ford have alluded to his Catholicism but relegate it to biographical contextualization.[6] Therefore, both Giles and Lourdeaux have made important correctives to this lack in understanding Catholicism in Ford's films. Furthermore, by emphasizing the Catholic dimension of Ford's films, both authors point to something very important about Catholicism in America, namely that it possesses a rich and complex imaginative dimension that has been inadequately understood in American cultural history. As Giles has argued, acknowledging the Catholic presence in the United States relativizes central concepts of American culture, including reason, nature, and the individual. Both authors, therefore, offer ways for thinking the meanings of Catholicism in America in a context of cultural relativity.

Yet, both Giles and Lourdeaux shy away from fully developing the significance of the Catholic imaginative dimension within Ford's films. Heavily utilizing post-structuralist theory, Giles sees Catholicism as primarily a residual force while Lourdeaux reads religious themes in terms of Irish ethnic identity. I argue that Catholicism manifests a stronger presence in Ford's films than either Giles or Lourdeaux acknowledge. Further, Ford's Catholicism represents an important, overlooked dimension of the cultural dialogue between Catholicism and American society in the twentieth century.

The Catholicism of Ford's films expresses a sacramental imagination along the lines that Andrew Greeley has identified in his empirical research into religious tradition and cultural identity.[7] It is less a matter of doctrine and explicit expression of ideas than a "distinctive style of imagining."[8] Catholicism here is an "imaginative and preconscious infrastructure."[9] In Ford's work this Catholic imagination is expressed through three recurring themes. The first is the central and paradoxical role of sinners in the unfolding of grace. Ford's heroes, Dallas and Doc Boone, Judge Priest, Abe Lincoln, and Tom Joad, are often either sinners themselves or identified with the cause of sinners. These sinful heroes mediate the sacred and secular, the spiritual and material impulses within social life.

The important role of mediation and ceremony constitutes a second theme of Ford's Catholic imagination. His films, particularly the Cavalry trilogy (1948-50), *Young Mr. Lincoln* (1939), *Judge Priest* (1934), *The Long Gray Line* (1955), continually delight in portraying the rhythms of social ritual such as parades, dances, military processions, and courtroom trials. These rituals reflect the fundamental mediated character of human and social existence in Ford's films. Communal rituals dramatize the possibilities of connection and reconciliation and suggest a theological vision that privileges relatedness and similarity over radical difference.[10]

The third important theme of Ford's popular Catholicism is communion. Group situations and institutional settings such as small communities, Western towns, military forts, and groups of people in transit, provide opportunities for characters to express an important value in Ford's world—living, even sacrificing, for others rather than for one's self. Thus, his films often dramatize communion by examining the tensions between the individualism of members of the respectable classes and the selflessness of the despised and lowly figures of society.

These themes echo McBrien's three characteristics of Catholicism as sacramentality, mediation, and communion. They run throughout Ford's films, but are particularly evident in three that I will explore in depth: *Stagecoach* (1939); *Fort Apache* (1948), and *The Sun Shines Bright* (1953).[11] *Stagecoach* was Ford's first Western in thirteen years and ushered in his "prestige period."[12] It was also his attempt to revitalize the Western film genre that had developed in the 1930s to a grade B form of entertainment. Although very much a product of the commercial context of the American film industry, *Stagecoach* also suggests deep artistic and critical aspirations as Ford sought to reclaim the Western as a viable film genre.

Fort Apache, however, was a straightforward effort at commercialism in the wake of the box-office failure of Ford's 1947 *The Fugitive*.[13] The production company Ford had founded with Merian C. Cooper after World War II needed a commercial success to survive. Ford, therefore, churned out a series of Western adventures, the first of which was *Fort Apache*.

The Sun Shines Bright was neither a commercial nor critical success yet was a film that Ford deeply wanted to make. He financed the film independently, suggesting the personal commitments he had to the project.[14] It is a film of small scale and tone. It is, at the same time, quite remarkable for its use of Catholic motifs in its portrayal of small-town Americana. These films, made in three different decades under different commercial contexts, suggest the range of expression that a sacramental imagination assumed in the films of John Ford.

Stagecoach expresses themes of sin and grace, mediation, and communion through the story of the group of people journeying through the hostile Western frontier to Lordsburg, Arizona. The real journey of *Stagecoach*, however, is less geographical than moral, one from intolerance and prejudice toward acceptance and forgiveness. It is a film about the triumph of the generosity of spirit over selfishness and isolation and creatively maps a Catholic moral landscape onto the mythic American West.

The group of stagecoach travelers and their journey are characterized by paradox. The representatives of respectable society who stand for virtues of propriety, thrift, and restraint—Mrs. Mallory; Gatewood, the banker; Hatfield, the chivalrous Southern gambler—are all ultimately moral failures. Gatewood is an embezzler of his own bank,

Hatfield has shot a man in the back, and Mrs. Mallory is too aloof and self-absorbed to care about anything but her own needs. Conversely, the sinners, Dallas, the prostitute, Doc Boone, the town drunk, and even Ringo, the outlaw, have no place in respectable society; yet, they all manifest values of compassion and acceptance. Similarly, characters such as Mrs. Mallory and Gatewood who assert their own interest contribute least to the collective good of the stagecoach, while those who think least of their own well-being, Dallas and Doc Boone, contribute the most to the coach's successful journey to Lordsburg.

One scene in particular accentuates the moral poverty of the privileged members of the stagecoach. It is the luncheon at Dry Forks, the first stop on their trip. Through careful framing and camera shots accentuating the table and the diners' relation to the table and each other, Ford constructs a dinner scene with strong sacramental resonance. The table itself stands in the middle of the room indicating the centrality of the lunch not simply as a moment for food but an occasion of communion. Furthermore, by focusing on the small gestures and details of the meal, the passing of plates, the holding of chairs, the spooning of food from bowls, Ford conveys the rich ceremonial character of the meal.

As the travelers enter the dining room, Mrs. Mallory heads to the front of the table while Dallas is depicted in the middle of the camera frame, suggesting the intimate connection between the meal and her character. Yet, as she notices Mrs. Mallory sitting down, Dallas quickly walks away from the table and sits at a side chair along the wall on the margin of the frame, the first indication of the divisions shaping the lunch meal. After the travelers have made plans to continue their journey and are ready to eat, Ringo calls Dallas back to the table, invites her to sit down, and holds her chair, which happens to be next to Mrs. Mallory. Cutting back and forth between the close-ups of Dallas and Mrs. Mallory, Ford uses the camera to underscore the social and personal tension that characterizes the meal.

Hatfield escorts Mrs. Mallory to the other end of the table. Both, in turn, are accompanied by Gatewood. Dallas and Ringo are left to eat in isolation. Then moments later, the camera from behind their shoulders zooms to a mid-shot of Mrs. Mallory and Hatfield looking at the two "sinners." The effect is to accentuate the distance at the table between Dallas and Ringo, and Mrs. Mallory and Hatfield. The luncheon scene dramatically renders the social and moral divisions among the group of stagecoach travelers and suggests how Ford used the failure of communion at the meal table to magnify the moral failure of proper middle-class social values.

At one point after the journey has resumed, Dallas notices Mrs. Mallory's discomfort and offers her shoulder to rest upon. Mrs. Mallory coldly declines. Meanwhile, Doc Boone continues to get drunk. At the next rest stop, Apache Wells, the travelers reach the dark point of their journey. They learn that the army troops have left the stop and the travelers are on their own to complete their journey to Lordsburg. Later that evening, bandits steal their spare horses. Finally, Mrs. Mallory, whose pregnant condition had become apparent, collapses as she begins her labor.

Yet, it is here that grace emerges through the selfless actions of Doc Boone and Dallas. The prostitute, who believed that it did not matter whether or not the coach made it to Lordsburg, comforts Mrs. Mallory through her labor pains. Doc Boone, the fatalist drunk, sobers up to deliver the baby. Their actions manifest a different understanding of virtue and agency from that of the other travelers. Through their very lack of individual power, they are able to express more humane and generous values than their respectable counterparts.

The scene at Apache Wells serves as an inversion of that at Dry Forks. The actions of the respectable characters had distorted the possibility of communion at the meal table. In sharp contrast, the compassion of the sinners asserts the possibility of more generous and humane values and practices.

The triumph of these values climaxes in Lordsburg with the union of Dallas and Ringo. When Ringo escorts Dallas to her home, at night through the town's streets, their walk signifies another inversion of respectable values. This walk calls to mind Dallas's and Doc Boone's forced march out of Tonto at the film's beginning. In that earlier scene, the sinners were escorted during the day, through the main street, under the stares and condemnations of the Ladies' Law and Order League. Ringo's and Dallas's walk is the opposite of that long walk marked by intolerance. Amidst the shadows of the red-light district, with the nighttime screams of pleasure and the noises of the saloons, emerges the expression of acceptance and genuine love. Ringo finally understands who Dallas really is and nonetheless reasserts his commitment to her.

Stagecoach, therefore, represents a signal moment in the Catholic cultural encounter with America. The heroes of *Stagecoach*, Dallas, Ringo, and Doc Boone, manifest characteristic traits of a Catholic sacramental imagination. They may be lowly and sinful in the eyes of respectable society, but they also realize the communal possibilities of social life. The line between saint and sinner, the film suggests, is in fact quite narrow. Indeed, *Stagecoach* suggests that such "sinful" characters have a unique role to play in society as carriers of the special gifts of compassion and selfishness that respectable members of community fail to practice.

The film expresses such perennial Catholic concerns in very American terms. The heroes Dallas, Doc, and Ringo are embodiments of traditional American virtues of tolerance and practicality. Even their names, in contrast to Mrs. Mallory, Hatfield, and Gatewood, suggest an American vernacular. Similarly, the Western genre of the film situated the story in a dominant American cultural narrative with which mass audiences would be familiar. Furthermore, by privileging characters who occupy marginal social status, *Stagecoach* resonated with populist themes that pervaded the 1930s American culture. At a time of continuing economic depression, the film offers a sharp critique of the individualist ethos of the marketplace. Indeed, the banker Gatewood, who mouths the platitudes of the business class, "what this country needs is a businessman for president," is portrayed as ridiculous. The character even possesses an uncanny resemblance to Herbert Hoover.

The relationship between Ringo and Dallas represents an important dimension of the dialogue between Catholic and American values. It also highlights the deeply gendered typology of Ford's world. Of the lowly heroes of the stagecoach, Ringo is the most individualistic in his fierce determination to avenge his family's murder. Like Mrs. Mallory and Gatewood, he too is committed to getting to Lordsburg for his own purposes. Yet unlike them, his own commitments do not prevent him from respecting Dallas and Doc Boone and recognizing the good they embody. *Stagecoach*, therefore, sanctions the American values of forceful self-determination and individual initiative. But it legitimates Ringo's individualism by distinguishing it from the hypocrisy and selfishness of other characters. It suggests the possibility that the individual can avoid self-absorption by combining achievement with a sensitivity toward the less fortunate coupled with a generosity of spirit.

Ringo and Dallas also reveal how the film transcends neat boundaries between Catholic and American. This transcendence rests upon traditional gender terms. It is not that the characters "Ringo" and "Dallas" correspond easily to static categories of "American" and "Catholicism," but rather that the boundary between Catholic and American identities becomes more permeable at the expense of reinscribing traditional gender roles. In simultaneously subtle, creative, and highly gendered ways, therefore, *Stagecoach* provided Catholics a popular cultural vehicle for both becoming American and sustaining a sacramental vision.

Fort Apache, made nine years later in 1948, in the aftermath of World War II, is a fictionalized telling of Custer's last stand. It is the story of a group of cavalry soldiers and officers in the West during the years after the Civil War that is composed primarily of Irish-Americans with names like O'Rourke and Mulcahy. Fort Apache receives a new commanding officer, Colonel Owen Thursday, who has little regard for either the fort or his men. Learning that the Apache leader Cochise has taken his people off the reservation, Thursday attempts to bring the Indians back. He believes this will be his ticket to glory and a return to the East. However, Thursday's arrogance and egotism lead him and his men into a disastrous massacre at the hands of Cochise.

Fort Apache is also a story about the importance of ritual, ceremony, and mediation. In this film, grace and communion are realized within institutional settings rather than through a group of people who are forced to struggle together as in *Stagecoach*.

Fort Apache itself exists as a mediating institution between society and wilderness, East and West. The film, therefore, explores the settlement of the West in communal rather than individualist term. The essential ceremonial character of the fort is conveyed through numerous scenes of ritual expression. Indeed, Colonel Thursday's first appearance at the fort interrupts a dance held by the troops in honor of Washington's birthday. Lt. Michael O'Rourke offers his card at the private residence of his commanding officer, Thursday. New recruits are initiated into the basic drills of army life. The procession of cavalry units from the fort into the Arizona desert are twice given elaborate portrayal.

All these representations of army ritual function to dramatize the fact that the fort's men are bound together as a community. Indeed, the extensive use of such rituals implies the nature of the fort as a communion. The men are committed both to their mission as guardians of law and order on the frontier and to one another.

The film's Catholic sensibility extends beyond the representation of the fort and suggests that the cavalry's tight-knit identity does not involve separation from its larger environment. Ford develops a sense of sacramental reality through the very cinematic rendering of the Western landscape itself. The forays taken by several of the officers, as well as the two cavalry campaigns into the open Arizona country, allow the film to highlight the spectacular buttes, vistas, and terrain of Monument Valley. Ford's camera often emphasizes characters riding *within* the rugged landscape, underscoring their existence as a part of the larger realities of the natural world. Further, the cinematography accentuates the wonder of this landscape rather than its threatening menace. Natural forces of earth and water, sky and mountain, light and shadow constitute an important presence in Ford's representation of the West, suggesting a Catholic sense of the beauty of the created.[15]

In addition to the natural beauty, the landscape also holds the presence of Native peoples. Ford's representations of Indians, while often sympathetic, nevertheless portray them in limited terms as either warriors or victims. The sacramental imagination, therefore, does trade upon long-standing stereotypes. However, it also complicates reductive interpretations of racist ideology in the movie, for this sacramentality also critiques the destruction of native peoples.

The cavalry's survival, as Captain Kirby York, a long-time officer at Fort Apache, understands, lies in its ability to live within the western territory and not simply as conquerors. As someone attentive to the ways in which small details can hold important meaning, Kirby York is able to read the signs of the Indian presence in the landscape, while Thursday is blind to them. In addition, York works for reconciliation between the army and Cochise. He recognizes the legitimate claims of the Indians who suffered enormously at the hands of the government agent and trader, Silas Meachum. It is, in fact, York who calls for and arranges a peace meeting between Cochise and Thursday.

In contrast to York, Thursday is incapable of understanding the importance of ceremony and mediation. Thursday can see only one aspect of the rituals of Fort Apache—their support of his authority as commander. He believes the rituals of Fort Apache and their power to create a cohesive identity among the soldiers are to serve his own purposes of military glory.

His limited and instrumental understanding of ceremony and ritual extends, with disastrous consequences, to his relations with Cochise. In a central scene that condenses the film's themes of mediation and reconciliation, Thursday and his contingent of cavalry officers meet Cochise and his representatives in the middle of the desert. York acts as mediator between Thursday and Cochise, making introductions between the cavalry officers and Cochise and his men. Speaking through a translator, Cochise informs Thursday that he and his people will not return to the reservation until the government agent Meachum is removed. If he remains, there will be war.

Outraged by this, Thursday dismisses the whole conversation and tells his translator, "No preliminary nonsense with him. No ceremonial phrasings. Straight from the shoulder I tell you. The recalcitrant swine, he must feel it." He orders Cochise and his people to return to the reservation or prepare to be attacked. Ford has the camera focus on York and the other cavalry men expressing their shock at Thursday's insensitivity to Cochise, their dialogue, and the ritual of reconciliation they are engaged in.

Thursday's arrogance seals the fate of the cavalry and he leads his men to their own massacre. The film ends, however, some time later with York, now commander of the fort, giving a speech to a group of reporters who sing the praises of Thursday as a true war hero. A portrait of Thursday in full military splendor hangs in the background. The reporters are eager to hear about Thursday, but York corrects them and tells them that the true heroes are the dog soldiers. The ghosts of cavalry officers on horseback are superimposed on the scene as York stares out the window, and says:

> They [the ordinary soldiers] aren't forgotten, because they haven't died. They're living, right out there . . . And they'll keep on living, as long as the regiment lives. The pay is thirteen dollars a month, their diet beans and hay—they'll eat horsemeat before this campaign is over—fight over cards or rot gut whisky, but share the last drop in their canteens. The faces may change, and the names, but they're there, they're the regiment, the regular army, now and fifty years from now.

York's words describe the regiment in terms akin to the communion of saints. They imply the special quality of men who live as a group far from society, without the reward and respect of that society, and who live not for themselves as individuals but for one another— their regiment. They will eat—beans and horsemeat—and drink together—"share the last drop in their canteens." York's emphasis on the dignity of these men in the ordinariness of their lives suggests their extraordinary significance. Because of the sacramental character

York ascribes to them, he suggests that these men can find worth in the work and backwater environments that Fort Apache represents. This quality separates the regular soldiers from Thursday.

York's final speech and the centrality of ceremony in the film suggest the identity of the fort as a communion where grace emerges through selflessness and an appreciation of the role of the ordinary as the vehicle of extraordinary value. Recognition of the sacramental imagination operating in *Fort Apache* prevents the film's meanings from being reduced to either a celebration of militarism or a tragedy of men caught in insane institutions. The communion of soldiers lends an attractiveness and value to their lives even amidst bankrupt leadership and the stupidities of war. Whether politically pleasant or not, *Fort Apache* does suggest the meaning and dignity men can forge with one another within the limits of institutional life.

In contrast to *Stagecoach*'s explorations of group interaction and *Fort Apache*'s chronicling of institutional life in the military, *The Sun Shines Bright* (1953) stages the themes of grace and sin, the role of mediation, and communion through the story of Judge Billy Priest. It is a remake of Ford's 1934 film *Judge Priest* starring Will Rogers. Though this version lacks the unique wit of Rogers, the sacramental themes of Ford's work are particularly evident in this re-telling of the Judge Priest story.

The film is set in Fairfield, Kentucky, in 1905. It centers on William Pittman Priest, the town judge, who, along with his political cronies, is running for re-election. Fairfield has a secret that ultimately threatens to ruin Judge Priest's chances for political victory. The daughter of the town patriarch and mother of Lucy Lee, one of the town's brightest young women, had left many years earlier in shame. The dishonor is so great that the patriarch refuses to acknowledge her existence or even his own granddaughter. Therefore, Lucy Lee lives without a true identity. When Lucy Lee's mother comes home and dies, Judge Priest has to decide whether to arrange for a dignified funeral for the woman and risk his own career, or continue to keep the town's secret. Ultimately, Priest does arrange the funeral and the town is able to reconcile itself to its past by showing mercy to its lowliest members.

The film is a story of how an individual's actions can mediate a community's encounter with grace. The sacramental nature of the main character, Judge Priest, offers an understanding of community that extends beyond that of Fairfield's respectable citizens. It is one rooted in a sense of the goodness of creation and an awareness that the sacred and the secular, the spiritual and the material, are often deeply intertwined. The tension between the judge as mediator of the town's law and his understanding that there can be no true justice without mercy gives the film its dramatic power. The judge's own sense of justice and compassion stems, in part, from his appreciation of the goodness in ordinary life. In a joke running throughout the film, Priest periodically asks for his whiskey in order to get his heart working again. The humor derives from the judge's fondness for alcohol, but it also suggests that he understands how whiskey can have a beneficial, rather than simply a corruptive character. Similarly, when a banjo-playing young man, U.S. Grant Woodford, is charged with vagrancy and brought to court, the judge orders him to take a job down at the wharves. Yet when Woodford plays his banjo, Priest is highly impressed and plays along on his trumpet. Before sending the young man to find work, he tells him not to work too hard, lest he injure his hands that play such wonderful music. Priest's final remarks to Woodford signal his awareness that the joy the man creates through his music is at least as important as thrifty work.

This scene indicates that, while Judge Priest may be lax in following legal decorum, he pursues a broader understanding of the law. In accordance with this more generous view of law, the judge makes room for the outcasts of society. Mallie Cramp, the town madam, at one point confides to Priest how much she appreciated his respect for her in his courtroom. Similarly, when the young black man, U.S. Grant Woodford, is accused of rape, Priest is skeptical of the charges and tells the young man that regardless of "race, creed, or color, justice will prevail in my courtroom." At the town jail, the judge stands between a lynch mob and Woodford. He incurs the wrath of white townsmen but also prevents a rampage of racist violence.

Priest's politics are also characterized by a blurring of lines between high principle and personal action to achieve larger ends. He does not shy away from the rough and tumble world of bargaining for votes. Indeed, he is a master practitioner of the art of local politics. Sensitive to the importance of small details and gestures, Priest takes advantage of every opportunity to promote himself. He hands out his political cards in his courtroom. While talking to the Grand Army of the Republic veterans and emphatically stating that he will avoid all mention of politics, he reminds the men to vote and hands them his cards as well. Aware of the importance of making a good impression on the members of the Women's Temperance Society at the town's election eve party, Priest and his friends swear off alcohol. What may seem like a confusion of politics and virtue in the eyes of his opponents is for Priest the precise mode of keeping politics rooted in the social experiences of the townspeople.

Priest's efforts at reconciliation extend beyond both courtroom and politics and entail bringing together the Confederate and Grand Army of the Republic veterans. He even helps the GAR veterans with their reunion meeting when their commander informs him that their flag has been stolen. Understanding that their meeting cannot properly begin without the symbolism provided by the flag, he escorts the national flag at the Confederate veterans' meeting over to the GAR room. While Priest is proud of his Southern and Confederate heritage, he also values the similarities of sacrifice, respect for tradition, and pageantry he and his Confederate friends share with the very different men of the Grand Army of the Republic.

The greatest test to Priest's commitment to communion occurs when Lucy Lee's mother returns home. Knowing her own degraded status in the community, the mother gets off the steamboat and is taken in by Mallie Cramp. She dies shortly thereafter. Mallie asks the judge to arrange a respectable funeral for her. "That poor thing was a good woman," she says. "She just sort of let life get the upper hand." Knowing that no one in town would help her with the funeral, she asks the judge's assistance. Priest understands that his help would cast him in a vulnerable position in the impending election, yet Priest agrees, saying, "Worry no more, Mrs. Cramp. The Lord will provide."

The day of the funeral is also the day of the election. At the height of the business day, Priest leads the funeral procession of Lucy Lee's mother down the main street, accompanied only by a carriage of Mallie and the other prostitutes. One of the town's respectable ladies, seeing this scene, exclaims, "No decent woman will speak to Billy Priest from now on." As the funeral procession passes by in quiet dignity, however, Priest's political cronies join him. Other townspeople slowly join in as well. Priest leads the procession through the center of town, past the mansion of the patriarch, and eventually to the outskirts of town to the black church where the funeral is held.

The combination of Priest and his disreputable friends, the prostitutes, and the blacks together creates a ceremony of the least likely that even the respectable citizens of town must acknowledge. For a brief moment, the town's hierarchy has been inverted. The lowly become the leaders and the social elites are the followers. A community of compassion and forgiveness is forged. At the end of the funeral, as Priest and Mallie marvel at the beautiful and well-attended funeral service, Priest reiterates what he had told Mallie earlier, "The Lord will provide." Indeed, Lucy Lee's mother is buried with dignity and respect as she had wanted. Yet the goodness of the Lord's abundance is realized only through Priest's courage to risk his own status and political future to insure a proper burial for one of the town's loneliest outcasts.

While Lucy Lee's mother is being buried, the election day activities proceed—the communion of grace and the forgiveness of sins are juxtaposed with the secular affairs of politics. Yet the two worlds are not strictly separated, for, ultimately, Judge Priest wins re-election, casting the tie-breaking vote for himself. As his name suggests, the judge is a secular priest mediating between the spiritual values of forgiveness and compassion and the material realities of local politics.

Through Priest, the community of Fairfield becomes a vehicle of grace. Indeed, the film suggests that the community achieves its greatest moments of glory and honor when it cares for its lowliest member. By having this grace emerge by way of a politician who risks his career to see that an outcast soul is properly buried, *The Sun Shines Bright* implies that compassion is more noble than perfection.

Stagecoach, Fort Apache, and *The Sun Shines Bright* are three examples of how Catholicism operates as an imaginative force in the work of John Ford. Like much of Ford's work, these films express both a deep identification with America and a revision of its popular culture. Parallels to Ford's engagement with America can be drawn with the Jewish-American composer, Aaron Copland, who worked at the same time as Ford and was also drawn to the American mythology of the frontier.[16] Both men are regarded as having created some of the finest American art in this century, and both came from ethnic and religious traditions outside mainstream American culture. Such similarities indicate that Ford's films were part of a larger cultural transformation in mid-twentieth-century America, as ethnic and religious outsiders increasingly came to redefine American identity and community.

Furthermore, working within the mass medium of film, Ford's Catholicism accomplished something akin to what liberal Catholic intellectuals such as John Ryan and John Courtney Murray sought, namely, a dialogue with the larger American society. Ford's films, therefore, are as important for understanding Catholicism in twentieth-century America as the works of more recognized Catholic thinkers.[17] Mass culture, in fact, provided an unlikely but highly creative place for a Catholic imagination to engage American society. Indeed, Ford's popular American Catholicism suggests a broader perspective to interrogate Catholic Americanization. His work reveals that creative Catholic thinkers could find a home in America by pursuing imaginative encounters with traditional forms of storytelling such as melodrama and adventure as much as they did by offering political support to the New Deal or sanctioning religious pluralism. Ford's films, therefore, suggest that the cultural process of becoming a Catholic American was far more complicated than we have realized.

Notes

[1] Paul Giles, *American Catholic Arts and Fictions: Culture, Ideology, Aesthetics* (New York: Cambridge University Press, 1992); Lee Lourdeaux, *Italian and Irish Filmmakers in America: Ford, Capra, Coppola, and Scorsese* (Philadelphia: Temple University Press, 1990).

[2] David Tracy, *The Analogical Imagination: Christian Theology and the Culture of Pluralism* (New York: Crossroad, 1981), pp. 405-456.

[3] Giles, p. 306.

[4] Lourdeaux, p. 15. On McBrien's three characteristics of Catholicism, see Richard P. McBrien, *Catholicism* (Minneapolis: Winston Press, 1981), pp. 1180-1183.

[5] Lourdeaux, pp. 88-89.

[6] See for instance, Tag Gallagher, *John Ford: The Man and His Films* (Berkeley: University of California, 1986); Joseph McBride and Michael Wilmington, *John Ford* (New York: Da Capo, 1988); Ronald L. Davis, *John Ford: Hollywood's Old Master* (Norman: University of Oklahoma Press, 1995). To various degrees these studies of Ford acknowledge Ford's Catholic background but give it little significance in their respective interpretations of his work. Gerald Mast also makes reference to Ford as a Catholic in his *A Short History of the Movies* (New York: Pegasus, 1971).

[7] Andrew Greeley, "Protestant and Catholic: Is the Analogical Imagination Extinct?" *American Sociological Review* 54 (August, 1989): 485-502.

[8] Andrew M. Greeley, *The Catholic Myth: The Behavior and Beliefs of American Catholics* (New York: Collier Books, 1990), p. 4.

[9] Greeley, "Protestant and Catholic," p. 486.

[10] Tracy, p. 408.

[11] This interpretation focuses on three films where Americanist images and narratives are prominent. It, therefore, argues that the characteristics of sacra-

mentality, mediation, and communion extend beyond the Irish ethnic focus that Lourdeaux has used to interpret Ford's Catholicism.

[12] On *Stagecoach* as part of Ford's "prestige period," see Gallagher, p. 143. See also McBride and Wilmington, p. 53.

[13] Davis, pp. 203-204 and Gallagher, p. 246.

[14] Gallagher, p. 454.

[15] Lourdeaux also points to Ford's depiction of Monument Valley as an implicit expression of a sacramental sensibility. See *Irish and Italian Filmmakers*, pp. 117-118. One of the least discussed aspects of Ford's Westerns set in Monument Valley is the extent to which characters keep *returning* to this wondrous landscape as if they, like we the viewers, enjoyed being amidst the beauty encountered there.

[16] On Copland, see MacDonald Smith Moore, *Yankee Blues: Musical Culture and American Identity* (Bloomington: Indiana University Press, 1985), pp. 130-160. On the central role of religious outsiders in creating American identity, see R. Laurence Moore, *Religious Outsiders and the Making of Americans* (New York: Oxford University Press, 1986).

[17] I develop these ideas in my dissertation, Anthony B. Smith, "American Catholicism and the Construction of a Public Tradition, 1932-1962" (Ph.D. dissertation, University of Minnesota, 1995).

"Into the Valley of the Human":
The Contribution of William F. Lynch, S.J.
to American Catholic Intellectual Life

It is perhaps somewhat inappropriate to speak of William Lynch's contribution to American Catholic intellectual life. To be sure, Lynch's three "early" books, *The Image Industries* (1959), *Christ and Apollo* (1960) and *Images of Hope* (1965), were widely read and very well received. Yet his other books, especially the "later" works, *Christ and Prometheus* (1970) and *Images of Faith* (1973), while well reviewed were not widely or carefully read.[1] Moreover, if one is to judge by the almost total absence of secondary literature that seriously engages his ideas, one would have to concur with the recent complaint of Nathan Scott about "the neglect [Lynch] has suffered."[2] Thus it would really be more accurate to speak of the *potential* contribution that Lynch's thought could make to American Catholic intellectual life. It is that contribution which the following brief papers suggest.

After a short note about Lynch's life, David Toolan presents some reflections on the relations between Lynch's thought and his life. That essay is followed by Jerry Bednar's discussion of some of the key intellectual "tools" employed by Lynch—analogy and imagination. Finally John Kane gives an introduction to Lynch's thought on Christ and culture.

The general title for this discussion employs one of Lynch's images—"into the valley of the human" (IH, 101). It hopefully suggests, in a preliminary way, the nature of his contribution to American Catholic intellectual life.

WILLIAM F. LYNCH (1908-1987)—A BIOGRAPHICAL NOTE

John F. Kane

Lynch came to national attention with the publication in quick succession, between 1959 and 1962, of four important and well-received books which ranged from a technical work on Plato to studies of cinema and literary theory and a collection of essays on aspects of contemporary American culture.[3] These were followed during the 1960s and early 1970s by books on mental illness and hope, on secularity and the religious imagination, and on faith, especially as it relates to culture and politics. Several of his books won national awards, two (*Christ and Apollo* and *Images of Hope*) were first reprinted in paperback editions in the New American Library's "Mentor-Omega" series and later reprinted again by Notre Dame Press.

In addition to his books, Lynch published more than seventy articles. He taught briefly at Fordham, was editor of *Thought*, Fordham's respected quarterly, from 1950 until 1956, and then taught at Georgetown where he directed the honors program and also taught at the Jesuit Woodstock seminary. He returned to full-time writing in 1962 as "writer in residence" at St. Peter's College (Jersey City). He lectured widely at colleges and universities throughout the country during the 1960s and 1970s, was an honorary visiting professor at Carleton College and at Muhlenberg College, and several times visiting professor at Princeton Theological Seminary. During his later years he founded and edited *New York Images*, a journal devoted to the interdisciplinary study of imagination and society. (Three issues appeared in 1984, 1985, and 1986.)

Lynch was born into an immigrant Irish Catholic family in New York City on June 16, 1908. He spent most of his life in or around New York, a city he loved deeply. After graduating from the Jesuits' Regis High School in 1926, he received a scholarship to attend Fordham where he graduated with a degree in classics in 1930. He worked for a year as a sportswriter for *The New York Herald Tribune* before returning to Fordham as an instructor in Greek and English. He joined the Jesuits in 1934, completed an M.A. in philosophy in 1939, and again taught at Fordham while working on his doctorate in classics, which he received in 1943. During these years and as part of Fordham's centenary celebration, he directed Greek-language productions of *Oedipus Rex* and *The Eumenides* that received national acclaim. He was assisted with original choreography and scores by Lincoln Kerstein and Martha Graham of the New York Ballet and by composer Virgil Thompson. He did his theological studies at Weston College (near Boston) and was ordained in 1945.

In 1960, *Time* called Lynch "one the most incisive Catholic intellectuals in the U.S."[4] In 1974, a *Boston Globe* review of *Images of Faith* referred to him as "one of the subtlest, soundest philosophical voices in the United States today."[5] Shortly after Lynch's death on January 9, 1987, fellow Jesuit Dan Berrigan described him as "a luminous spirit whose work lifted American Catholicism more than a few notches in the direction of intellectual maturity. . . . a Jesuit in the grand manner, rare as radium and twice as bright. Grandly human, grand in learning, a man of scope and sensibility."[6] More recently, Nathan Scott described Lynch's work as "one of the most remarkably sensitive and original explorations of the interior life in the literature of our period."[7]

SOME BIOGRAPHICAL REFLECTIONS ON WILLIAM F. LYNCH'S THOUGHT

David S. Toolan

Bill Lynch's project was essentially that of a cultural critic. He was concerned about how artists—writers, dramatists, film-makers—shape (or misshape) "the body of sensibility," what Joseph Campbell would have called the myths we live by. Another way of putting this would be to say that he was a critic of the imagination—of the inadequate and dehumanizing images or story-lines by which we live (or stop ourselves from living). And in this regard Bill Lynch carried on a one-man campaign against all forms of one-sidedness that force us into stark, either/or choices between, say, freedom and authority, the right-wing and the left-wing, individual and society, flesh and spirit, or the infinite and the finite. In our folly, we may polarize things, but reality, as he insisted in *Images of Hope*, is not fundamentally conflictual.

The themes of his books—a one-sided Apollonian imagination, a one-sided Promethean activism, or the "gnostic" imagination that asks us to jump out of our skin to attain some form of transcendence—illustrate a failure to recognize, as Jerry Bednar has said, that contraries belong together. If in any work of art or of theology, one pole is absolutized, Lynch argued, the multifaceted human spirit is flattened, and the result is both bad art and bad theology.

Against all such false imaginings, he opposes a christological imagination—an imagination that invites us to enter more deeply and richly into time. As he put it in *Christ and Apollo* in criticizing T. S. Eliot's notion of reaching a "still point" outside of time. "We need not utterly change our ways and thoughts to know [God]; we need not utterly jump out of our skins to get to him."[8]

The principle here—that time needs no redeeming, indeed, that the Eternal is to be found in the step-by-step rhythms of time and the "realistic imagination"—is something that Lynch learned, I believe, from the method of prayer in the *Spiritual Exercises*. This has nothing to do with a slavish, external imitation of Christ. It means using your creative imagination in prayer—inserting yourself into a biblical scene, applying your five senses so that you taste and feel yourself there as an active participant in Christ's archetypal story. If you let your imagination go, the biblical stories do not unfold exactly as they do in the text. No, the story unfolds as the Spirit directs, exactly targeted to where you are in your life. It invites you to step deeper into your own life, to pay attention to the movements of the Spirit in time. And this, I would say, is the secret source of all of Bill Lynch's criticisms of "fantasy"—a false, Platonizing or gnostic transcendence that seeks an escape from the temporal process. For him, Christ has hallowed time and earthiness.

In his writings, Lynch's critique of the absolutizing, either/or imagination is generally focused on the secular world beyond the church. Yet it was impossible to know the man, as I did, without realizing that he was also wrestling with his own demons of perfectionism, the fierce moralism of Irish-American ghetto Catholicism, and a Jesuit spirituality deeply infected by American Pelagianism. One of the great dangers of the *Spiritual Exercises*, with its constantly repeated question after each meditation, "What can I do for Christ?", is that it can itself be one-sided, turning many a young idealist into a willful workaholic. In any case, I am fairly confident that it was the moralistic perfectionism and absolutizing of his own Catholicism that led Bill Lynch, in the late 1950s, to a major psychological breakdown.

Years later, all he would need to hear at a Jesuit dinner table was someone dropping a cliché like "do your best"—and he would explode. (He had a ferocious temper.) Doing his best under the lash of "never enough" had nearly broken him and, of course, led, when he emerged from the abyss, to that wonderful book, *Images of Hope*, widely read at the time by psychologists and widely ignored by theologians. Similarly, he could never hear of Karl Rahner's hypothesis of a "final option" at the moment of death without protesting that this was an example of inhuman grandiosity and the gnostic imagination. The very thought, as you are perhaps dying of cancer and not exactly in top form, that you would have to pull yourself together and DO SOMETHING, makes this a momentous decision. Well, this expectation was preposterous and inhuman, something only a romantic German, or an American Pelagian, could concoct.

Such fantasies play to the activist American temper just at the moment when it is time for something else—a letting go. As Lynch once put it,

> The American is not equipped . . . with an imagination, with a set of images, which would tell him it is all right to lie down in good time and die, dependently leaving it to God to raise him up again. Therefore he must, like Sammy, run.[9]

One of the great gifts that Bill Lynch left me was that he let me take part in his dying. In late 1986, I had just become the superior of our local Jesuit community when Bill fell very ill and spent about two months in Manhattan's Lennox Hill hospital. I would visit him every day, and step by step he took me with him in the process of dying. His body was failing him, but his active imagination, a theme that was utterly central to his thought, was alive and well.

In *Images of Hope*, he speaks about the healing power of being able to imagine a future, especially regarding dying and becoming finally dependent on a power not our own. During the last month of his life, to the great frustration of the doctors who wanted some straight answers from him about his symptoms, he moved into a twilight zone. It was as if he were experimenting in passing over into another region—not so much vertically "up there" as ahead, in the unknown future. It was sheer play, and I found it wonderful to enter into these spaces with him.

For instance, one day, as I entered his hospital room, he called out, "Give me your pants!" "What's happening?" I asked. "I'm taking a trip on a train," he answered, "and I need clothes." I said, "Why don't you check out whether you really need them." So he retired back into that twilight zone for a bit and then returned with a big grin. "I don't need clothes!" he said. "I can come as I am!" Then another problem: "I need money; give me some money," he said. So I asked, "Why don't you check that out too?" And again he checked it out and came back, again with a surprised smile: "The trip is free; there's no charge!"

It was extraordinary to explore this territory with him. He could describe where he was. On train trips, on other voyages. And he was always asking you to join him, come with him. He'd say: "COME! COME!" His own literal-minded nurse would rebuke him: "Father Lynch, you're not going anywhere; you're going to get well." She insisted on feeding him fantasy. But he would have none of it. "COME!" The African-American nurse for the patient next to him understood, was on his wave-length. "Father Lynch," she'd cheerily say, "I'll come, I'm ready when you are." In January of 1987, he was ready, faithful to the time of the end—or the next beginning.

Let me end my remarks with what seems to me the crucial question for us. Some of the old battles Bill Lynch fought are now won. We're at a different place now. But he opened up many fruitful lines of inquiry, especially regarding the imaginal shape or misshape of our lives. So the question is: where can we go with such lines of inquiry and criticism today? How might we run with his ideas now, in our situation?

I have but one suggestion, one regarding the national abortion debate. Knowing Bill, I cannot help but think he would find the way we are posing the issue as an either/or choice between an absolutized pro-choice position and an absolutized pro-life position. Here, Bill might note a failure of the imagination, and thus a terrible oversimplification on both sides. Can't we do better?

THE CONTOURS OF THE VALLEY:
WILLIAM F. LYNCH, S.J., AND THEOLOGY

Gerald J. Bednar

William Lynch's journey into the valley of the human was a march into the common finite dimensions of everyday life. It was a courageous march because so many would rather ignore the finite, and go straight-away to the infinite. As David Toolan has shown, Bill Lynch's valley contained many shadings, many mixtures of both light and darkness. Others who looked only for the light or only for the dark would miss the finite contours where people were meant to live with each other and with their God. How did Lynch survey that valley? Two of his important tools can be treated here: the analogical imagination and faith as imagination.[10]

The Analogical Imagination

The imagination, for Lynch, simply describes the activity whereby people make images. Such an activity is so wide-ranging that it becomes apparent that the imagination draws on all of the faculties, feelings, experiences, and life histories of those who imagine.

> It is not a single or special faculty. It is all the resources of man, all his faculties, his whole history, his whole life, and his whole heritage, all brought to bear upon the concrete world inside and outside of himself, to form images of the world, and thus to find it, cope with it, shape it, even make it. The task of the imagination is to imagine the real. However, that might also very well mean making the real, making the world, for every image formed by everybody is an active step, for good or for bad.[11]

The concrete world is thus mediated to the person through the imagination. The imagination is at play as soon as anything is perceived. The imagination is not confined to "re-presenting" our world, it "presents" it as just or unjust, reputable or reprehensible, or as being any one way rather than another.

Lynch was convinced that a person gains knowledge by "insertion" into one's culture. The broader the insertion, the better. This means that the more resources that go into our images, the better.[12] For example, if theologians want reliable guidance on theodicy, they should draw on all available resources—not only philosophy and theology, but also drama, poetry, novels, autobiography, music, and so on. Distortions occur when only one approach is used—only philosophy, or only theology, or only psychology. Poor Johnny One Note can't explore the wonders of music very well except in that one note, that one key. Lynch wants us to explore the full range of the chromatic scale—

with all its potential for probing the diverse dimensions of human experience.

What does the term "analogical" add to the idea of imagination for Lynch? Unlike many who define analogy in terms of a relationship in which one thing is "like" something else, Lynch uses the term "analogy" to describe what is *both* the same *and* different. The same and the different are received "according to a proportion" (*ana logon*) with each component of the thing contributing its charm to the making of that thing.[13] If Poor Johnny One Note had an analogical imagination, he could range throughout all the scales and keys available to any musician. The analogical enables a person to account for the different aspects of a reality in a single image. In other words, Lynch insisted on keeping together in thought and image that which is already found together in reality.

Among the most interesting and threatening things found in reality are "contraries." Lynch defines contraries as those features in any particular finite existent that are in some way opposed to each other, but are always found together.[14] Their nature is such that they cannot exist apart from each other. For example, any physical object has a left side and a right side. Although these are opposing aspects of a thing, they cannot exist independently of one another. All sorts of contraries can be considered: the one and the many, the same and different, the inside and the outside, good and bad, and so on.

There are also such things as contradictories. These are opposing features that can never be found together: good and evil, or love and indifference, might be examples.[15]

Lynch thought it essential to use the analogical imagination to show how contraries can and must be conceived as coexisting together in any particular thing. Analogy holds both terms of the contraries in proper proportion.[16] While an analogical image may highlight one aspect of a reality, it never allows that aspect to act as if it could exist on its own.[17] For example, while one may develop persuasive images of the Interior Castle of one's life, those images cannot be treated as if they could exist without the Exterior Castle.

With Lynch's understanding of the analogical, contraries can be kept together without the fear of falling into reductionism which diminishes a reality by becoming infatuated with only one of its elements. Lynch recognized the temptation to reductionism as a function of what he called the "absolutizing instinct." The absolutizing instinct is that inclination in us that prompts us to invest absolute value in one particular aspect of a reality.[18] For example, everyone recognizes that faith includes a psychological dimension, but the reductionist concludes that faith can "really" be explained only in terms of psychology. The psychological, in that case, is invested with absolute value. Other dimensions of faith, such as the religious and the ontological, are missed. Lynch noted that Freud and his followers could have reached a more complicated and a more satisfying understanding of faith had they employed an analogical imagination. The same can be said of theologians.

Lynch recognized how difficult the analogical imagination had become for people in our culture. When Lynch saw modern drama, he noted that many times one contrary was favored to such an extent that the less favored contrary was muted almost out of existence. Usually, playwrights tried to explain away the finite.[19] Craft images to convince people that they really have only the infinite within them, and they are eager to hear more. But those images are forgotten almost as soon as the closing curtain falls because, Lynch would contend, too often those images have failed to account for the finite.[20]

Bring on a playwright who is insightful enough to tell us the obvious, that we are finite, and you will have a much different story— perhaps even a classic. The job of the playwright is to show us our finite dimension in a way that gives us some distance from it, so that we can bear to take a good honest look at it.[21] When this is done with some skill, then our finitude can strike us with power because its contrary, the infinite, cannot be far behind. When there is no cheating, when the hero or heroine is brought face to face with death, time, exhaustion, birth, and other limit experiences, then the power of the infinite can be seen in its proper proportion, in its proper perspective, analogically. Those experiences are the vehicles of the divine. To exclude the finite is to exclude the infinite.[22] They are contraries, and belong together.

Another characteristic of the analogical imagination is that it "moves with every change in reality. . . . It does not try to impose one single form of its own upon the world."[23] In other words, the analogical imagination is sensitive to the varying ways in which entities may be received into the world. It will resist the preconceived notions of what anything "has" to be. Lynch respected each entity's right to "emerge" into its own maturity on its own terms. A thing does not have to look outside of itself to find the laws according to which it should be acting. It has within it all it needs to be what it is.[24] As it grows to its maturity, we stand to learn from it. But that cannot happen if we impose our preconceptions on it. For example, theologically, the analogical imagination will enable a society to shift its image of femininity according to the various ways that real women come to express their humanity. Thus, finite entities can be said to have a certain autonomy. They only need to obey the law that is within them making them what they are.[25]

So, thus far, we have seen that Lynch proposed that we adopt an analogical imagination. By this he means an imagination that can fashion images that are ontological reachings into reality. Those images, in other words, hold together in proper proportion the various aspects—especially the contraries—of whatever is imagined.

Faith as Imagination

Lynch explored the relationship between faith and experience. Too often theologians have treated faith and experience as if experience were a phenomenon so divorced from faith that it could serve as an independent criterion of faith. But under Lynch's conception, faith itself is a way of experiencing or imagining.[26] Faith is a way of composing the experiences we have throughout our lives.[27] Lynch reminds us that there is no such thing as a "pure" image or a "pure" experience. It is always touched by a way of receiving those experiences or images.[28] Some look at the world and receive it as a gift. Others look at the same world, and see only the absurd. The difference is not in the data, but in two different ways of taking in the same data. Lynch, therefore, treats faith as imagination. Faith is the pattern or the paradigm by which anyone composes the reality he or she encounters. Faith is a way of imagining things.

Because faith is a way of living and experiencing, it is historical. It moves through time, which is to say that faith is dramatic. So too should its images be dramatic.[29]

Through the action (drama) of the imagination, our rational, predictable, rather neat, theoretically constructed world meets the "diffraction" of reality. Lynch proposes that once an idea is posited in the real world through action, it meets a certain resistance, and can never "remain itself . . . because under the weight of the world it diffracts and breaks up" somewhat as a beam of light breaks apart as it passes through a prism.[30] Allow the best laid plans to begin to take shape.

Once they hit the prism of reality, they oftentimes break into such varied and unanticipated pieces that immediately adjustments must be made:

> It becomes an adventure. Now only the imagination can take over its course. More often everything goes ordinarily, with the usual diffraction of an idea as it enters the world, as enter it must. But almost as often it does not. The message of Romeo to Juliet enters crookedly and tardily; we should not say that it does not get there, it does not get there as intended by some pure and loving intelligence, but gets there late and madly. The original word or event becomes splashes of fragmentation or sorrow, diverted from its pure lines and intentions by the rougher lines of the people in between the pure idea and the world.[31]

Lacking the benefit of diffraction, the imageless thought can be just as false as the thoughtless image. Both the logic of the rational and the diffraction of the dramatic must be brought to bear on the various ways we deal with reality.[32] Furthermore, the *pathos* of diffraction, the suffering that occurs when we act on our ideas, constitutes an important moment in our effort to learn (*mathos*), to reach some resolution when faced with difficult issues. Drama, *pathos*, *mathos*: Action, suffering, and learning form a methodological tool to probe human advancement.[33] Faith's concepts, therefore, need to pay attention to the ways in which they enter the world, the suffering they engender, and the possible learning that can result from that kind of suffering. Often enough, the Christian's drama will involve the *pathos* of irony (life through death, riches in poverty, strength in weakness), and will require patience to see the resolution, the learning, the *mathos*, eventually take shape.[34]

Faith's images are powerful because images can do so much. Images do not simply portray something. They are also accompanied by a feeling. Consider the image of a baby that has been brutalized. What happens when a Christian hears an image like that developed along those lines? Most would wince at such an image. In a certain sense, one can say that "images feel."[35] They also can grow leery, they can evoke loyalty or betrayal, they can love or hate, and coax us to believe or to grow suspicious. They can also lead us into reality, or farther away from it. Images also think.[36] For example, how many times in the Gospels do Jesus' parables challenge our hackneyed logic with quite a different logic of their own? Consider the laborers who come into the fields at different times, yet all receive the same pay (Matt. 20:1-16). That image is informed by a different rationality than many employ.

Faith as imagination also accounts for the unity of love of God and love of neighbor. The vertical and horizontal are contraries.[37] The horizontal dimension puts the believer in touch with other people in a certain sort of way. This horizontal dimension implies that faith has a body.[38] It is the level on which faith becomes incarnated. Faith must be embodied in our actions, our images, thoughts, prayers, and so on, and that embodiment will affect not only our ability to reach each other, but also our ability to encounter God.

Faith not only has a body, it has a body of sensibility.[39] Faith's body reacts variously to the varying forms of reality it encounters. Faith is not rigid. It does not respond univocally to every event it confronts. It responds to some events with compassion, to others with humor, to others with admiration, and so on. This means that faith is flexible according to a sensibility.[40] Faith as imagination is analogical and, therefore, attends to the proper proportion, or blend, of sensibilities that would be appropriate. That sensibility takes on a body anytime any of the faithful act and react appropriately to those in front of them. That body is at times as obvious as the great institutions of the church, such as Catholic Charities, and at times as subtle as the wink of encouragement that one person may give another in trying circumstances.

Furthermore, Lynch urges that faith and incredulity should not be separated in the body of sensibility of faith. This incredulity of faith does not defeat faith (for that kind of incredulity would be its contradictory), but it opens faith to wider horizons. This incredulity makes us humble enough to know that we do not know exactly what we are talking about. This use of the analogical in theology keeps faith and incredulity in proper relation to each other. If they were not, Lynch contends that we would be left with only an ideal in which to believe, and the concrete reality of faith would be unlivable.[41]

In the final analysis, the only livable place for us is the finite. Lynch was convinced that our salvation lies in the finite contours of the valley of the human where Christ came to dwell among us. The finite does not negate the infinite, it is its contrary, its dwelling place on earth. As such, Lynch's thought offers many riches for those who would critique the finite valley of the human that we call our culture.

OF CHRIST AND CULTURE—BUILDING FAITH'S BODY

John F. Kane

Writing at one point in his book *Christ and Apollo* about the fragmentation characteristic of our times, Lynch refers to the "separated
religiosity" of those Catholics "who believe that 'ideas' and some
strange version of dogma they have concocted is the only thing that
matters . . . by the saving of souls they mean . . . the saving of the top
of the head."[42] Then he adds this comment:

> God knows, we must always fight for the purity of dogmatic
> truth, but even here we must not be guilty of that dichotomy
> which would make dogma reside in the pure mind and give it no
> relation to human reality, to sensibility, or to all the mighty
> energies of the imagination's bloodstream. If we do this, if we put
> all our eggs into saving the "intelligence" . . . then the culture
> engineers . . . will take over the rest. And the people, having been
> given half a Christ, will be left in a hell of sensibility.[43]

The comment is at least as significant today as when it was made in
1960 and it goes to the heart of Lynch's fundamental project. He certainly read and knew theology and was, as he puts it, concerned for
"the purity of dogmatic truth." Yet he was not primarily concerned
with academic theology. If one wants to think of his contribution in
terms of theology, it's perhaps best to see him working at a "secular"
or a "political" theology, or perhaps at a "theology of culture." Yet
since many still remember him primarily for his books on literature
and cinema, let me hasten to add that he was not concerned about
culture only in some restricted sense of "the arts" any more than he
was concerned about the separated discipline of theology. He was,
rather, concerned about giving "a whole Christ to the people"—relating doctrine and the resources of faith to "human reality, to sensibility, or to *all the mighty energies of the imagination's bloodstream.*"
His contribution was directed, to use an image central to his last book,
toward that larger "body of faith"[44] that is human culture—understood
not as some separated artistic realm, nor simply as an ideological su-

perstructure to the real thing, but as the real human thing itself, that real and embodied sensibility which is as much the "bloodstream" of social as of personal life. Well before Vatican II, Lynch was concerned to call theology and church out of an intellectual and spiritual ghetto—not only to bring the resources of faith to the critique and construction of human sensibility and politics, but also to bring the rich, diverse, maddening, mean, and beautiful body of human sensibility and action, the lifeblood of the human city, into the realization of the fullness of Christ. As he saw it, this building of the body of sensibility and faith was especially the vocation of intellectuals. He was thinking not so much of theologians or even academics, but of artists, writers, and other leaders in public and cultural life—and not only, nor even primarily, "religious" or Christian artists and writers.[45] Still Christian intellectuals do have a crucial role. Thus, one way of understanding Lynch's "contribution to Catholic intellectual life" is in terms of his call to Catholic and Christian intellectuals for the development of what could be called a distinctly lay rather than a clerical theology. He wanted a focus on the meaning of Christ centered in the world rather than in the church, in the larger body of human faith that moves analogously through every sphere of existence. Catholic intellectual life needs this call and challenge at least as much today as thirty years ago. The need arises from current Catholic struggles over clerical restoration in which all sides seem focused and polarized on narrowly ecclesial issues, and even more from the growing retreat of intellectuals, including theologians, into various narrow and separated specializations.

Lynch's own writings not only provide one significant model for such thinking and building (or, as he would have it, such imagining) of the full body of faith, but also make specific major contributions to the task. For instance, his critical discussion of cinema and of literary theory in *The Image Industries* and *Christ and Apollo* remains remarkably relevant.[46] So, too, the more directly political-cultural essays in *The Integrating Mind* and the extensive discussion of personal and social illness in *Images of Hope*. Yet, his two later books, *Christ and Prometheus* and *Images of Faith*, deserve special attention, partly because they have been the least read and discussed, but also because they provide such dramatic exemplification of his major themes and purposes. The first is Lynch's effort, through the central images of Prometheus and Christ, to provide a more adequate image of the secular. The text offers a way of imagining and affirming the great human-promethean project of autonomy and rationality, while simultaneously developing an internal critique of its dehumanizing promethean*isms*. The second, *Images of Faith*, is Lynch's effort, through the figures of Christ and Dionysius, to provide a new and more adequate image of human faith. In this case, faith has a body that shifts and changes as it moves through the stages and times of life in that complex and difficult imagining we call history.

As with all his writings, in these books one finds a complex, often dense, invariably demanding movement of thinking and imagining. Perhaps it makes sense to speak of a pattern of thought and images since I often have the sense that Lynch's writing is an artistic weaving. Different threads or strands enter in various combinations and directions to produce no neat theory or easily summarized set of ideas, but a different way of moving and putting things together, a renewed or transformed fabric of thought and imagination. At least his writings affect me, not as some clear theory or one more set of ideas does, but more like a shift in focus and perspective, a change of sensibility. And that, I think, is precisely his goal, his "fundamental project"—to build, by critical analysis of prevailing ideas and images and by the suggestive elaboration of alternatives, a *body of sensibility* that brings "Christ" into fruitful collaboration with "all the mighty energies of the imagination's bloodstream" and all aspects, however secular or worldly, of the life of the people.

I have been writing too much in generalities. Let me give a specific illustration of Lynch's contribution. I will beginning to follow one of the central threads in the fabric of his thought—his discussion of time and temporality.

Immediately, of course, I am faced with an irony Lynch would have appreciated. Irony, especially what he calls "the irony of Christ," is a central category in his discussion of faith and time in *Images of Faith*. At the moment, it is ironic that I want to write of Lynch's ideas about time and have so little time (and space) to do so. Yet at root is a more fundamental irony, faced not only by every speaker (and writer), but by all of us in every aspect of our lives. I want to make a point and you, I hope, want me to get to the point. Yet there is no way for us to get there in this very human and temporally defined world than by the definite temporal process of moving one step at a time, one word after another, through specific and partial images and ideas, inflections and gestures.

Lynch wrote continually, in a variety of ways, about such movement and temporal process—on stage, in story, in actual life and history.[47] Two of the most basic sources for his understanding of time are classical Greek drama and biblical narrative, especially the gospel presentation of the real temporal movements and stages of the life of Christ. So fundamental for him is the dimension of time, and so connected is his understanding of time to Christ, that he could write at one point in his final book:

> I repeat that everything I have ever written asks for the concrete movement of faith and the imagination through experience, *through time*, through the definite, through the human, *through the actual life of Christ*.[48]

He returns continually to discussion of the various temporal images and rhythms which affect and can dominate our actual movement through life. They include the images and rhythms presented in the arts and popular culture through story and sound, music and movement. In addition, the actual rhythms and images of the city as found in the workplace or the public square have a place in Lynch's discussion.[49] Thinking even more broadly, he includes the images and rhythms by which we move through the time and stages of our personal lives.

So fundamental for us is the reality of time that we have great need of a sensibility which enables us to live with humanity and real hope and faith *in and through time*, through the passages of our lives and the dramatic movements of our often tumultuous history. What we do *not* need are fantastic gnostic rhythms and images which simultaneously dismiss the real and ordinary time of our lives and of history, as if a barren wasteland of repetition and endlessness ("tomorrow and tomorrow and tomorrow . . ."), and urge an impossible transcending of the limitations of temporality. Yet, Lynch argues, our sensibility is to a great extent captivated by many variations on such gnostic images and rhythms. Thus we as a people need to pay serious, critical attention to the state of such images and rhythms, and to building a more adequate temporal sensibility. As Christians we need to ask what Christ has to contribute to this situation, not just to time and history abstractly considered or to dogma "in the top of the head," but to the concrete sensibility, the images and rhythms of temporality that prevail in our lives and are embodied in our culture.

Lynch's writing is an ongoing discernment and critique of such prevalent gnosticism, which he calls by this and many other names.[50] In fact, his discernment is so good and so constant that it's often tempting to understand him simply as a superb culture critic. In *Christ and Apollo*, he analyzed the gnostic patterns in writers as different as Proust and Poe, in the supposedly Christian sensibilities of Eugene O'Neill and Graham Greene, and even in the more authentically Christian sensibility of a T. S. Eliot. *Christ and Prometheus* is an extended analysis of the gnostic and romantic pseudo-magnificences of "progress" and "possibility" that haunt and dehumanize the modern secular project. At the same time, remarkably similar gnostic sensibilities pervade humanistic fears and religious denunciations of that project. And in *Images of Faith*, using the figure of Dionysius as the powerful primal energy of faith that moves us into life and time, Lynch explores the gnostic tendencies which continually pervert that movement. He finds them, for instance, in those many programs and ideologies, whether secular or religious, right or left, which attack some abysmal present, promise a glorious alternative, and demand revolutionary change. He calls this "revolution without imagination" and without irony. Yet gnostic tendencies are equally present in the many forms of contemptuous irony which disdain all politics and programs. This dialectic of contempt and glory, of scorn and the will to power, prevails as much in personal life as in politics, in the manic-depressive patterns not only of so many addictions, but also of so many spiritualities and theologies.

Yet Lynch is not just another angry critic of prevailing sensibilities. If *Images of Faith* can be read as a sustained critique of Nietzsche's Dionysius and the prevalence of that gnostic figure in contemporary culture, it is more fundamentally a retrieval and affirmation of a different Dionysius, just as *Christ and Prometheus* retrieves a different Prometheus. For Christ, according to Lynch, is neither the enemy of Prometheus and Dionysius, nor simply their savior who comes from the outside and at the last minute. Rather the God, who created and sustains these magnificent human energies, embraces and enters them again and again and again to move them not away from but "into the valley of the human." God moves them into the passage through the limited definiteness of time and the movements of lives and history where alone they find reality and truth and power.

The supreme irony, then, is that the very real glory of Prometheus and Dionysius, and the still greater glory of Christ, are actually to be found only in the poverty of time and the limited partiality of its stages and passages. The irony of Christ is his reality, the irony of incarnation. The greatness and glory of messiah and kingdom are realized in the poverty and particularity of the actual stages of the life of Jesus, even unto real death.[51] Or, put more positively and accurately, the irony is that real power and glory are no gnostic fantasy, but the insight of truth, the beauty of love, and the power of good realized as the energies in us of Prometheus and Dionysius move through the limited stages of time even unto death. In this dramatic movement, the supreme ironist is their companion, mentor, and savior. As "firstborn," he has already made this passage, embraced time, affirmed its goodness, and restored for us, against every gnostic fantasy, confidence in its real power.[52]

"It is completely false to say that Christ redeemed time. For time has never needed redeeming."[53] "Human time is a divine construction, narrow indeed but powerful as all real being is (and dreaming is not), all of its phases important . . . none of its phases to be omitted without paying a price."[54] But if time needs no redeeming, we do. For there is that in us, in Prometheus and Dionysius, which strains against the poverty and limitation of time and is willingly seduced by the gnostic fantasy of some short cut, some leap transcending time's slow and often difficult stages. Our culture and sensibility are shot through with these rhythms and images of such transcending. For this redemption, even as for creation itself, time is God's instrument. Thus even God needs, as we do, a body of sensibility, of rhythms and images, guiding the movement and revealing the meaning of the human and redemptive passage through time. And Christ, in the actual stages and ironies of his life, is the fundamental image of that passage, the touchstone of that body of sensibility.

Yet the meaning of that image must be reappropriated, re-imagined, time and again, in the diversity of periods and cultures and lives, in all the dimensions of our lives, lest we end with "only half a Christ and a hell of sensibility." Lynch's own contributions to such re-imagining for our time and sensibility are many. The final section of *Images of Faith*,[55] for instance, is a difficult and rewarding imagining of the movement of dionysian energy from childhood aspiration and expectation through encounter with the unexpected to the building of more realistic trust and confidence, and then again through encounter with suffering and the tragic even unto the real loss and nothingness of death. It is a modern *Imitation* as the magnificent energy of Dionysius is tutored by the ironies of Christ in its passage through time to real insight, power, and glory. The image of faith encompasses moving, suffering, and growing through the stages and passages of life and thus provides a real alternative to Nietzschean and other contemporary forms of gnosticism. The intricate detail of Lynch's act of imagination requires more explanation than possible here.

Let me, instead, end with a short cut. Recently the film *Braveheart* won many awards. The story of a Scottish peasant hero depicts his life through battles, through love and loss, to sacrificial death at the hands of his enemies and posthumous victory in national independence from England. The subtle but clear appeal to Christian symbolism is evident throughout, especially in the climactic betrayal by an ally, crucifixion-like execution, and hint of resurrection in the apparition of the hero's previously murdered wife. Yet in fact the film's sensibility is pervasively gnostic. The intensity and excitement of its rhythms lift one in typical Hollywood fashion out of ordinary time into some Valhalla of heroic action as never once touched the real earth or was lived by any real hero. The carnage of battle and the finality of death are shown, yet only in images which shock and horrify but effectively deny real battle and real death. The beauty is breathtaking, both in lingering close-ups of the two heroines and magnificent panoramas of Scotland's peaks and valleys. Yet the love of beauty and the beauty of love in this film's images are finally little more than "cheap grace"— unearned, undiscovered, unreal. The film's climax maintains the gnostic fantasy with no real crucifixion, no real death, and thus no resurrection. It all happens by sleight of hand—the suggestion of pain without real pain, the apparition of resurrection before any death, robbing death of its reality and sting. The movie provides abundant "cheap grace," but no real power and glory.

The much acclaimed film is, I think Lynch would say, unfortunately typical of our impoverished and gnostic sensibility. It gives again evidence of our need for the building of a more authentically human sensibility. Lynch's great contribution is his detailed elucidation of that need.

Notes

[1] Lynch's works will be referred to by the following abbreviations and editions: CA = *Christ and Apollo* (Notre Dame: University of Notre Dame Press, 1975); IM = *The Integrating Mind* (New York: Sheed and Ward, 1962); IH = *Images of Hope* (New York: Mentor-Omega Book, New American Library, 1966); CP = *Christ and Prometheus* (Notre Dame: University of Notre Dame Press, 1970); IF = *Images of*

Faith (Notre Dame: University of Notre Dame Press, 1973). Lynch's other books are *An Approach to the Metaphysics of Plato Through the Parmenides* (Georgetown University Press, 1959) and *The Image Industries* (New York: Sheed and Ward, 1959).

² Nathan A. Scott, "Religion and the Imagination: Some Reflections on the Legacy of William F. Lynch," *Thought* 66 (1991): 151. Some of that neglect will be remedied by the publication of Gerald Bednar's *Faith as Imagination: The Contribution of William F. Lynch, S.J.* (Kansas City: Sheed and Ward, 1996).

³ See note # 1 (above) for a listing of Lynch's books.

⁴ "Downward to the Infinite," *Time* (23 May 1960): 82.

⁵ Herbert A. Kenny, "Faith and the Ironic Imagination," *Boston Sunday Globe*, 27 January 1974.

⁶ Daniel Berrigan, S.J., "Father William Lynch Dies, 'Jesuit in the Grand Manner'," *The National Catholic Reporter*, 23 January 1987, p. 4.

⁷ Scott, "Religion and the Imagination," p. 156.

⁸ CA, p. 152.

⁹ IH, p. 212,

¹⁰ See Gerald J. Bednar, *Faith as Imagination*.

¹¹ Lynch, CP, p. 23. (See note 1 from the introduction for a complete listing of Lynch's books.)

¹² "Theology and the Imagination," *Thought* 29, no. 112 (Spring 1954): 76-79; Lynch, IM, pp. 110-111, 117-118. "The Life of Faith and Imagination: Theological Reflection in Art and Literature, *Thought* 57, no. 224 (March 1982): 9; "Theology and the Imagination II: The Evocative Symbol," *Thought* 29, no. 115 (December 1954): 544.

¹³ "Theology and the Imagination," pp. 67, 82-86. CA, pp. 133, 149; "The Task of Enlargement," *Thought* 51 (December 1976): 350-351; "Adventure in Order," *Thought* 26, no. 100 (Winter 1951-1952): 39. Lynch also explained the analogical in terms that avoid the univocal (which views everything as the same) and the equivocal (which views everything as different). The analogical describes what is both the same and different. It is the "new." The analogical image will reflect the same and the different in proper proportion. CA, Chapters 5 and 6.

¹⁴ *An Approach to the Metaphysics of Plato*, pp. 26-27; CA, pp. 141, 151; Lynch, IF, pp. 84, 89; IM, p. 15. IH, pp. 229 ff.

¹⁵ CA, p. 142, n.; IF, p. 84.

¹⁶ CA, pp. 149-152.

¹⁷ "Theology and the Imagination," pp. 82ff.

¹⁸ IH, pp. 105 ff.

¹⁹ "Theology and the Imagination," pp. 67-68; "Theology and the Imagination II: The Evocative Symbol," *Thought* 29, no. 115 (December 1954): 546.

²⁰ See CA, pp. 85-88 for examples.

²¹ "A Dramatic Making of the Human," *Humanitas* 14, no. 2 (May 1978): 168-169. "The Drama of the Mind: An Ontology of the Imagination," *Notre Dame English Journal: A Journal of Religion in Literature* 13, no. 1 (Fall 1980): 21.

²² CA, pp. 12-18, 91-92; "Theology and the Imagination," pp. 67-68.

²³ William F. Lynch, "Foundation Stones for Collaboration Between Religion

and the Literary Imagination," *Journal of the American Academy of Religion*, 47, no. 2, Supplement (June 1979): 343.

[24] CP, p. 129.

[25] IM, p. 72 ff.

[26] IF, pp. 5, 17.

[27] IF, p. 7.

[28] IH, p. 244; IF, pp. 18, 53; CP, p. 76.

[29] IF, pp. 53, 59, and Chapter 4.

[30] Lynch, "The Imagination of the Drama," *Review of Existential Psychology and Psychiatry* 14, no. 1 (1975-1976): 3-4.

[31] Ibid., p. 4.

[32] IF, pp. 36-38, 53, 56, 60-61, 68.

[33] CP, p. 24.

[34] IF, pp. 14, 24, 83ff, 94-102, "Theology and the Imagination," p. 67.

[35] "The Life of Faith and Imagination," pp. 9-10.

[36] Ibid., pp. 9-14, 16; IF, pp. 60-61.

[37] CP, pp. 137-140.

[38] IF, pp. 53-74.

[39] IF, pp. 63-64.

[40] IF, p. 78.

[41] IF, pp. 91-93.

[42] CA, p. 139.

[43] CA, p. 39.

[44] See, IF, pp. 53-74. By "body of faith," he did not mean "body of Christian faith" (either as a metaphor for "church" or as a call to building or recovering a "Christian culture"). He affirmed and welcomed the necessary emergence of an autonomous, secular, human culture. (This is the central argument of *Christ and Prometheus*.) Yet he was convinced that "Christ" and the resources of Christian faith and thought had much to offer the larger task of building the cultural embodiment of human faith.

[45] Lynch's efforts as editor of *Thought* and his attempt at the end of his life to found *New York Images* exemplify his understanding of the role and vocation of "intellectuals" in the creation of culture. His great concern was the separation of "intellectuals" (artists, writers, academics, opinion leaders) from their rootedness in the life of the people. (See IM, pp. 117-18, IF, pp. 107-108.) When the intellectuals become "a social class, preoccupied with themselves" (IF, p. 107), then the realm of popular culture is colonized by the worst commercial interests and manipulated by those he called "the cultural engineers." Lynch's strongest remarks in this regard are to be found in *The Image Industries*.

[46] Jesuit film critic Richard Blake is, I believe, simply wrong when he suggests that Lynch's film criticism has been superceded by more sophisticated relations between religion and the screen arts. See Richard A. Blake, *Screening America* (New York: Paulist, 1991), pp. 36-40, 98.

[47] One of his earliest published articles is "Of Rhythm and Its End," *Spirit: A Magazine of Poetry* 6, no. 5 (1939): pp. 148-151. For his more developed ideas, see

especially: CA, pp. 31-64, 169-177; IM, pp. 18-37; CP, pp. 6-21, 56-63, 75-98; IF, pp. 19-33, 109-175.

[48] IF, p. 81 (emphasis added).

[49] See, for instance, his important comments on the need for public ritual: IM, pp. 121-130 and CA, pp. 177-184.

[50] See, for example, CA, pp. 3, 33 ff.; IH, pp. 137-145; CP, pp. 43 ff., 105 ff.; IF, pp. 41 ff., 88 ff.

[51] IF, pp. 77, 88 ff.

[52] On Christ's passage through time see CA, pp. 13 ff., 49 ff., 176, and IF, pp. 55, 109.

[53] CA, p. 51.

[54] CA, p. 41.

[55] IF, pp. 109-175.

The Limits of Parody:
An Analysis of *American Catholic Arts and Fictions: Culture, Ideology, Aesthetics* by Paul Giles

Una Cadegan

Most students of academic scandal are probably already familiar with Alan Sokal, the physicist who recently published an article in the leftist social-science journal *Social Text* claiming that postmodern theory had finally undercut science's basis for believing in objective reality. Sokal simultaneously published an essay in *Lingua Franca*, the *People* magazine of academe, admitting that the *Social Text* article was a hoax, designed to expose the poverty of cultural studies analysis and to urge academic leftists to more activist forms of cultural criticism. Sokal's antics have given rise to extended comment on the American Studies H-Net discussion list, and the main characteristic of almost twenty printed pages of reaction has been a stunning lack of humor. Almost nobody gets the joke, or thinks there is a joke to be gotten, and Sokal has been called everything from an adolescent to a liar.

I begin with this example for two reasons. First, it is a reminder to me not to be too humorless myself in this analysis of *American Catholic Arts and Fictions*.[1] Second, and more importantly, the *Social Text* hoax raises questions about the nature and limits of satire and parody, questions at the heart of my reaction to Paul Giles's big book.

Good postmodern etiquette requires that I begin by locating myself on the scholarly map in order to make clear why my reactions are as they are. As a cultural historian, I have always been most interested in literature, but I was not trained in an English department and full disclosure compels me to admit that I am a terrible literary critic. I am interested in literary texts not solely as aesthetic objects but as artifacts of particular people acting in particular times and circumstances. My method is primarily ethnographic; I attempt so far as possible to understand a culture, the framework of meaning from within which people operate, in the terms they themselves would use. I try in the process to be cognizant of what postmodernism teaches us about the limits of such understanding, without thereby becoming paralyzed.

My analysis of Giles is therefore an explicitly interdisciplinary one. This is in some ways an unfair perspective from which to evaluate the book, because Giles is frankly and openly a literary critic, interested primarily in aesthetics. But by including the word "culture" in his title, by making "theology" one of his primary analytical categories, by including among his evidence works produced over the course of a century and more, he invites the attention of readers whose methods include those of anthropology, theology and history, at the very least. With the overlap and interplay of (at least) these four fields in mind, I ask my major question: what does Giles's book contribute to the field of American Catholic studies?

Not surprisingly, perhaps, as an anthropologist, as an historian, Giles is a very fine literary critic. By foregrounding the aesthetic dimensions of his material, Giles obscures some of the crucial ways in which culture more broadly considered operates in both the works he examines and in those he excludes. He re-reads the aesthetic history of American Catholicism, but discounts the related and equally intriguing history of American Catholic aesthetics. The former project—reintegrating American Catholic writers and artists into the canon of American literature—is of great value and deftly carried through. However, by dismissing the institutional embodiments of the theological frameworks that interest him, he distorts his subject in ways that many students of American Catholic history and culture will find frustrating.

In two genuinely intriguing ways, Giles's book opens out new directions for American Catholic studies. The most apparent strength of the project undertaken in *American Catholic Arts and Fictions* is the boldness of its collage. A table of contents that includes Orestes Brownson and Henry James alongside Andy Warhol and Robert Mapplethorpe piques the kind of interest that not only sells books (a not unworthy goal) but also generates alert inquiry. How is he going to pull this one off? the potential reader wants to know. And, for the most part, the collage is more than a ploy; Giles makes the case for an enormous variety of artists all belonging in something like the same

category. I was persuaded that a similar "slipperiness" and "elusive-
ness" characterize both Jay Gatsby in F. Scott Fitzgerald's novel and
the blandly parodic silk-screens of Andy Warhol, and that the formal-
istic immobility of Robert Mapplethorpe's portrait photographs does
indeed raise some of the same questions about individuality and temporality as does Nathaniel Hawthorne's *The Marble Faun*. So, while I
have some concerns about how and why Giles delimits his criteria for
inclusion in his alternative canon, it hangs together in coherent and
useful ways.

The second way in which this book holds real potential for American Catholic studies is in its fashioning of a critically astute language
that describes the alternative trajectory of American Catholic intellectual culture. "It will be the contention of this book," Giles says, "that
there is, in fact, a viable American Catholic intellectual tradition—
conceived in a widely cultural rather than theological sense—but that
this tradition has been obscured from view precisely because it rejects
the traditional American equation of intellectualism with 'questioning' or with 'nonconformity,' in the broad sense of that term" (52).
This assertion will likely not come as news to anyone long involved in
the study of American Catholic history. Further, it is a conclusion at-
tainable by means of good old-fashioned Enlightenment objectivity—
taking all of the available data into account—and does not necessarily
require the use of deconstruction or any of the other resources in the
arsenal of poststructuralism.

Nonetheless, it seems to have been the radical distancing characteristic of a postmodern stance toward knowledge and tradition that
made possible Giles' reconfiguration of American literary history.
Questioning the most basic assumptions of American literary history
enabled him to see the extent to which those assumptions were shaped
by primarily Protestant notions of the independent autonomous self,
striving for transcendence by means of a romantic quest to escape
from the constrictions of community and society. This recognition in
turn highlights for Giles the existence of an alternative tradition, shaped
by Catholicism, in which selfhood is communally molded and defined,
and fulfilled by immanence rather than transcendence. And if the
method that enabled these insights for Giles also provides a language
through which scholars of American Catholicism can talk to their more-
theoretically- and less-theologically-inclined colleagues, then it is
something for which to be grateful.

On the other hand, though, that same postmodern distance serves as an entry point for a discussion of what Giles's analysis does not take into account. Throughout the book, he is cautious almost to the point of absurdity not even to appear to be making anything like a truth-claim, a caution most evident in his continual use of quotation marks around the word "Catholic." He is so consistently careful to disclaim any assertion that a given writer or filmmaker is "really" "Catholic" that one begins to wonder just how terrible a fate that might be. This reticence toward religious language begins more and more to resemble Victorian reticence toward sex; by the time Giles says that "the structure of burlesque ensures that everybody comes to resemble everybody else in the sight of that entity Derrida would term (God)" (322), one cannot help but wonder whether he has at some point been threatened with expulsion from the academy for the forthright use of God-talk.

Giles's delicacy concerning the language of religion and belief is evidence of his openness, the same openness that enables him to see the distinctiveness of American Catholic literary traditions. In this sense, his openness serves him well. In another sense, though, openness becomes for him a central criterion by which to judge not only literary works but also critical perspectives and, it seems, whole cultures. In using openness, a resistance to easy answers and premature closure, as an aesthetic criterion, Giles is applying a commonplace of contemporary criticism. As just one other example, David Robey says in his Introduction to Umberto Eco's *The Open Work* that "although open works are not the only kind of art to be produced in our time, they are the only kind that is appropriate to it; the conventional sense and order of traditional art reflect an experience of the world wholly different from ours, and we deceive ourselves if we try to make this sense and order our own."[2]

Giles goes to great length to demonstrate that the Catholic authors whom he considers accomplished as artists keep things sufficiently open. For example, he wants us to know that Flannery O'Connor's work is engaged in an "interesting tension with the premises of neo-scholastic Catholic theology" (360). In the self-assured tone that characterizes even the deconstructively self-aware critic (we might call it the critical/magisterial "we") Giles goes on to say that "we find also in O'Connor . . . a typically postmodernist understanding of the arbitrary and discontinuous nature of any kind of system. Unlike the utopian modernists, postmodernists tend not to cherish idylls of an ultimate, clean, well-lighted place. The allure of final closure has vanished out of sight" (392). Maybe it is the metaphor of "sight" here that brings to mind O'Connor's story "Greenleaf," in which the complacent Mrs. May is gored through the heart by a bull. At the story's end, caught in the bull's "unbreakable grip . . . [s]he continued to stare straight ahead but the entire scene in front of her had changed—the tree line was a dark wound in a world that was nothing but sky—and she had the look of a person whose sight has been suddenly restored but who finds the light unbearable."[3]

Or, similarly, in "The Displaced Person," the monumental Mrs. Shortley, in her death throes, has "a peculiar lack of light in her icy blue eyes. All the vision in them might have been turned around, looking inside her."[4] A little further on, Mrs. Shortley, "her huge body rolled back still against the seat and her eyes like blue-painted glass, seemed to contemplate for the first time the tremendous frontiers of her true country."[5] Anecdote is not argument, but I think I could marshall enough examples from O'Connor to suggest that her fiction is concerned with something usefully, if tentatively, identifiable as "closure." Whether it is "alluring" is an entirely different question.

The problem with Giles's choosing an essentially aesthetic criterion to dominate his discussion, however, is that it clouds his ability to do the history, anthropology, and theology that his subject requires. Before looking at each of these areas in some detail, I will take a minute to offer my own self a caveat. As a person engaged in interdisciplinary work, and very much aware of its difficulties and pitfalls, I want to avoid putting myself out of business by asking so much from one book that no one person could possibly do it all. So I highlight the gaps in Giles's work in the spirit of James Joyce's supposed reply when someone asked him what he was doing in writing *Finnegans Wake*: "I'm creating jobs for graduate students as yet unborn."

As an historian, I would take Giles to task on two counts, one historiographical and one having to do more specifically with types and uses of primary evidence. I should say first that Giles recounts the history and predicament of U.S. Catholicism with a great deal of accuracy and sympathy. However, there are some gaps. He cites only one secondary source each on the Modernist controversy and on Dorothy Day, the Catholic Worker, and the role of Mystical Body theology.[6] This shallowness in historiography is probably the explanation, also, for an apparent conflating on his part between "Americanization" generally considered and the Americanist controversy, specifically. The two phenomena overlap, surely, but his argument requires some distinctions, as well, which he never makes.

Second, and more seriously, Giles's discussions of culture and ideology require more external documentation than he has provided. To be fair, let me reiterate my realization that he is primarily interested in literary analysis. But since so much of his topic comprises the tenets by which works have been included in the canon of American literature, one wishes he had devoted a little more energy and evidence to the process of canon formation. By what networks of professional support and advancement, for example, did Theodore Dreiser's works come to be seen as essential, when virtually every critic who has ever written about him admits that aesthetically his style is abysmal? Note that I am not suggesting that we cease reading Dreiser; but I am saying that his work is *prima facie* evidence that aesthetic criteria are not the only ones operating here. Similarly, Giles dismisses writing that he takes to be "stereotypical" in its depiction of Irish-American culture. In this category, though he does not deign even to mention her, I suppose he would include probably the best-selling Catholic author of the century, Kathleen Norris, a popular novelist of the mid-twentieth century. As a cultural historian, I would like to see some argument made about why positive stereotypes are "sentimental" and "self-congratulatory," while at the same time he seems to accept *Studs Lonigan* as an ethnographically pure transcription from life.

Which brings me to my point about anthropology. Giles claims to be interested in culture, to be "dissolving theology into anthropology" (9). But his interest is highly selective, apparently driven not by the anthropologist's desire to understand a culture as its inhabitants understand it, but by an elitist appraisal that includes what he thinks worthy and excludes what he thinks uninteresting. Again, this may make for fine literary criticism, but it makes for very thin ethnography. For example, his assertion that "the most typical writers (in the sense of telling us most about a common culture) are nearly always the best writers, not the worst" (24), comes near to being nonsensical. Those who are "best" and can "tell us the most" are by definition atypical; further, if "worst" means, as it seems to, "most popular," then anyone interested in the fullness of the common culture has at least to take the worst into account, rather than assuming that the best both includes and surpasses it.

Giles is willing to be something of an advocate for Catholic *writ-*

ers, whose works reveal as provisional and culturally determined the previously unchallenged "American-ness" of the Protestant pastoral, with its vision of the disembodied romantic self free of all constraint. What he is unwilling to grant is that there is also an alternative tradition of Catholic *criticism* that conceives of the relationship between culture and aesthetics in terms even more different from those of the twentieth-century academy. Or, to be more precise, he is willing to grant that there is such an enterprise, but it interests him not at all. "The Jesuit critic Harold C. Gardiner," he says, " . . . represents this didactic approach at its least attractive" (23). Whether a scholar need be "attracted" by what he or she studies is an interesting question, but here Giles is dismissing an extensive institutional enterprise with direct bearing on his own subject. One of the most powerfully dismissive terms in the contemporary critical lexicon, "didactic" is used to close down precisely the issues it might be used to open. As the most elementary of examples, what is it, one might ask, that Gardiner was presuming to teach?

Giles thinks he already knows. His charge: "Texts that not only emerge from within the framework of Catholic orthodoxy but also choose simply to reproduce that framework as a fait accompli tend to lack subtlety" (23), the direst of failings among those who prefer the stance of ironic detachment, and one, by the way, that I would have to in large measure concede. But again, trying to be a good ethnographer, I would pursue the question by asking, if these texts *lack* subtlety, what might we say they *possess*? What they possess is a deep and, yes, often unsubtle conviction that views about literature and views about theology are more continuous than discontinuous, more related to each other than separate from each other. Giles sees this less as a conviction than an inadvertent amalgam of unlike elements. Self-consciously Catholic literary critics, he argues, "elide philosophical assumptions into literary judgments without knowing it. Their competing philosophies are seen not as competing philosophies but as absolute truths, with their opinions on literature emerging as a by product of these deeply-held but unstated beliefs" (204). Deeper exploration of the sources he dismisses as unattractive could have offered Giles extensive evidence that the philosophical assumptions of most Catholic critics are anything but unstated.

For example, in an article entitled "Free Verse," in the April 2, 1921 "Literature" section of *America*, Conde B. Pallen makes clear his position on the subject in his opening lines.

"Shredded prose" is an apt description, if not an exact definition of what its advocates call free verse. That it is free, as free as madcap caprice, may be granted; that it is verse, which is built on metrical units, is to be denied. People may speak of a square circle, but there is no such thing; contradictions in terms are only a way of registering the impossible. . . .
The free-verse movement, like many other radical movements of the day, is a reaction from law and order. . . . Like free verse, cubism and futurism have flared up, the dawn of new things, only to be consumed in the lurid flame of their own incandescent folly. Free verse is only another *ignis fatuus* blown from the miasmic jungles of disorder. You cannot escape the law. God made the world in measure, weight and number, and in measure, weight and number it will endure.[7]

We may say many things about this particular critical perspective, but what we cannot say is that the critic is unaware that his literary judgments are based on his philosophical precepts.

Similarly and, to coin a phrase, more subtly, Moira Walsh, film critic for *America*, wrote in 1964 about the need for a mature and sophisticated approach to film criticism. She acknowledged that opinions had shifted over time as to whether ignorance of evil was the best protection from it. But "in this age," she argues, "good and evil, truth and falsehood, are so deceptively and inextricably woven together in our affluent, materialistic, post-Christian culture that unwitting corruption is the almost inevitable consequence of ignorance."[8] Thus it was necessary that the Catholic film-review enterprises judge "films in the rational, humanistic, Christian terms that befit an art form with a right and even a duty to confront the actualities of human existence."[9] If such an approach presented problems for people used to an older, more directive approach, then, another critic said, their very discomfort was evidence of the old system's "arrogant disregard of conscience and of a properly motivated commitment," and the solution lay in educating and enlightening the average moviegoer: "There is a world of difference between a film that holds up to view a situation that is obviously reprehensible morally and a film that says such a situation is desirable and worthy of emulation. Moviegoers must learn to tell the difference."[10]

Giles seems to be surprised that self-consciously Catholic critics use theological criteria in their judgments about literature. Rather than see this tendency as part of his own evidence, he castigates them for it; rather than explore the critical counterpart to his alternative literary canon, he relegates Catholic critical schemas to the critical limbo of "their own particular metanarrative impulses" (204). However, while Giles may prefer to set critics such as Gardiner, Pallen, and Walsh aside as merely mechanically orthodox, I suggest that in the interplay of their overlap and disagreement, in their oppositional relationship to dominant ideologies, and in the potential they offer for the study of change and refinement in a critical tradition over time, the work of such critics awaits the cultural historian like one great big playground.

This dismissal of the complexities of Catholic institutional literary culture (itself ironic, since Giles is always looking for complexity) is related to the points I want to make about theology. Exactly what Giles means when he uses the word is unclear. He wants theology to be seen as "a fluctuating signifier, a series of fictional constructions" (31), which is a satisfactory definition for his purposes, and he uses it with satisfying deftness in places. For example, he uses Gerard Manley Hopkins to unsettle, of all people, Jacques Derrida. Specifically, in their self-conscious use of metaphor, Giles argues, Hopkins's texts deconstruct themselves, but in a way that emphasizes not difference "as Derrida would have preferred," but similarity, i.e., analogy, in good Catholic fashion. By refusing to "essentialize difference," Hopkins out-deconstructs Derrida (392).

But when anyone starts taking theology too seriously, Giles gets a little nervous. We have already seen his attempt to persuade us that Flannery O'Connor was not really taken in by the narrow rigidity of neo-scholasticism, and he is quick with such reassurance whenever theology appears to stop fluctuating and attaches itself to belief and commitment. It's a full-time job. For example, Giles would like to situate Eugene O'Neill comfortably as someone who "draws upon the expressionist techniques of modernist drama so as to undercut the bland optimism of quotidian life" (132). To do so, however, he needs to explain away the conspicuously odd choice O'Neill made to submit the manuscript of his 1932 play *Days Without End* to Martin Quigley and Daniel Lord (of movie censorship fame) for their review. Such unartistic obsequiousness requires that Giles come up with a neat critical maneuver to save O'Neill for his canon of "real" artists. So of a play that, he admits, ends with the protagonist "kneeling at the foot of the cross in 'ecstatic mystic vision,' " Giles nonetheless asserts: "The play's religious implications are not unambiguous, insofar as it is hinted that the desire to embrace God, like the contrary desire to embrace death that John displayed previously, could be seen in a psychological sense as a self-fulfilling prophecy, thus making religious belief a form of psychotherapy rather than theology" (132). Whew, that was a close one. Almost as tough to explain away as Hemingway's conversion (118).

By redefining theology so that it has little or nothing to do with belief, commitment, and accountability to a tradition and an institution, Giles risks misrepresenting both the history and culture of many of his subjects. I will give three brief examples. The first has to do with how he uses the notion of analogy; the second with the relationship between faith and doubt; the third with the relationship between sacrament and sacramentality.

First, as far as I understand the notion of analogical thinking, I think Giles uses it deftly to help characterize the ways in which American Catholics have presented an alternative view of American society. He also points out places where Catholics indulge in "univocal" thinking (315, e.g.), which he calls the opposite of the analogical. Although I am no more of a specialist in Aquinas than Giles is, as I understand the doctrine of analogy, univocal thinking is not so much its opposite as one of two potential distortions. In specifying what we know about God, we can be too certain that our way is *the* way, too certain that the things we say about God are the only right things to say. Giles points out, rightly, that this perspective is rejected by Catholic tradition. What he never mentions, though, is the equal distortion of equivocal thinking—what I understand to be the paralyzing inability to say anything about God with any confidence, any certainty.

There is a tentativeness in analogical thinking, but it is a confident tentativeness. If self-consciously Catholic authors are willing to embrace openness, it is because they have a fair amount of confidence about who is going to do the closing, along with a self-conscious humility about whom the final word belongs to. This stands in contrast to Giles's position, which requires openness and indeterminacy as a basic artistic stance. He stakes out as his own position one that Catholic theology (i.e., taken as a volitional position and not just as a residue) would describe as equivocal. This location helps to explain Giles's insistence that parody is "the most appropriate art form within which to express this metaphorical paradox" of being "neither totally of the world nor totally out of it" (388).

Giles's sense that parody is a form particularly congenial to Catholic writers is useful and accurate, so far as it goes. However, when we move beyond form to content the picture gets more complex. The reason many academics have reacted so humorlessly to Sokal's hoax article is that his parody is perceived as a mockery of something—namely, cultural studies—which they believe should be taken seriously. Sokal claims to be parodying cultural studies for a higher good; that is, for its own stated goal of social change through realization of inequities in power. The question of why one parodies is the one Giles finesses a little reductionistically. That Catholics have been more skeptical toward what we might call the univocity of American myth than Protestants is, I think, true; but Catholicism taken as a whole cultural stance is historically, even in the U.S., as skeptical toward equivocal thinking as toward univocal. Catholic writers and other artists reject easy transcendence not because they reject transcendence *per se* but because God is present in the material world and does not need to be sought elsewhere; rejecting romantic self-transcendence is necessary precisely because the self is never thereby really transformed. And, Catholic writers and artists deflate the elite not because everyone is equally undignified but because everyone's dignity is infinite. Giles omits or brackets or displaces the second term of each of these contraries.

My second point about Giles' use of theology has to do with another set of contrary terms: faith and doubt. In this case, though, rather than eliminating the second term he uses it to challenge the coherence of the first. That is, for Giles, the existence of doubt seems to discredit the experience of faith; ambivalence poses a threat to certainty. Giles can, of course, find in the rhetoric of mid-twentieth-century U.S. Catholicism confident equations of faith with certainty. But a wider historical perspective would have revealed bigger barrels and much livelier fish. For example, Giles draws an interesting comparison between Flannery O'Connor and Jean Genet as writers who explore the idea that the sinner may be closer to and more aware of grace than the righteous. But he goes on to say that in this process "ideas of `belief' or 'disbelief' cease to be relevant as wholly distinct categories, for neither writer is susceptible of being finalized by theological proof" (363). The comparison is illuminating in its way, but it risks ascribing O'Connor's complexity to her artistry, which has somehow won a battle with the simplistic (and artistically deadening) certainty of belief. O'Connor would have opposed neither her faith to her work ("I write the way I do because [not though] I am a Catholic. This is a fact and nothing covers it like the bald statement.") nor faith itself to doubt: "When I ask myself how I know I believe, I have no satisfactory answer at all, no assurance at all, no feeling at all. I can only say with Peter, Lord I believe, help my unbelief."[11] Jackson Lears links modernist ambivalence with the same scriptural precedent, displaying the wider historical sensitivity in which Giles is lacking: "This attitude, in its aversion to static systems, is a thoroughly 'modern' one. But in a more profound sense, it is as old as the Biblical cry: 'Lord, I believe; help thou mine unbelief.' "[12] Flannery O'Connor's ambivalence owes at least as much to distinctively Christian traditions such as the dark night of the soul as it does to a protopostmodernist commitment to indeterminacy.

None of this is to accuse Giles of being insufficiently devout; but it does suggest that he needs to pay more careful attention to the devotion of others insofar as it is part of his data. Perhaps the most significant relationship obscured by Giles's stance of indeterminacy is that between the "cultural residue" of sacramentality and the actual practice of the sacraments. He uses the word "transubstantiation" over and over again to describe the propensity of Catholic writers and artists to transform things into other things. But, almost without exception, nowhere in 531 pages does he mention the Eucharist. The exceptions tend to be biographical—F. Scott Fitzgerald was a practicing Catholic until the age of 21 (170), John Berryman served mass daily for several years (233)—although Giles seldom specifies the implications, either personal or artistic, of a given writer's decision to leave, join or rejoin "the Church."

It is here that, whether for believer or distanced analyst, theology and ethnography meet. If Giles wants to argue that transubstantiation is a metaphor distinctively appropriate to Catholic writers, then he needs to acknowledge its groundedness in that particular discourse. To make of it a purely formal category (though its formal use is surely part of the overall picture) is to disconnect it from the experience that gives rise to it in the first place. Transubstantiation is a powerful critical tool for understanding Catholic traditions in writing because the Eucharist is a powerful element of the experience of belief, even for those who have rejected its literal theological content. Giles brackets this experience in much the same way that he uses quotation marks and parentheses to distance himself from what others mean by "Catholic" and (God). For many of the people about whom he is writing, participation in the sacraments—particularly in the Eucharist—is not a legalistic "adherence to external laws and objects" (445) but an acknowledgment of the connection of the material world with the reality of God. Giles does not have to accept this formulation, but his analysis of a number of writers would have been richer had he been able to suspend his own disbelief enough to take into account the full range of his subjects' belief.

Giles's critical resources provide him with few tools for dealing with the relationship between doctrine and experience, except insofar as it is something to be escaped in order to become a good artist. That a deep and intellectually nuanced understanding of doctrine, nourished by sustained, sometimes ambivalent immersion in an admittedly flawed community (Flannery O'Connor said it seems to be a fact that we have to suffer as much from the church as for it)[13] could actually give rise to good art is something Giles's critical system is unable seriously to consider.

When Giles specifies what deconstruction can do, here is what he says: deconstruction can "help the rational mind to preserve a more paradoxical awareness of the discrepancy between its own lucidity and every form of religious conditioning or assertion of metaphysical truth" (19). When I am presented with this choice, I feel a little like Robert Frost in the poem "New Hampshire":

> Lately in converse with a New York alec
> About the new school of the pseudo-phallic,
> I found myself in a close corner where
> I had to make an almost funny choice.
> "Choose you which you will be—a prude or puke."[14]

Frost is disinclined to choose:

> Nothing not built with hands of course is sacred.
> But here is not a question of what's sacred;
> Rather of what to face or run away from.
> I'd hate to be a runaway from nature.
> And neither would I choose to be a puke
> Who cares not what he does in company,
> And, when he can't do anything, falls back
> On words, and tries his worst to make words speak

Louder than actions, and sometimes achieves it.
It seems a narrow choice this age insists on.[15]

I am stretching Frost a little here, but I think Giles is presenting us
with a similar choice, and one almost tiresome in its familiarity: take
belief seriously, or be a good artist. Be committed to a tradition, or
"ironically detach [oneself] from the imposition of all grand conceptual systems" (530). Here's how Robert Frost declines to choose:

Well, if I have to choose one or the other,
I choose to be a plain New Hampshire farmer
With an income in cash of say a thousand
(From say a publisher in New York City).[16]

My analogous rejection of the choice Giles presents would appeal, as
a beginning, to a more nuanced understanding of tradition. There is
much fruitful reflection on the topic by theologians, of course, but I
could also point to a recent article by folklorist Henry Glassie, who
says of tradition: "A continuous process situated in the nothingness of
the present, linking the vanished with the unknown, tradition is stopped,
parceled, and codified by thinkers who fix upon this aspect or that, in
accord with their needs or preoccupations, and leave us with a scatter
of apparently contradictory, yet cogent definitions."[17] The thinkers
Glassie refers to are not solely or even primarily academics, but include, among others, the storyteller/historian in a small Ulster town
and a Turkish calligrapher. They are actors in time who choose to bear
an historical responsibility to those who come before and after them.
"Nor must history and culture be ranged beyond the reach of men and
women," Glassie concludes. "The big patterns are the yield of small
acts. History, culture, and the human actor meet in tradition."[18]

To the extent that Catholicism is not a "residue" that still occasionally "interpellates" its subjects, but "volitional, temporal action," Giles
prefers not to take it into account. But this is not to say that his book is
not useful; quite the opposite, because in no sense has the last word
been said on any of these subjects. As Robert Frost (who must have
known something about deconstruction, although he never uses the
word) concludes his very long poem: "It's restful to arrive at a decision, / And restful just to think about New Hampshire. / At present I
am living in Vermont." I take this to mean that the project in which we
are engaged will give us good work to do for a very long time.

Notes

[1] Paul Giles, *American Catholic Arts and Fictions: Culture, Ideology, Aesthetics* (New York: Cambridge University Press, 1992). All page numbers for references will be cited in the text.

[2] Umberto Eco, *The Open Work* (Cambridge, MA: Harvard University Press, 1989), p. xiv.

[3] Flannery O'Connor, *Collected Works* (New York: The Library of America, 1988), p. 523.

[4] Ibid., p. 304.

[5] Ibid., p. 305.

[6] On the first he cites Gabriel Daly, *Transcendence and Immanence: A Study in Catholic Modernism and Integralism* (Oxford: Oxford University Press, 1980); on the second, James T. Fisher, *The Catholic Counterculture in America, 1933-1960* (Chapel Hill: University of North Carolina Press, 1989).

[7] Conde B. Pallen, "Free Verse," *America* 24 (April 1921): 578-79.

[8] Moira Walsh, "Right Conscience About Films: II" *America* 110 (May 1964): 685-86.

[9] Moira Walsh, "A Right Conscience About Films," *America* 110 (May 1964): 658.

[10] Msgr. Thomas F. Little, "The Modern Legion and Its Modern Outlook," *America* 113 (December 1965): 744-45. Walsh and Little were both writing at the moment when the Legion of Decency was being re-formed into the National Catholic Office for Motion Pictures.

[11] Letters to A., 20 July 1955 and 2 August 1955, *Collected Works*, pp. 942, 944.

[12] T. J. Jackson Lears, *No Place of Grace: Antimodernism and the Transformation of American Culture, 1880-1920* (New York: Pantheon, 1981), p. 312.

[13] Letter to A., 20 July 1955, *Collected Works*, p. 942.

[14] Robert Frost, *Selected Poems of Robert Frost*, ed. Robert Graves (New York: Holt, Rinehart and Winston, c. 1963), p. 106.

[15] Ibid., pp. 107-8.

[16] Ibid., p. 108.

[17] Henry Glassie, "Tradition," *Journal of American Folklore* 108 (fall 1995): 395.

[18] Ibid., p. 409.

Paul Giles and the Tar-Baby

Peter A. Huff

"Do please, Brer Fox, don't fling me in dat brier-patch."
—Joel Chandler Harris

In recent years, historians of American Catholicism have engaged in serious soul-searching about the status of their discipline. In 1993, Jay Dolan observed a remarkable "lack of confidence" in current works concentrating on the U.S. Catholic past.[1] At the same time, Leslie Woodcock Tentler argued that American Catholic history remains a marginal practice in the historical profession.[2] Three years later, Philip Gleason endorsed Tentler's thesis and reminded his colleagues that, despite its desire to recover the muted voices of the national heritage, multiculturalism still shows little interest in retrieving the "Catholic voice" in American history.[3] Likewise, Jon Butler maintained that the use of Catholic models in American religious history represents nothing less than "Historiographical Heresy."[4] Curiously, along with bold experimentation in methodological strategy, a degree of anxiety characterizes contemporary endeavors in U.S. Catholic historical scholarship.

In spite of the pensive mood that hangs over American Catholic historical writing, the study of the American Catholic cultural experience seems to be enjoying something of a renaissance in at least some quarters of the international academy. Thanks in large part to scholars in literary and material culture studies—that is, "outsiders" unaffiliated with the Catholic historical establishment, the study of American Catholic literature and art is gaining considerable legitimacy. Just as American studies breathed new life into literary and historical research during the 1950s and 1960s, the new movement of Catholic cultural studies may be the force to reinvigorate the examination of the American Catholic heritage in the next century.

One impressive work in this new field is Paul Giles's *American Catholic Arts and Fictions* (1992). A study of Catholic contributions to literature, film, and the visual arts in the United States, the book traces the development of American Catholic creative life from the nineteenth century to the late twentieth century. A formidable exercise in interdisciplinary research, it is an ambitious treatment of over a score of writers, film makers, and artists—ranging from Orestes Brownson, F. Scott Fitzgerald, and Flannery O'Connor to Mary McCarthy, Robert Mapplethorpe, and even Alfred Hitchcock.

Such a roll call of creative minds may, however, bewilder the reader familiar with conventional wisdom regarding the lackluster performance of the Catholic artistic tradition in America. Scholars trained in the ritual practice of bemoaning the inferiority of American Catholic arts and fictions will also be hard pressed to explain how Giles can devote more than five hundred pages to a cultural failure. After all, isn't the American Catholic artistic tradition a legacy of provincialism and smug piety masquerading as art?[5]

Giles's response to that question is evident in the four major assumptions that shape his work. Regarding popular art, faith and creativity, the nature of Catholic art, and the Catholic imagination's impact on American culture, the assumptions set in motion a fascinating series of individual and comparative studies. At the same time, however, they raise significant questions about the proper methodological strategies for the interdisciplinary study of American Catholic culture.

In journals such as *Religion and Literature*, *American Literature*, *Horizons*, *Modern Language Quarterly*, and *Journal of Religion*, Giles's book has already received critical praise and serious analysis. The purpose of this critique is to evaluate the four main presuppositions that shape *American Catholic Arts and Fictions*. Though arguments over first principles may, as Newman warned, turn into "a sort of night battle, where each fights for himself,"[6] they do highlight important issues at stake in an area of research. In this particular case, the stakes involve the integrity of the American Catholic experience itself.

Good Art, Bad Art

First, Giles presupposes a clear distinction between popular art and high art. He admits that working-class Catholics have long been nourished by popular art, but he deems the "mediocre fiction" of the Catholic ghetto and the "populist sentimentality" of the mid-twentieth-century cinema unworthy of consideration. This sort of judgment, now quite baffling to many scholars in American and religious studies who are becoming increasingly sophisticated in their study of mass culture, allows Giles to bypass much that critics have found so annoying: the apologetic novel of the nineteenth century, the genteel verse of Victorian poets, and the "fiction with a parochial purpose" that characterized American Catholicism at the turn of the century.[7]

Giles's text also provides little for the reader interested in a hermeneutics of Catholic popular culture in the twentieth century. He writes about American Catholic arts and fictions with only a handful of words tossed in the direction of a Frank Capra movie or a Cardinal Spellman novel, and he assiduously ignores kitsch best-sellers of the calibre of the *Joshua* novels by Joseph Girzone. Given his decisions regarding, in his words, "good" and "bad" art, Giles skirts many of the problems that have nagged other interpreters of American Catholic imaginative life.[8] While he cannot be faulted for failing to write a book he did not intend to write, he is accountable for explaining the aesthetic principles governing his selection and exclusion of subjects.

By contrast, Anita Gandolfo's study of new Catholic fiction in America carefully avoids such elitism.[9] In her attempt to understand the postconciliar Catholic experience in America, she treats not only the critically acclaimed works of John F. Powers and Walker Percy but also the "thesis-ridden" fiction of Andrew Greeley, William Kienzle, and Ralph McInerny. Her willingness to give such "lowbrow" authors serious attention allows her to hear the variety of voices offering "fictionalized solutions" to the challenges facing Catholics in contemporary America.

For his part, Giles thinks that Jack Kerouac or Mary McCarthy "or indeed Flannery O'Connor can reveal more about the Catholic experience in the United States than many wearisome issues of the *Catholic Digest*."[10] To be sure, such figures can disclose a great deal about Catholic America. In *The Catholic Counterculture in America*, James Fisher has demonstrated the significance of Kerouac as a window into American Catholic experience.[11] The same case could be made for Allen Tate, whose troubled post-conversion life hardly lived up to the expectations of critics who hailed him as the American Newman.[12] But these figures do not necessarily reveal more of the American Catholic experience than the films and light fiction consumed by millions of rank-and-file Catholics. Arguably the unbiased observer might gain greater insight into American Catholicism from a Greeley romance or a Father Dowling mystery than from, say, Andy Warhol's iconography or Mapplethorpe's sadomasochism.

Good Art, Bad Catholics

A second presupposition guiding Giles's work is the assumption that Catholic faith inevitably leads to the stifling of imagination. Spiritually inclined writers and artists have long been wary of Catholicism, associating the tradition with the Index of Forbidden Books and censorship of motion pictures. Once the patron of the arts, the church in the modern age has seemed too content to sacrifice aesthetic value on the altar of public decency. Consequently converts from Newman to Wallace Stevens have wrestled with the church's nasty reputation for suppressing free expression. Even sympathetic insiders, promoting Catholic involvement in the arts, have suggested that the worth of Catholic art often exists in inverse ratio to the piety of the artist.

Giles is not the first to indict American Catholic art for its saccharine view of human nature and its tendency to lace literature with homiletics. After his conversion in 1938, Merton blasted the Catholic literary establishment for those very offenses. "A bad book about the love of God," he said, "remains a bad book." In contrast to Giles, however, he argued that American Catholic literary life suffered from a deficit of faith not a surplus. He attributed the mediocrity of Catholic letters to a bourgeois suspicion of sainthood.[13]

Likewise, Tate, after his 1950 conversion, scorned Catholic culture in the name of orthodoxy. Questioning Cardinal Spellman's attempt to suppress controversial films, Tate suggested that censorship pointed to a "latent heresy" within the American church. The Legion of Decency's crusade against female nudity in movies, while ignoring the broader "vulgarity of the Hollywood view of life," was like "one heresy combatting another." Similarly, in reaction to the sentimental piety of the American Catholic novel, especially Spellman's *The Foundling*, Tate exposed the practical heresy of the ostensibly orthodox writer. The responsibility of the orthodox artist is not to protect delicate sensibilities from the realities of worldly existence but "to portray the human experience as it is, whether he likes it or not."[14]

Unmoved by the testimony of the literary converts, Giles states the stereotype in its canonical form: orthodox belief and pious practice yield bad art—at least as far as the American tradition goes. Continental figures such as Bloy, Bernanos, Mauriac, and Rouault discovered a way to unite traditional devotion and artistic achievement, but practicing American Catholics have failed to make an impressive showing on the world's art scene.

In light of this presupposition, the reader is again bound to ask how Giles can write so extensively of American Catholic arts and fictions. The trick, it appears, is to assemble writers and artists only tangentially and sometimes even unwillingly associated with Catholic tradition. In order to warrant his selection of subjects, Giles resorts to the most technical of justifications—citing the Catholic baptism, family background, ethnic neighborhood, and Catholic education of each author and artist. After the first chapters, it is clear that a better title for his study would be *American Ex-Catholic Arts and Fictions*. If converts make the best Catholics, Giles is quite certain that lapsed or "apostate" Catholics make the best artists.

The American Catholic Frame of Mind

This conclusion reveals a third assumption informing his study. Giles's work presupposes that "Catholic art" possesses substantive meaning. Making such a claim, he enters a long conversation on the nature of Catholic art. For many observers, Catholic art simply means Catholic propaganda.[15] For others, it means art sporting "Catholic decor."[16] Some critics locate the Catholicity of art in its adherence to certain principles of aesthetics: the artist need not be Catholic; the object need not refer to Catholic beliefs or cultures.[17] Still others define Catholic art experientially—that which is informed by "the experience of being a Catholic."[18] At the same time, a number of Catholics spurn the entire idea of Catholic art. If it exists, Catholic art is simply art produced by someone who happens to be Catholic.[19]

For his part, Giles brings to the conversation a distinctive proposition. According to him, what makes an American Catholic art or fiction Catholic is neither its creator's involvement in the life of Catholicism nor his or her intent to produce a work of Catholic dimensions. Rather, Catholic art reflects a type of creative consciousness—a "Catholic cast of mind" unfettered by the quotidian realities of creed and commitment.[20]

A significant dimension of the text is Giles's attempt to show that this Catholic imagination represents an alternative aesthetic tradition in U.S. cultural history. According to Giles, the study of American literature has usually meant the interpretation of texts from the privileged perspective of a Protestant hermeneutics. Just as the history of American Protestant traditions represented the transformation of Puritan impulses in secular directions, so the American literary legacy received its energy from the unsolved problems of the nation's Protestant heritage. It continued in post-Puritan fashion the same quest initiated by the first "errand into the wilderness." In other words, the nation's literary tradition has functioned as one chapter in the master narrative of the American Protestant myth. Catholic literature exists outside the great American code.

In his critique of this reading of U.S. literature, Giles uses Richard Chase's *The American Novel and Its Tradition* as a representative text.[21] From the academic generation that fostered myth criticism and American studies, Chase functions as a perfect example of the interpretive pattern Giles criticizes. His book, which enjoyed a quarter century of classroom use, places American fiction in the context of the country's attempt to come to terms with the mythic power of its Puritan past. In it Chase constructed a usable history of the American novel consistent with the consensus histories of American religion written by his contemporaries Winthrop Hudson, Sydney Ahlstrom, and H. Richard Niebuhr.[22]

A strength of Giles's book is his critique of such "Protestant" readings. He is absolutely right when he denies that Puritanism and post-Puritanism constitute the only angles of vision available to the American artist. In his attempt to deliver this insight, however, he overstates the case by absolutizing a Catholic imagination operative in American culture.

Catholic intellectuals have long endeavored to define the nature of the Catholic *mentalité*. Tate contrasted the Catholic tradition's "symbolic imagination" with the "angelic" imagination of secular modernity.[23] William Lynch recommended what he called the "analogical" or "Christic" imagination in opposition to the "Apollonarian" vision of technological society.[24] These constructs have been supplemented by Tracy's rehabilitated "analogical imagination" and Greeley's "liturgical imagination."[25] They have also been joined by interpretive models designed to capture the distinctively Catholic imagination of America—only a few of which have asked whether the nation also plays host to a Southern Baptist imagination or a Mormon imagination or a Black Muslim imagination.[26]

When Giles himself addresses the issue of a Catholic imagination, he concentrates on a cluster of features. He describes the American Catholic sensibility as sacramental and analogical, a world view rooted in a milieu of "institutional grace." The aesthetic parallel to the Incarnation, the American Catholic approach to art sticks with the particularities of concrete reality. For this reason, the iconographic qualities of film and the visual arts provide a natural outlet. In addition, the Catholic imagination betrays no trace of Emerson's gnostic escape into abstract transcendence. It seeks no pastoral utopia free from urban ugliness and injustice, nor does it crave antinomian privileges of perfection and exceptionalism. Rather, the opposite of Tillich's "Protestant principle," the Catholic imagination resides in the imperfect world of the American city where good and evil are confused, national identities scrambled, and solitude is an alien luxury. American Catholicism, for Giles, informs a native imagination communal by instinct, universal in vision, ritualist in behavior, and immune to the reformist impulses of Protestant America. Though he sneers at Hollywood's cheap stereotype of American Catholicism as urban, ethnic, and often criminal, Giles endorses the myth at the same time he tries to subvert it.

Giles's typological understanding of the American Catholic imagination accords with other models of "Catholic substance." In doing so, it depends more upon theological convention than critical analysis. The myth of the sacramental Catholic versus the word-oriented Protestant is a theological fiction. As John Bossy has shown, the Tridentine Mass and Counter-Reformation polyphony represent the triumph of logocentrism in Western religion just as much as do Reformation traditions of public preaching and private Bible reading.[27] Likewise, the tracts of nineteenth-century devotional Catholicism and the postconciliar vernacular Mass reflect the print-centered spirituality of modern Catholicism. At the same time, evangelical altar calls, Pentecostal healing lines, Mormon temple rites, and the ceremonial handling of serpents to a Country-Western beat display sacramental spiritualities in non-Catholic Christianities.[28] Colleen McDannell's *Material Christianity* reveals iconographic imperatives in American Christianities other than Catholicism.[29]

In addition, Giles's Catholic imagination fails to reckon with the "migrations of the holy" in American pluralism. What is the relevance of Giles's sacramental model for contemporary Catholics whose "liturgical imagination" may soon be a relic of the past? How does his vision of "institutional grace" square with the anti-institutional strategies currently restructuring American Catholicism? Given the state of Catholicism in Walker Percy's suburban servitude, one must question the accuracy of Giles's static notion of a sacramental Catholic imagination.

In areas where Giles's study is more original, it is also more problematic. When he introduces the final trait of the American Catholic imagination—its "all-embracing skepticism"—he sneaks "Protestant principle" back into his profile of Catholic art. According to Giles, the universalism of U.S. Catholicism has created a sensibility that interrogates all claims to ultimacy—an imagination "influenced more by . . . Renaissance relativism than by medieval absolutism."[30] This quality, he contends, is the factor that moves American Catholic art toward comedy, parody, and burlesque. Unlike its sober Protestant counterpart, obsessed with righteous empires, the Catholic imagination takes mischievous delight in unmasking all purported authorities.

To illustrate this skepticism Giles cites Flannery O'Connor: "What kept me a skeptic in college was precisely my Christian faith." For Giles, this sentence validates his hunch about the relativism in the American Catholic tradition and helps to explain why it generates a centrifugal force spinning artists out of the orbit of conventional belief. Giles also thinks it exposes the gulf between continental Catholicism and the American experience: "In many twentieth-century European Catholic writers . . . there is a sense of exile and nostalgia for the lost enchanted garden, a garden associated with the social order and ecclesiastical authority of an Age of Faith. But this medieval ideal has never existed anyway in the United States."[31]

As engaging as this hypothesis is, it clearly outruns the evidence. Numerous studies have shown American Catholics, at various points in their history, to be preoccupied with the "mythic" Middle Ages.[32] More importantly, O'Connor herself refutes Giles. In the 1962 letter he cites, O'Connor was hardly recommending relativism. Rather, writing to Alfred Corn, a young man concerned about modernity's challenges to Christianity, she acknowledged that Christian belief takes tough hits in the university classroom. Suggesting Chardin, Gilson, and Newman for his reading, she even encouraged him to find Christian books to balance "anti-Christian" texts he would encounter. Finally, she advised, "Learn what you can, but cultivate Christian skepticism." In another letter to Corn, not mentioned by Giles, O'Connor continued to play the spiritual director. Writing on the eve of Vatican II, she confessed her own relationship to Catholic authority: "I don't find it an infringement of my independence to have the Church tell me what is true and what is not in regard to faith and what is right and what is wrong in regard to morals. Certainly I am no fit judge."[33]

Neither postmodern skeptic nor latter-day Renaissance relativist, O'Connor stands as a prophetic witness against Giles's American Catholic cast of mind. For her, Christian skepticism was not the application of Enlightenment critique to the canons of tradition nor a postmodern strategy of self-criticism designed to mitigate tensions between religious belief and secular inquiry. Rather, her Christian skepticism was a project of radical questioning with aims opposed to Giles's understanding of American Catholic creativity. What she proposed was the deliberate mockery of Renaissance and Enlightenment pretensions by the needling authority of unreconstructed and unrepentant Christian orthodoxy—the very thing that Giles says turns a good Catholic into a bad artist.

Perhaps because he recognizes the subversive potential of her presence, Giles assigns O'Connor only a bit part in his study. According to the index, her name appears in the text fewer times than James Farrell's or Frank O'Hara's. As far as Giles is concerned, the woman who was arguably the greatest American Catholic writer of the twentieth century, the redneck Thomist who read the *Summa* every night and got her kicks from giving liberals "a nasty dose of orthodoxy," has little to say about the American Catholic imagination.[34]

Inside the American Catholic Mind

O'Connor's awkward position in Giles's project highlights the book's fundamental assumption concerning the way in which the American Catholic imagination has functioned in American culture. Drawing from Marx, Feuerbach, Weber, Durkheim, Geertz, and Harvey Cox, Giles first argues that modern religious consciousness has often assumed a subtle, secular form. Then he maintains that the Catholic imagination has undergone such a secular transformation. Finally, applying the theory to the American scene, Giles asserts that a secularized Catholic consciousness, operating as an occult "subliminal force" in the minds of (mainly former) Catholic artists, has animated the U.S. Catholic aesthetic tradition.

This method informs the major premises of Giles's book and implies three additional claims—sociological and psychological. First, Giles's argument hinges on a unique theory of secularization. Theorists before him have occasionally referred to religion as the object of secularization, imagining, as Bonhoeffer did, a "non-religious" Christianity. But it is never clear what Giles himself means by a secularized (i.e., non-religious) Catholicism. His narrative "tracing the transformation of religion" seems to approximate what O'Connor called the "vaporization of religion in America."[35]

Second, Giles's method entails the claim that former Catholics never escape the mythic structure of their background. According to this view, the post-Catholic never shakes a psychological connection with the church.[36] Anecdotal evidence states that Protestants may "deconvert" with little or no continued influence from their religion of origin. When it comes to Catholics, legend says that the household gods of Catholic myth haunt lapsed or apostate Catholics to such a degree that they never successfully enter a new religion or establish a non-religious identity free from Catholic karma. Catholics who leave the church ironically end up "thinking with the church" after all. Once a Catholic, always a Catholic.[37]

Though empirical data offers partial support for such beliefs, the claim that former Catholics retain an innate Catholic consciousness remains unsubstantiated. It is one thing to suggest that ex-Catholic artists occasionally draw upon a rich tradition such as their native Catholicism, but it is quite another to claim that former Catholics function as ill-fated carriers of an aesthetic virus regulating their creativity. Can we, by extension, find a Catholic consciousness lurking in the careers of ex-Catholics such as Timothy Leary and G. Gordon Liddy?[38] Linked to Foucault's "positive unconscious,"[39] Giles's approach borders on religious imperialism and racial determinism. Like other exercises in deconstruction criticism, it portrays artists as victims of "inherent structures [and] psychological forces" beyond their control.[40] To paraphrase Rahner, Giles's artists are anonymous Catholics.

Third, Giles's psychological method assumes it is possible to identify an artist's germinal state of mind. "We should not be bound by the intentional fallacy," he says,[41] and in part he is right. When the New Critics condemned what they called the intentional or genetic fallacy as literary heresy, they overreacted to a scholarly establishment entrenched in historical studies. But when literary history seeks the unconscious sources of a class of artistic works, the discarded prejudices of antique New Criticism deserve reexamination. "Critical inquiries," as Beardsley and Wimsatt once observed, "are not settled by consulting the oracle."[42]

Speaking of the Catholic imagination as an "unconscious influence," Giles resorts to what Kuklick long ago condemned as "a crude Cartesian view of mind."[43] In spite of his safeguards, the "specter of 'myth'"[44] hovers over his project just as it possessed Chase and the architects of myth criticism. Writing the history of American Catholic arts and fictions, as Perry Miller wrote the history of the New England mind, Giles assumes the role of a postmodern phrenologist feeling the bumps on the American Catholic head. A mental infrastructure in the minds of people separated from the body of Catholicism, Giles's Catholic imagination can be found anywhere and credited with anything. Its postmodern credentials only aggravate its impressionistic quality.

The Brier-Patch

To conclude this critique, it may be helpful to turn to the work of an American Catholic author whom Giles does not treat: southern writer Joel Chandler Harris. Anyone familiar with the Uncle Remus stories of the Victorian convert will remember the famous animal fable of Brer Rabbit and the Tar-Baby. Thought by many to be an African survival, the narrative tells the story of how the trickster Brer Rabbit foils Brer Fox's attempt to trap him with a tar-and-turpentine dummy. Through wit and words—and a bit of reverse psychology—Rabbit out-foxes his adversary and convinces Fox to throw him into the nearby brier-patch where, the reader learns, Rabbit was "bred en bawn."[45]

A provocative metaphor in traditional southern discourse, the brier-patch has come to represent the lesser of two evils in an imperfect world. A prickly and uncomfortable place, it is a far better location for an uppity rabbit than a sticky death trap overseen by a natural predator. Indeed, despite its obvious limitations, it even feels like home.

In cultural criticism one must choose between Tar-Babies and brier-patches. Disconnecting Catholic arts and fictions from America's legacy of popular art and the ethos of ordinary Catholicism, Giles has estranged the Catholic tradition from its natural environment. Separated too far from the rectory drama, the detective novel, the "golden age" movie, the Catholic Book Club, and organs such as *Catholic Digest*, American Catholic arts and fictions assume an unfamiliar aspect. Divorced from the myth, ritual, and evolving reality of living Catholicism, they become absolutely alien.

Fed up with the vulgarity of American Catholic letters, Allen Tate indicted the nation's Catholic tradition for packing heaven with barbarians. Unwilling to recount the earthly history of those barbarians, Giles has transformed the study of American Catholic art into the study of fugitive Catholics influenced by a secularized Catholicism. Until the Catholic tradition spawns enough artists with the spiritual credentials of O'Connor and the artistic abilities of Fitzgerald, the study of American Catholic arts and fictions will have to perform much of its research in the brier-patch where they were "bred en bawn."

More importantly, Giles's project has lodged the study of American Catholic art in the viscous grip of another Tar-Baby. Despite his allegiances to deconstruction theory, his argument threatens to revert to structuralism at every turn. Ironically this approach makes the American Catholic tradition appear more homogeneous than it really is. Giles's anxiety over the place of converts and true believers in his narrative reveals his resentment toward the tradition's natural heterogeneity and his failure to grasp the plurality of visions contained within "orthodoxy." Fixing the essence of his "Catholicism" in a secular sacramentalism skeptical of all absolutes, he has reified his own categories into archetypes and concealed the diversity within American Catholic culture. As a result, he obscures what Dewey would have called "that sense of an enveloping undefined whole" accompanying Catholic experience.[46]

Ultimately this quest for an elusive "something" at the heart of the Catholic tradition arrests the effort to construct a satisfactory model for the study of American Catholic writers and artists. Giles runs into the same roadblocks that frustrated Tate, Lynch, and the others who sought the singular genius of the Catholic imagination. After accusing Tate and other "didactic" critics of subjecting the Catholic imagination to a neo-Thomist captivity, Giles constructs his secular Catholic mind along lines curiously similar to the "analogical imagination" that reigned in mid-century Catholic criticism. In the end, his postmodernism mimics Catholic high modernism.

Giles's performance in *American Catholic Arts and Fictions* is bold and sassy like Brer Rabbit's. With its publication the study of American Catholic arts and fictions attains a new level of methodological sophistication and critical virtuosity. At a fundamental level, however, it offers a distorted picture of the Catholic contribution to American art. Its basic premises are unexamined assumptions and in some cases even cliches about American Catholic culture. Perhaps a visit to the brier-patch will correct its limitations.

Notes

[1] Jay P. Dolan, "New Directions in American Catholic History," *New Dimensions in American Religious History*, ed. Jay P. Dolan and James P. Wind (Grand Rapids: Eerdmans, 1993), p. 172.

[2] Leslie Woodcock Tentler, "On the Margins: The State of American Catholic History," *American Quarterly* 45 (March 1993): 104-127.

[3] Philip Gleason, "Recovering the Catholic Voice in American History," B. K. Smith Lecture in History, University of St. Thomas, Houston, 21 March 1996.

[4] Jon Butler, "Historiographical Heresy: Catholicism as a Model for American Religious History," *Belief in History: Innovative Approaches to European and American Religion*, ed. Thomas Kselman (Notre Dame: University of Notre Dame Press, 1991), pp. 286-309.

[5] See Paul R. Messbarger, "The Failed Promise of American Catholic Literature," *U.S. Catholic Historian* 4 (1985): 143-158. Arnold J. Sparr, "From Self-Congratulation to Self-Criticism: Main Currents in American Catholic Fiction, 1900-1960," *U.S. Catholic Historian* 6 (1987): 213-230.

[6] John Henry Newman, *Fifteen Sermons Preached Before the University of Oxford* (London: Longmans, Green, and Co., 1898), p. 201.

[7] See volumes in the series *The American Catholic Tradition*: Willard Thorp, *Catholic Novelists in Defense of Their Faith, 1829-1865* (New York: Arno Press, 1978) and James A. White, *The Era of Good Intentions: A Survey of American Catholics' Writing Between the Years 1880-1915* (New York: Arno Press, 1978). See also Paul R. Messbarger, *Fiction with a Parochial Purpose: Social Uses of American Catholic Literature, 1884-1900* (Boston: Boston University Press, 1971).

[8] Paul Giles, *American Catholic Arts and Fictions* (New York: Cambridge University Press, 1992), pp. 278, 296-298, 530.

[9] Anita Gandolfo, *Testing the Faith: The New Catholic Fiction in America* (New York: Greenwood Press, 1992).

[10] Giles, *American Catholic Arts and Fictions*, p. 23.

[11] James Terence Fisher, *The Catholic Counterculture in America 1933-1962* (Chapel Hill: University of North Carolina Press, 1989).

[12] See Peter A. Huff, *Allen Tate and the Catholic Revival: Trace of the Fugitive Gods* (New York: Paulist Press, 1996).

[13] Thomas Merton, *The Sign of Jonas* (New York: Harcourt, Brace and Company, 1953), p. 59 and *Run to the Mountain: The Story of a Vocation*, ed. Patrick Hart (San Francisco: Harper Collins, 1995), p. 420.

[14] Allen Tate, letter, *New York Times* (1 February 1951): 24. Allen Tate, lecture, Assumption University, 1958. Princeton University Libraries. Allen Tate, "Orthodoxy and the Standard of Literature," *New Republic* 128 (5 January 1953): 24.

[15] See David Jasper, *The Study of Literature and Religion* (Minneapolis: Fortress Press, 1989), pp. 56-63.

[16] Bill Oliver, "Faith and Fiction in a Secular Age," *U.S. Catholic Historian* 6 (Spring/Summer 1987): 118.

[17] See Jacques Maritain, *Art and Scholasticism*, trans. J. F. Scanlan (New York: Charles Scribner's Sons, 1930). Flannery O'Connor, *Mystery and Manners*, ed. Sally and Robert Fitzgerald (New York: Farrar, Straus, and Giroux, 1969).

[18] Gandolfo, *Testing the Faith*, p. xii.

[19] See J. F. Powers, "The Catholic and Creativity," *American Benedictine Review* 15 (March 1964): 63-80.

[20] Giles, *American Catholic Arts and Fictions*, p. 507.

[21] Richard Chase, *The American Novel and Its Tradition* (Garden City, NY: Anchor, 1957).

[22] The tradition is not without its present-day proponents. Richard Ruland and Malcolm Bradbury's *From Puritanism to Postmodernism* (New York: Viking, 1991) identifies the contemporary milieu of American literature as the "world of ultimate Protestantism" (p. 423).

[23] Allen Tate, *Essays of Four Decades* (Chicago: Swallow Press, 1968), pp. 401-446.

[24] William F. Lynch, *Christ and Apollo* (New York: Sheed and Ward, 1960).

[25] Andrew Greeley, "Catholics, Fine Arts and the Liturgical Imagination," *America* 174 (18 May 1996): 9-14.

[26] See Joseph J. Feeney, S.J., "The Varieties of the American Catholic Religious Imagination: A Contemporary Taxonomy," *Thought* 66 (June 1991): 206-220.

[27] John Bossy, *Christianity in the West 1400-1700* (Oxford: Oxford University Press, 1985).

[28] See Paul K. Conkin, *Cane Ridge: America's Pentecost* (Madison: University of Wisconsin Press, 1990).

[29] Colleen McDannell, *Material Christianity: Religion and Popular Culture in America* (New Haven: Yale University Press, 1995).

[30] Giles, *American Catholic Arts and Fictions*, pp. 507-508.

[31] Giles, *American Catholic Arts and Fictions*, pp. 507, 525.

[32] Philip Gleason, *Keeping the Faith: American Catholicism Past and Present* (Notre Dame: University of Notre Dame Press, 1987), pp. 11-34. William Halsey, *The Survival of American Innocence: Catholicism in an Era of Disillusionment, 1920-1940* (Notre Dame: University of Notre Dame Press, 1980), pp. 61-83.

[33] Flannery O'Connor, *The Habit of Being: Letters of Flannery O'Connor*, ed. Sally Fitzgerald (New York: Farrar Straus Giroux, 1979), pp. 476-478, 488-489.

[34] O'Connor, *Habit of Being*, p. 510. See Ralph McInerny, "Flannery O'Connor, Hillbilly Thomist," *American Spectator* (July 1983): 22-23. Marion Montgomery, *Why Flannery O'Connor Stayed Home* (La Salle, IL: Sherwood Sugden, 1981).

[35] O'Connor, *Mystery and Manners*, p. 161.

[36] Giles's view bears a striking resemblance to G. K. Chesterton's notion of the "psychological" Christian. See *The Everlasting Man* (New York: Image Books, 1962), p. 168.

[37] On this topic Giles relies upon Peter Occhiogrosso, *Once a Catholic* (Boston: Houghton Mifflin, 1987). See also Andrew M. Greeley, *The Communal Catholic*

(New York: Seabury Press, 1976) and *The American Catholic* (New York: Basic Books, 1977). Dean R. Hoge, *Converts, Dropouts, Returnees: A Study of Religious Change Among Catholics* (Washington, D.C.: United States Catholic Conference, 1981). John D. Barbour, *Versions of Deconversion: Autobiography and the Loss of Faith* (Charlottesville: University Press of Virginia, 1994).

[38] See James Fisher, *The Catholic Counterculture in America*, p. 253.

[39] Michel Foucault, *The Order of Things: An Archaeology of the Human Sciences* (New York: Pantheon, 1970).

[40] Thomas C. Foster, *Form and Society in Modern Literature* (De Kalb, IL: Northern Illinois University Press, 1988), p. 49.

[41] Giles, *American Catholic Arts and Fictions*, p. 30.

[42] W. K. Wimsatt, *The Verbal Icon* (Lexington: University of Kentucky Press, 1954), p. 18.

[43] Bruce Kuklick, "Myth and Symbol in American Studies," *American Quarterly* 24 (October 1972): 437.

[44] Giles, *American Catholic Arts and Fictions*, p. 21.

[45] See Edwin Anderson Alderman and Joel Chandler Harris, eds., *Library of Southern Literature*, 17 vols. (Atlanta: Martin and Hoyt, 1909) 5: 2123-2125.

[46] John Dewey, *Art as Experience* (New York: Capricorn Books, 1958), p. 195. See E. M. Adams, "Art, Culture and Humanism: Religion for Our Times," *Religious Studies and Theology* 13-14 (December 1995): 17-30.

Part III

LOCAL THEOLOGIES

Religion, Secularization, and Cultural Spaces in America

Jon H. Roberts

The concept of secularization, which is often employed to describe the changing relationship of religion to society and culture in the West, has long interested me, but I have never really approached the subject head on. The College Theology Society's invitation to consider American religious intellectual traditions seemed to be an ideal opportunity to take a fresh look at the concept of secularization. Accordingly, I eagerly began examining the massive theoretical literature on this topic.

At the hands of sociologists, and to a lesser extent historians, the concept of secularization has enjoyed a checkered past.[1] The concept first attained prominence in the work of nineteenth-century proponents of the Enlightenment project—people such as Auguste Comte and Herbert Spencer. These thinkers, most of whom were of a positivist bent, predicted the steady decline and eventual demise of supernaturally based religious "myths" in the face of increasing rationality and scientific rigor. In subsequent years, other sociologists, such as Emile Durkheim and Max Weber, though less belligerent in their opposition to traditional patterns of religious belief and less eager to invoke secularization in support of "counter-religious ideologies," nevertheless employed the concept in support of a variety of evolutionary narratives of social change.[2] At the hands of these sociologists, secularization became a concomitant of the technical rationality associated with the development of industrial capitalism and the scientific rationality associated with the developing scientific world view. During the 1950s and 1960s, the concept was retained by sociologists such as Talcott Parsons and Peter Berger. These scholars regarded secularization as an important component of the paradigm of "modernization" to which they had committed themselves. Within that paradigm, which stressed the structural differentiation of life, religion was basically limited to the realm of individuals' private lives.

More recently, some sociologists have criticized secularization as a theoretically flabby, even incoherent, concept. In fact, since the middle of the 1960s, about as much space has been devoted to a consideration of whether secularization is a coherent theory as to whether it has actually occurred.[3] A variety of difficulties have been cited. These include the problem of clearly distinguishing between what is religious and what is secular, the suspect nature of data relating to religious belief and church membership, the tendency to exaggerate the religiosity of the period chosen as the starting point, and the tendency to underestimate the religiosity in subsequent periods.[4] Indeed, critics assert, secularization has come to mean all things to all people and is actually, as one sociologist has put it, "a *doctrine* more than it is a theory."[5] By 1965 use of the term had become so problematic that the eminent sociologist of religion David Martin suggested that "*secularization* should be erased from the sociological dictionary."[6]

I must confess that I find Martin's invitation to wield the eraser quite beguiling. As a historian, I have been trained to view theoretical concepts with a jaundiced eye. Indeed, demolishing the models, paradigms, and generalizations of social scientists is often viewed as an integral part of the historian's vocation. The prospect of being able to claim respectable sociologists as allies serves to give the idea of discarding the concept of secularization added appeal. Still, however tempting it might be to adopt a slash and burn approach to secularization, I have been unable to avoid the lingering suspicion that something of major significance happened between the seventeenth century, when theological categories provided the framework for much of the abstract thinking that occurred about human experience, and the twentieth century, when the relative absence of religious discourse has prompted suggestions that a "culture of disbelief" dominates the American public arena.[7] If the appropriate term for that "something" is not secularization, then I do not know what else it might be. Nor am I not alone in my hesitation to abandon use of that term. Thirteen years after suggesting that the term be eliminated, David Martin published his most important book in the sociology of religion: *A General Theory of Secularization.*[8]

This is not to say, of course, that clear definitions are unnecessary. Obviously, in order to ascertain whether secularization has occurred, it is necessary to know what the "it" is. Toward that end, I suggest that we view secularization simply as a process signifying a decline in the relevance of the transcendent and divine in integrating and legitimating life within modern culture. This definition is consistent with Max Weber's view that secularization involves the "disenchantment of the world."[9] It is also consistent with Peter Berger's conception of it as a "process by which sectors of society and culture are removed from the domination of religious institutions and symbols."[10] Finally, in my judgment, my proposed definition is sufficiently sharp-edged to be both analytically useful and historically testable.

With this definition as a starting point, a historian might begin to evaluate whether and to what extent secularization has actually occurred by envisioning culture as a series of dimensions, or "spaces." The spaces that I have in mind include familiar and often overlapping components of the cultural landscape where discourse about meaning and the nature of reality characteristically occur. These include such realms as politics, the law, socio-economic interactions, the family, community life, religious institutions, the popular media, technology, the natural world, and even the nature of human beings as amalgams of mind and body. The discourse relating to the transcendent—the "God-talk"—that occurs within a cultural space at any given time is a measure of how compelling recourse to the divine seems to be within that space.[11] In turn, the location and the pervasiveness of religious discourse within a society's culture are related to the religiosity of that culture. In this view, secularization refers to a relative decline in the extent to which cultural spaces are occupied by God-talk. The historian's task would thus consist of analyzing how perceptions of the presence—or absence—of God have changed over time within cultural spaces.

It is worth highlighting some of the implications of this approach to secularization. First, it avoids equating that concept with either loss of belief or the declining status of organized institutions of religion. While such phenomena may indicate secularization, I am not persuaded that continued belief or even continued high church membership in themselves provide solid grounds for denying that secularization has occurred. Secularization is a concept that refers to the intensity and the relevance of a system of belief, not its reality or its ecclesiastical institutionalization. Second, this approach is more sensitive to changes in patterns of thought and discourse—in other words, the cognitive arena—than it is to institutional change within society. What this implies is the continued need for social historians and sociologists to lend their voices to the conversation about secularization. Third, nothing in the historical analysis of secularization implies that the process, if it has occurred, is necessarily irreversible. Conceivably the history of discourse about the divine can be non-linear. Re-sacralization can occur. Similarly, viewing the issue "spatially," it seems clear that the boundaries of secular and sacred are quite permeable; no obvious advantage is to be gained by rigorously construing either dimension. Finally, it seems reasonable to assume that at any given time, there will be differences in the degree and extent to which cultural spaces are congenial to discourse concerning the divine and the transcendent. Hence, a truly adequate evaluation of the process of secularization in the United States would involve a systematic examination of all the spaces within American culture.

Unfortunately, such an examination would require considerable space. Accordingly, I would like to examine briefly the changing role of God-talk in two cultural spaces: the natural world and the social arena. My hope is that by tracing the changing role of discourse concerning the divine in those two spaces, I can provide at least some broad hints as to the kind of analysis that I have in mind for others as well.[12] I should also note the focus will be on the American intellectual community, loosely interpreted.

The groundwork for the possibility of secularization was laid very early in the history of Western civilization. From biblical times onward, partisans of the Judaeo-Christian tradition emphasized a sharp ontological distinction between the God who created the universe and the universe that was created.[13] In a fundamental sense, that is to say, God was conceived as transcendent over, though intimately involved with, the cosmos and the human beings who occupied it.

The post-Reformation Protestants who comprised most seventeenth-century European immigrants, brought this view of a "wholly other," yet providentially involved, God with them. The pre-modern, pre-industrial world from which they came, with its vagaries of weather, disease, famine, and seemingly random acts of violence, was sufficiently unpredictable and tragic to imbue them with a lively sense of their contingency. Most also believed, however, that appearances to the contrary notwithstanding, the events that impinged upon their lives were not truly random. Rather, such events attested to the existence of a cosmic plan designed by a transcendent, albeit inscrutable, Deity. This view led John Calvin to declare that "not a drop of rain falls without the express command of God."[14] To be sure, not all Europeans living in British North America were equally devout in proclaiming that faith or in worshipping this providential Deity, but there seems to be convincing evidence that recourse to transcendent meaning and providential purpose was fundamental to the world view of virtually everyone.[15]

As Europeans were settling North America, of course, the Scientific Revolution was in full swing. One of the very foundations of that revolution was the notion that the orderliness of the natural world was an expression of God's will.[16] Not surprisingly, many educated individuals in Europe and America alike found the ideas central to the scientific world view—in particular, the congeniality of nature to reasoned empirical inquiry and the concept of natural law—enormously attractive. Those ideas seemed to make it possible to reconcile belief in God's transcendence with belief in a measure of rationality, regularity, and order within the cosmos.[17]

During the eighteenth century, the venerable belief in an inscrutable Deity who personally directed natural events underwent further erosion in the face of a growing commitment to scientific reason and natural laws. Those concepts, so central to the Enlightenment, fostered the idea that God was a rational Being who had chosen to create and sustain the universe in accordance with a pattern intelligible to human beings.

This shifting body of ideas did not entail loss of belief in God's governance of the cosmos. Not only were the scientists most intimately associated with the Enlightenment, such as Isaac Newton, eager to affirm God's providential oversight and intervention, but other participants in the cultural dialogue concerning the meaning and significance of the natural world invoked supernatural emblems and divinely ordained final causes in framing their discussions of nature.[18] The eminent New England divine Cotton Mather, for example, concluded his detailed discussion of the nature of snow by reminding his readers that by virtue of the atoning agency of Christ, his readers' sins had become as white as snow.[19] Similarly, Jonathan Edwards concluded from his intricate description of the nature and purpose of a spider's web that it clearly revealed "the exuberant Goodness of the Creator Who hath not only Provided for all the Necessities, but also for the Pleasure and Recreation of all sorts of Creatures, and Even the insects and those that are most Despicable."[20] At a somewhat different level, Christian apologists increasingly appropriated the design and order disclosed by science in fashioning arguments demonstrating God's existence and in reinforcing appreciation of God's wisdom and goodness.

If, however, nothing in principle prevented partisans of the scientific view of nature from paying homage to nature's God, nevertheless natural laws embraced by science constituted a series of halfway houses that allowed nature to be described without invoking the Deity. It is important to emphasize that there was nothing logically necessary about this. Actually, nothing in the concept of natural law *per se* speaks to the issue of whether that law expresses inherent properties of matter, properties conferred on matter by God, or "energy" emanating from the immediate activities of an immanent Deity. For students of secularization, the really decisive move was not the affirmation of natural law but the decision to give matter causal efficacy and to distinguish "secondary" causes, which were commonly regarded as agencies within nature by which God normally effected His purposes, from the divine First Cause.[21] That decision made the distinction between divine and natural agency ontologically significant.

Not everyone accepted that view. For example, Jonathan Edwards, convinced, as he put it, that "there is no proper substance but God himself," held that matter was the product of the constant and immediate activity of God and that the laws of nature were simply expressions of the way in which the Deity habitually chose to act.[22] Writing about a century later, Francis Bowen, an intellectual whose wide-ranging interests stood him in good stead as editor of the erudite *North American Review* and as Harvard's Alford Professor of Natural Religion, Moral Philosophy and Civil Polity, declared that "what are called *secondary* causes are really no causes at all, but only mark the occasions on which events and changes take place, all of which are brought about by the direct agency of a power, that is wholly foreign to this world."[23]

Edwards and Bowen, however, were atypical. After about 1675, an ever-increasing number of theologians and natural philosophers alike described the cosmos in ways that implied that the power to act was an essential property of natural phenomena. Although most of those thinkers continued to affirm that the operation of secondary agencies was governed by divine purpose and that finite entities were constantly preserved "in being and vigour" by God's *concursus*, they assumed that those agencies possessed real power.[24] Leonard Woods, Andover's Abbot Professor of Theology, gave expression to the prevailing view when he asserted that just "because there is only one *supreme* cause it does by no means follow that there are no subordinate causes." On the contrary, he maintained, the Deity had established "many subordinate causes, . . . all having a measure of efficiency."[25]

It would be a mistake, however, to attribute the triumph of belief in the causal efficacy of natural phenomena to nothing more than the influence of the scientific world view. By the nineteenth century, the speculations of Friedrich Schleiermacher and a number of other German theologians had alerted many American religious thinkers to the dangers of pantheism.[26] Any blurring of distinctions between nature and the supernatural appeared to some embattled Christians to be a theologically dangerous compromise with that heresy.[27]

Prior to about the last quarter of the nineteenth century, the affirmation of an ontological distinction between material and divine agency seemed relatively unimportant, because religious thinkers tended to focus their attention on more anomalous instances of divine intervention rather than on the pervasive presence of God in law-like processes. In large measure this decision was a function of their confidence that such instances abounded in nature. Of particular importance in this regard was the appearance of successive groups of ever more highly developed species during the course of the history of life. The appearance and disappearance of plant and animal species seemed to show, as the eminent geologist and Congregationalist clergyman Edward Hitchcock put it, that "the Deity has always exercised over the globe a superintending Providence."[28]

The plausibility of relying on "special" instances of divine intervention within the natural world largely depended on the inability of scientists to describe central features of natural history in terms of natural agencies. By the middle of the nineteenth century, however, scientists had become increasingly confident that ultimately *all* natural phenomena could be described in terms of "secondary" causes. This confidence was given a dramatic boost by the two major achievements of nineteenth-century science, the articulation of the principle of the conservation of energy and the promulgation of a credible theory of organic evolution. By the end of the nineteenth century, it seemed possible to describe the structure and operation of the entire cosmos in terms of a series of chains of cause and effect. Just as important, by mid-century scientists were increasingly gravitating toward the idea that the very aim of their inquiries, as the Wesleyan natural historian

William North Rice put it, was "to narrow the domain of the super-natural, by bringing all phenomena within the scope of natural laws and secondary causes."[29]

The imputation of causal efficacy to secondary agencies, coupled with the growing scope of scientific explanation in terms of those agencies, made it increasingly possible to describe the natural world without resorting to God. Not that large numbers of people, even within the intellectual community, ceased believing in God, rather, by the late nineteenth century, sustained analysis and discussion of nature without invoking the Deity had become possible. The theistic approach to the natural world was not commonly denounced or even rejected; it was simply increasingly disregarded.[30]

At this point, I should probably address myself to a couple of obvious rejoinders to the picture that I have been constructing. First, since 1875, the idea that science can provide the best, or even an adequate, approach to the natural world has been strongly contested by a number of American religious intellectuals. Arguably, the most notable forms of the protest can be found in opposition from members of three groups: Protestants such as J. Gresham Machen who were committed to "muscular" views of biblical authority; liberal Protestants, who adopted a radical formulation of divine immanence that invoked God as "the efficient cause and constant mover of all things"; and Roman Catholic Neoscholastics, who enjoined people to use a set of categories for thinking about reality—essence and existence, substance and accidents, act and potency, and so forth—that constitute a real alternative to the scientific world view.[31]

A second criticism of the view that I have proposed is that Americans have quite clearly encountered the natural world in ways that neither invite nor require the kind of thinking about causes and scientific intelligibility that I have been focusing on. That is to say, they have engaged in a more immediate, often aesthetic, appreciation of the natural world that frequently leads to invocation of the divine.[32]

I would respond to these suggestions by emphasizing that secularization does not imply the total absence but simply a *decline* in the religious discourse within a given cultural space. That there are subcultures of conservative Protestants, liberal Protestants, and Neoscholastics who continue to posit theological interpretations of nature is undoubtedly true. It is also perfectly reasonable to assume that some Americans have retained a lively sense of the beauty and theological significance of the natural world. Nevertheless, even the most cursory analysis of public discourse since 1900 will suggest that fewer and fewer members of the American intellectual community, at least, have continued to call attention to the link between nature and nature's God. The fact that the declining status of God-talk in discourse about nature has been neither a smooth nor uncontested affair does not gainsay the fact that it has occurred.

The way that American intellectuals have interpreted social interactions also suggests an increasingly secularized pattern. During the seventeenth century, most colonists of British North America were apparently too intent on making their way in the social arena to do much thinking and talking about it. Accordingly, in that period much of the discourse concerning the social order in British North America centered in the colonies of New England. In those colonies, social thought was strongly informed by providentialist assumptions similar to those that obtained in analyses of the natural world. John Calvin, a patron saint of the Puritans who established New England, was one of many Protestant reformers who insisted that the multitude of individual interactions within society constituted the fabric of a moral order governed by a sovereign and inscrutable Deity.[33] Although he acknowledged that depraved and fallible human beings were frequently incapable of fathoming God's purposes, he adamantly rejected the notion that the world was the product of magic and luck.[34]

The New England Puritans joined Calvin in emphasizing that human beings would never, as the clergyman Increase Mather put it, "be able fully to understand by what Rules the Holy and Wise God ordereth all events Prosperous and adverse which come to pass in the world. His ways of Providence are unsearchable."[35] Paradoxically, however, the Puritans, like Calvin himself, denied that a providential interpretation of history absolved human beings from the responsibility of living their lives in accordance with the dictates of God's will. Rather, even in Puritan New England, a sizable number of intellectuals coupled their acknowledgments of the bondage of the will to sin and the sovereignty of God with the claim that on some level, at least, human beings possessed a measure of freedom.[36] Moreover, as time went on the "Arminianizing" of American theology continued apace.

Free will, however, only provided the basis for the *ability* of human beings to act in accordance with the divine plan. For guidance as to what that divine plan actually was, the Puritans believed, individuals were to look to the Scriptures. Applying this view to society as a whole, the authorities of Massachusetts Bay during the early years of settlement embraced a series of principles governing commerce—principles such as the "just price" and limitations on the amount of interest rates on loans.[37] As it happened, the enforcement of those principles proved short-lived. The New England merchants, whom the principles were to regulate, had little sympathy with the Puritan social ideals of order, stability, and discipline, and they chafed under the restrictions that had been imposed upon them.[38] Ultimately, the increasing dependence of New England communities on the economic contributions of those merchants forced the Puritans to abandon most of their attempts to regulate the economy in accordance with their perception of the dictates of God's will.

If, however, the laws of New England less clearly reflected the views of Puritan social theory by the end of the seventeenth century, the major tenets of Christian theology continued to play a fundamental role in grounding the thought and discourse of British North Americans concerning the social order. Indeed, in some respects, the emphasis that Christians placed on social interactions assumed increased importance in the eighteenth century. Historians have commonly regarded that century as a period when personal piety increasingly gave way to moralism in American formulations of Christian theology. It certainly seems to be the case that an increasing share of public discourse turned from questions relating to religious devotion and salvation to questions relating to character and social obligation.[39] Or perhaps it would be more accurate to say that increasingly, individuals' acts of righteousness in their treatment of others became the measure of the quality of their Christian devotion, and their moral behavior became the most convincing evidence of their salvation.

At the same time that relationships among individuals were assuming increasing importance within Christian theology itself, partisans of the Enlightenment were contributing to changes in the way that social interactions were being conceptualized. The same emphasis on mechanistic causality that was refashioning visions of the natural world also played a role in reshaping conceptions of the social order.[40] Divine providence did not disappear; it remained a subtext in a good deal of American discourse concerning the social order. By the eighteenth century, however, providentialists found it necessary to reconcile divine oversight with not only the seemingly incorrigible belief in moral responsibility but also a growing confidence that it would be possible to discern intelligible patterns of social interaction akin to the laws of nature. Not surprisingly, most believers dealt with this situation by subordinating discussion of "special" providence to the claim that social interactions could be described within the rubric of divinely ordained moral law.[41]

In discussing the mechanics of the social order, most thinkers, Christian and non-Christian alike, equated "causes" with individual motives and "effects" with human behavior. And since they continued to interpret both motives and behavior within the context of moral philosophy, they characteristically defined social phenomena as the product of individual moral agents viewed collectively.[42]

Although it is possible to discern efforts on the part of such notable eighteenth-century American intellectuals as Benjamin Franklin to formally separate discourse concerning moral philosophy from theological dogma, most thinkers who participated in the public dialogue concerning the nature of society allied themselves with the Scottish common-sense philosophers in maintaining that aspirations for a more "scientific" view of social interaction only made sense within the confines of a theistic view of reality. Indeed, the widespread insistence on describing the social order within a religious framework is one of the reasons why historians have characteristically emphasized the American Enlightenment's moderate tone.

During the period from about 1775 to 1870, much of Americans' discourse about the appropriate nature of their society was dominated by the classical liberal emphasis on the desirability of human freedom and unfettered social mobility. At the same time, however, most Americans who participated in what we might call the "public culture" of the United States continued to emphasize that this freedom and mobility took place within the framework established by divinely ordained moral law. Of particular importance in this regard were the numerous thinkers who taught moral philosophy in American colleges. Those moral philosophers, who dealt not only with ethical issues but also with subjects that would later comprise the social sciences, expressed views concerning human nature and human society that were embraced by a spectrum of intellectuals from Thomas Jefferson to the Unitarian clergyman William Ellery Channing to ardent Protestant evangelicals such as Francis Wayland.[43] Drawing primarily on the work of Scottish thinkers such as Frances Hutcheson, Thomas Reid, and Dugald Stewart,

American moral philosophers maintained that a careful examination of human experience and the dictates of "common sense" would disclose the existence of moral law, a network of principles that had been ordained by God to regulate human relationships. Obedience to principles such as thrift, industry, temperance, and sexual morality often brought happiness in this life. By contrast, violation of those principles brought a sundry set of woes: poverty, ill health, and ultimately, the torments of hell.[44]

If participants in public discourse concerning the American social order believed that the substance of the moral law had been codified in the Scriptures and confirmed by the experience of countless saints and sinners, most also held that God had implanted the ability to make moral judgments within human nature itself. As a result of that "moral sense," or conscience, human beings were unique among God's creatures in being able to make moral distinctions.[45]

Affirmations of moral law and humanity's ability to discern it played an important role in American culture prior to about 1870. To begin with, the matrix provided by moral law enabled Americans to discern at least some order within their often seemingly chaotic social experience. In addition, in a period characterized by assaults on tradition, hierarchy, and a wide variety of institutional mechanisms such as established churches that had long fostered order within society, the notion of discoverable moral law and a moral faculty implanted within each human being provided American thinkers with an important intellectual justification for encouraging public virtue.[46] Finally, by establishing a link between virtue and happiness on the one hand, and sin and woe on the other, moral law provided Americans with a kind of "social theodicy" that helped explain why some people achieved success while others suffered.

Notwithstanding the functional import of the idea of a divinely ordained "moral economy," however, references to God's role within the cultural space relating to social interaction became increasingly less common during the course of the nineteenth century. There were several reasons for this. First, the analogy between natural law and moral law was not entirely felicitous. Only a cursory examination of human experience indicates that the laws comprising God's moral order were considerably more variable than those describing the natural world. Villains, after all, prospered, while saints endured trials that would have made Job wince. What this suggested, the moral philosophers maintained, was that God governed the fortunes of human beings in accordance with their individual needs and natures.[47] However, although this position may have satisfied those already convinced of the presence of moral law, some Americans remained perplexed. Their perplexity was doubtless intensified in the wake of the carnage generated by the Civil War and the vagaries of industrialization. Those Americans who did not simply throw up their hands and ascribe human destiny to luck and fate proved willing to give a hearing to views of the social order that sought either to ignore or to dispense altogether with the role of the divine.[48]

Second, nontheistic interpretations of society became increasingly credible in the late nineteenth century. In that period theories providing for the gradual evolution of moral ideas undermined the intellectual imperative for describing social interactions in terms of a divinely ordained moral law.[49] In addition, in a rapidly changing social environment, the norms governing human interaction appeared to be subject to almost constant renegotiation and alteration. To some Americans, at least, this suggested that those norms were human rather than divine creations.

Third, even many thinkers who remained committed to a belief in a rough correlation between virtue and happiness found it relatively painless to retain notions of a moral economy while detaching them from their providential underpinnings. Hence, many participants in the public dialogue concerning society continued to emphasize the importance of good character and applauded prosperity, while ignoring the transcendent foundation that had originally grounded those concepts. As early as the 1840s, a number of clergy in the United States were expressing concern about a growing tendency on the part of Americans to extol material progress without acknowledging the divine scheme of redemption on which behavior leading to that progress was ostensibly based.[50] Within the rhetorical structure of American discourse, "character" increasingly substituted for "virtue" and "obedience to moral law." While those terms did not denote radically different ideas, in practice the former term—"character"—tended to be more conducive to secular renderings. By the late nineteenth century, even those who still invoked religion in discussing the social order, such as partisans of the Social Gospel, were focusing less on the agency of God than on the treatment that human beings and institutions extended to one another.

Finally, the very nature of society in the period after 1870 became so complex that the notion that the social universe could be adequately described in terms of the motives and consequences of individual actors became ever less credible.[51] The faith in the existence of laws describing social interaction remained intact. Indeed, it even intensified in the scientistic climate of the late nineteenth century. Most educated Americans now deemed it necessary, however, to turn to an increasingly specialized group of "social scientists" for an understanding of what those laws were and how they shaped social interaction.

This is not to say that the cultural space occupied by social thought during the late nineteenth and early twentieth centuries was completely bereft of God-talk. To the contrary, investigation of the origin of social science in the United States has revealed that religious concerns motivated a sizable percentage of social scientists in the half century after 1870.[52] Nevertheless, a pattern similar to that which occurred in discussions of the natural world can be discerned in discussions of the social order and the activities of human beings within it. Even the large number of Americans who retained their belief in a close connection between character and success and "sin" and failure devoted little attention to the precise role of God in this process.

As social scientists fought doggedly during much of the twentieth century to attain the status for their disciplines that they believed had been accorded to the natural sciences, most of them made a concerted effort to avoid making normative judgments that could be construed as religious in nature. Increasingly, public dialogue about society was dominated by the voices of those intent on avoiding discussion of the transcendent in their discussion of the dynamics of the social order.

My brief examination suggests that secularization has occurred in the cultural spaces relating to dialogue concerning the natural world and society. Some students of American society have acknowledged that many cultural spaces have become desacralized and that religion has become an increasingly private matter, but they have insisted that "relocation" is a more appropriate term than secularization for describing the situation.[53] In my judgment, there are several difficulties with this position. First there appear to be no clear grounds for evaluating the relative importance of religion within the lives of individuals over time. What kind of evidence accessible to investigators would count? On the face of it, it would certainly seem most plausible to assume that the more vital religion is in the lives of individuals, the more pervasive religion will be as an influence within the life of the culture that those individuals inhabit. More important for our purposes, though, is the fact that an assessment of the importance of religion in the private lives of individuals is not synonymous with an appraisal of its importance in the life of the larger culture. If one is interested in the extent of religion's cultural influence, is it possible to interpret the increasing privatization of religion as anything other than a symptom of secularization?

I do not exclude the possibility that resacralization can occur within cultural spaces. Recently, for example, the transcendent seems to be making something of a comeback in the cultural space occupied by discourse concerning social interaction. It would certainly be difficult to understand the numerous cultural issues that manifest themselves within the American political arena—prayer in school, abortion, attitudes toward homosexuality, and the like—without acknowledging the important role of religious concerns. Similarly, in "New Age" religion, it is possible to discern an approach to the natural world that constitutes a significant alternative to the scientific world view. On the other hand, it seems to me that it is necessary to exercise a good deal of caution in interpreting these phenomena as strong evidence of resacralization. Much of the discourse relating to socio-political issues that focuses on religion consists of the partisan rhetoric of the "Christian right." Many of their opponents have treated religion as it has been thus manifested more as an object of contempt than as a framework within which social inquiry can proceed. Significantly, too, much of the discussion of social interaction has centered on "family values." Although this is clearly an area of widespread interest and concern, more broad-ranging analysis of the socio-economic order continues to occur without much reference to the transcendent. Nor has New Age religion's take on the natural world yet struck deep roots within the larger culture. Finally, it is worth noting that most recent religiously based dialogue concerning the social order and the natural world has remained at the grassroots level, unheralded and often opposed by American intellectuals. I suspect that before a significant change occurs in the allegiance of the American intellectual community to the kind of scientific world view that has largely eliminated God-talk from many cultural spaces, a radically different way of religiously envisioning the data of human experience will need to occur. Surely this would involve an intellectual revolution of epic proportions, and it is difficult to anticipate just what such a revolution would look like. But that, of course, is precisely what is most characteristic of revolutions, intellectual and otherwise.

Notes

[1] A good survey of the history of the term is David Lyon, "Secularization and Sociology: The History of an Idea," *Fides et Historia* 13 (Spring-Summer 1981): 38-51. My discussion of the changing fortunes of the concept draws to a considerable extent on this article.

[2] The term "counter-religious ideologies" has been used by David Martin, albeit in a more present-minded context than I have employed it. See David Martin, "Towards Eliminating the Concept of Secularization," in *Penguin Survey of the Social Sciences, 1965*, ed. Julius Gould (Baltimore: Penguin Books, 1965), pp. 169, 176.

[3] Olivier Tschannen, "The Secularization Paradigm: A Systematization," *Journal for the Scientific Study of Religion* 30 (1991): 395.

[4] Martin, "Towards Eliminating the Concept of Secularization," pp. 169-182, esp. 172-173; Jeffrey K. Hadden, "Toward Desacralizing Secularization Theory," *Social Forces* 65 (1987): 587-611, esp. 599-600; Mary Douglas, "The Effects of Modernization on Religious Change," *Daedalus* 111 (1982): 5; Larry Shiner, "The Concept of Secularization in Empirical Research," *Journal for the Scientific Study of Religion* 6 (1967): 207-210; Steve Bruce, *A House Divided: Protestantism, Schism, and Secularization* (London: Routledge, 1990), pp. 7-16, esp. 9-10. It is worth noting that Bruce rejects the objections he discusses as decisive.

[5] Hadden, "Toward Desacralizing Secularization Theory," p. 588.

[6] Martin, "Towards Eliminating the Concept of Secularization," p. 182.

[7] Stephen L. Carter, *The Culture of Disbelief: How American Law and Politics Trivialize Religious Devotion* (New York: Basic Books, 1993). See also Andrew Delbanco, *The Death of Satan: How Americans Have Lost the Sense of Evil* (New York: Farrar, Straus and Giroux, 1995).

For the dominance of theological categories during the colonial period, see Fred Anderson, *A People's Army: Massachusetts Soldiers and Society in the Seven Years' War* (Chapel Hill: University of North Carolina Press, 1984), pp. 217-218; and David D. Hall, *Worlds of Wonder, Days of Judgment: Popular Religious Belief in Early New England* (Cambridge, MA: Harvard University Press, 1989), pp. 14-17.

[8] David Martin, *A General Theory of Secularization* (New York: Harper & Row, 1978).

[9] Max Weber, "Science as a Vocation," [1918], *Daedalus* 87 (1958): 133.

[10] Peter L. Berger, *The Sacred Canopy: Elements of a Sociological Theory of Religion* (1967; Garden City, NY: Anchor Books, 1969), p. 107. My conception of secularization is also quite close in spirit to the discussion in Thomas Luckmann, *The Invisible Religion: The Problem of Religion in Modern Society* (New York: Macmillan Publishing Co., Inc., 1967), pp. 39-40; Karel Dobbelaere, "Seculariza-

tion: A Multi-Dimensional Concept," *Current Sociology* 29 (Summer 1981): 5; and Bryan Wilson, *Religion in Secular Society: A Sociological Comment* (Baltimore: Penguin Books, 1966), p. 14.

Some ways of describing secularization are notoriously difficult to measure. How, for example, do we define—and then measure—piety? Often the primary source of discussions of this alleged phenomenon is complaints about others from those who view their own piety as the measure of religious devotion. Nor is church attendance a self-evidently valid measure of religiosity. There might well be functions that motivate people to attend church that have little to do with expressions of religious conviction. Still, these problems may not be insuperable, and efforts to address them speak to the sensible conviction that change has occurred over time in a culture's religiosity.

[11] The notion of the nature of religion is admittedly a thorny one. I share the view of many American cultural historians, such as Andrew Delbanco, who recently observed that "the essence of religious faith is the idea of transcendence." Delbanco, *Death of Satan*, p. 228. I would also acknowledge, however, that this may well be a culturally bound definition.

[12] For a perceptive discussion that focuses on the legal and political arenas, see Carter, *Culture of Disbelief.*

[13] Peter L. Berger, *The Sacred Canopy*, pp. 113-121.

[14] John Calvin, *Institutes of the Christian Religion* [1959], trans. Henry Beveridge (1845; Grand Rapids, MI: Eerdmans, 1975), Bk. I, ch. 16, section 5. See also ibid., Bk I, ch. 16, section 1-2, 4, 8; ibid., Bk. I, ch. 5, section 11.

[15] Edmund S. Morgan, "The American Revolution Considered as an Intellectual Movement," in *Paths of American Thought*, ed. Arthur M. Schlesinger, Jr. and Morton White (Boston: Houghton Mifflin Company, 1963), p. 12.

Recently Jon Butler has noted that Christian practice in the seventeenth century was quite "insecure," but his argument focuses primarily on the issue of institutionalized religion rather than belief. Jon Butler, *Awash in a Sea of Faith: Christianizing the American People* (Cambridge, MA: Harvard University Press, 1990), p. 38.

[16] For a representative statement of this position, see M. B. Foster, "The Christian Doctrine of Creation and the Rise of Modern Natural Science," *Mind*, n. s., 43 (1934): 446-468.

[17] Perry Miller, *The New England Mind: From Colony to Province* (Cambridge, MA: Harvard University Press, 1953), p. 437; Perry Miller, *Errand into the Wilderness* (Cambridge, MA: Harvard University Press, 1956), pp. 225-226.

[18] Isaac Newton, for example, declared that "a God without dominion, providence, and final causes, is nothing but Fate and Nature" (Isaac Newton, *The Mathematical Principles of Natural Philosophy*, trans. Andrew Motte, 2 vols. [1729; London: Dawsons of Pall Mall, 1968], II: 391).

[19] Cotton Mather, *The Christian Philosopher* [1721], ed. Winton U. Solberg (Urbana: University of Illinois Press, 1994), pp. 67-69.

[20] Jonathan Edwards, "Of Insects" [1715], in Clarence H. Faust and Thomas H. Johnson, *Jonathan Edwards: Representative Selections, with Introduction, Bibliography, and Notes*, rev. ed. (New York: Hill and Wang, 1962), p. 7.

[21] John Dillenberger, *Protestant Thought and Natural Science: A Historical Interpretation* (Garden City, NY: Doubleday, 1960), pp. 67-69; Perry Miller, *The New England Mind: The Seventeenth Century* (New York: Macmillan, 1939), pp. 224-226, 231-235.

[22] Jonathan Edwards, "Of Being," in *The Philosophy of Jonathan Edwards from His Private Notebooks*, ed. Harvey G. Townsend (Eugene, OR: University of Oregon Press, 1955), pp. 15-20, quotation on p. 17.

[23] [F. Bowen], "Brougham's Natural Theology," *North American Review* 54 (1842): 138-139. See also Francis Bowen, *The Principles of Metaphysical and Ethical Science Applied to the Evidence of Religion*, rev. ed. (Boston: Hickling, Swan & Brown, 1855), pp. 95, 99-100.

[24] Joseph Haven, "Place and Value of Miracles in the Christian System," *Bibliotheca Sacra* 19 (1862): 339; [Robert L. Dabney], "Geology and the Bible," *Southern Presbyterian Review* 14 (1861): 271-272; C. H. Hitchcock, "The Relations of Geology to Theology," *Bibliotheca Sacra* 24 (1867): 475; John Harris, *The Pre-Adamite Earth: Contributions to Theological Science* (Boston: Gould, Kendall, & Lincoln, 1849), pp. 100-101; S. W. Culver, "Natural and the Supernatural—How Distinguished and How Related," *Baptist Quarterly* 8 (1873): 362-368; [Samuel John Baird], "The Providential Government of God," *Biblical Repertory and Princeton Review* 30 (1858): 319-320, 325-328, 341-342; Henry Ware, *An Inquiry into the Foundations, Evidences, and Truths of Religion* (Cambridge, MA: John Owen, 1842), pp. 157-158; Anonymous, "The Reign of Law," *Biblical Repertory and Princeton Review* 42 (1870): 76; E. Nisbet, "Darwinism," *Baptist Quarterly* 8 (1873): 218-223; James McCosh, *The Method of the Divine Government, Physical and Moral* (New York: Robert Carter & Brothers, 1851), pp. 191-193, 204.

[25] Leonard Woods, "Divine Agency and Government, Together with Human Agency and Freedom," *American Biblical Repository*, 2nd ser., 12 (1844): 412. A similar position prompted Charles Hodge, Princeton Seminary's influential Professor of Exegetical, Didactic, and Polemic Theology, to maintain that in the ordinary course of affairs, "the agency of God neither supersedes, nor in any way interferes with the efficiency of secondary causes." Charles Hodge, *Systematic Theology* (1871; New York: Scribner, Armstrong, and Co., 1873), I: 600. See also ibid., pp. 575, 595-597, 621, 690.

My discussion in the preceding paragraph is a close paraphrase of a passage in which I discuss the issue at greater length in Jon H. Roberts, *Darwinism and the Divine in America: Protestant Intellectuals and Organic Evolution, 1859-1900* (Madison, WI: University of Wisconsin Press, 1988), pp. 101-102.

[26] [Albert Baldwin Dod], "Vestiges of Creation," *Biblical Repertory and Princeton Review* 17 (1845): 553; [Lyman Atwater], "The Positive Philosophy of Auguste Comte," *Biblical Repertory and Princeton Review* 28 (1856): 61, 87; McCosh, *Method of the Divine Government*, pp. 222-225.

[27] A representative statement of this position was enunciated by the Reverend William W. Patton of Chicago. In 1862 Patton warned readers of the *Methodist Quarterly Review* that opponents of the idea that "material forces are brought into being as permanent agencies" were implicitly endorsing pantheism. Convinced that it was a short step from denying that real efficacy belonged to "physical

causes" to rejecting the view that human beings possessed freedom of will, he concluded that the ascription of all causal efficacy to God was "theologically suicidal." William W. Patton, "The Tendency of Scientific Men to Skepticism," *Methodist Quarterly Review*, 4th ser., 14 (1862): 552-553. See also Woods, "Divine Agency," pp. 411-413; Hodge, *Systematic Theology*, I, pp. 579-580.

²⁸ Edward Hitchcock, *Elementary Geology*, 8th ed. (New York: Newman & Ivison, 1852), p. 284. See also L. W. Green, "The Harmony of Revelation and Natural Science: With Especial Reference to Geology," in *Lectures on the Evidences of Christianity. Delivered at the University of Virginia During the Session of 1850-1*, ed. W. H. Ruffner (New York: R. Carter & Bros., 1852), p. 463. I have discussed this and related issues at much greater length in Roberts, *Darwinism and the Divine in America*, pp. 9-13.

²⁹ William North Rice, "The Darwinian Theory of the Origin of Species," *New Englander* 26 (1867): 608. See also ibid., p. 618; George F. Wright, "Recent Works Bearing on the Relation of Science to Religion. No. II—The Divine Method of Producing Living Species," *Bibliotheca Sacra* 33 (1876): 480; [Francis Ellingwood Abbot], "Philosophical Biology," *North American Review* 107 (1868): 379-380; Asa Gray, *Darwiniana: Essays and Reviews Pertaining to Darwinism*, ed. A Hunter Dupree (1876; Cambridge, MA: Harvard University Press, 1963), pp. 78-79; Asa Gray, *Natural Science and Religion: Two Lectures Delivered to the Theological School of Yale College* (New York: Charles Scribner's Sons, 1880), p. 77. I have discussed this crucial development in the history of science and Christian apologetics at greater length in Jon H. Roberts, "Scientific Culture, Religion, and Higher Education in America, 1870-1930," in John F. Wilson et al., *Religion and the Modern American University* (Princeton: Princeton University Press, forthcoming).

³⁰ For a more fully developed statement of this theme, see Roberts, *Darwinism and the Divine*, pp. 233-242.

³¹ The liberal affirmation of God's immanence is from F. H. Johnson, "Theistic Evolution," *Andover Review* 1 (1884): 372.

³² It could be argued, for example, that much of what passes for the environmentalist ethic is driven by a sense of the natural that has little to do with the categories of science.

³³ Calvin, *Institutes*, Book 1, ch. 16, section 9.

³⁴ Ronald J. VanderMolen, "Providence as Mystery, Providence as Revelation: Puritan and Anglican Modifications of John Calvin's Doctrine of Providence," *Church History* 47 (1978): 30-32. Keith Thomas, *Religion and the Decline of Magic* (New York: Charles Scribner's Sons, 1971), pp. 78-112.

³⁵ Increase Mather, *The Doctrine of Divine Providence Opened and Applyed* [1684], quoted in Lester H. Cohen, *The Revolutionary Histories: Contemporary Narratives of the American Revolution* (Ithaca, NY: Cornell University Press, 1980), pp. 28-29.

³⁶ Philip Greven, *The Protestant Temperament: Patterns of Child-Rearing, Religious Experience, and the Self in Early America* (New York: Alfred A. Knopf, Inc., 1977), pp. 87, 218.

³⁷ Bernard Bailyn, *The New England Merchants in the Seventeenth Century*

(Cambridge: MA: Harvard University Press, 1955), pp. 20-23, 32-34.

[38] Ibid., pp. 39-40, 105-111, 134-142.

[39] Donald H. Meyer, *The Democratic Enlightenment* (New York: G. P. Putnam's Sons, 1976), p. 65. The classic study is Joseph Haroutunian, *Piety Versus Moralism: The Passing of the New England Theology* (1932; New York: Harper & Row, 1970).

[40] Gordon S. Wood, "Conspiracy and the Paranoid Style: Causality and Deceit in the Eighteenth Century," *William and Mary Quarterly*, 3d ser., 39 (1982): 413-414.

[41] I should probably make it clear at this point that I am not suggesting that American religious thinkers dispensed altogether with the idea of "special" providence. They continued to believe, for example, that God interacted directly with individual souls on the spiritual plane. See James Turner, "Morality, Natural Law, and Unbelief: Some Roots of Agnosticism," *Perspectives in American History*, n. s., 1 (1984): 366. I am simply maintaining that in thinking about social interactions, most American intellectuals increasingly gravitated toward the notion that God worked by means of more lawlike processes that fell within the rubric of "general" providence.

[42] Wood, "Conspiracy and the Paranoid Style," pp. 416-417.

[43] William G. McLoughlin, ed., *The American Evangelicals, 1800-1900: An Anthology* (1968; Gloucester, MA: Peter Smith, 1976), p. 4.

[44] My thinking on this issue has been strongly informed by Turner, "Morality, Natural Law, and Unbelief," pp. 359-378, esp. 366-367.

[45] There are a number of useful works on moral philosophy. See, for example, D. H. Meyer, *The Instructed Conscience: The Shaping of the American National Ethic* (Philadelphia: University of Pennsylvania Press, 1972).

[46] For a good discussion of this theme, see Mark Noll, *The Scandal of the Evangelical Mind* (Grand Rapids, MI: William B. Eerdmans Publishing Company, 1994), p. 87, *passim.*

[47] Charles D. Cashdollar, "The Social Implications of the Doctrine of Divine Providence: A Nineteenth-Century Debate in American Theology," *Harvard Theological Review* 71 (1978): 268.

[48] For the increasing tendency to ascribe human destiny to luck and fate, see Delbanco, *Death of Satan*, p. 143.

[49] This story is ably told in Turner, "Morality, Natural Law, and Unbelief," pp. 371-373.

[50] Mark Y. Hanley, "The New Infidelity: Northern Protestant Clergymen and the Critique of Progress, 1840-1855," *Religion and American Culture* 1 (1991): 203-226.

[51] An excellent discussion of this issue can be found in Thomas L. Haskell, *The Emergence of Professional Social Science: The American Social Science Association and the Nineteenth-Century Crisis of Authority* (Urbana: University of Illinois Press, 1977).

[52] See, for example, Arthur J. Vidich and Stanford M. Lyman, *American Sociology: Worldly Rejections of Religion and Their Directions* (New Haven: Yale University Press, 1985); and John M. O'Donnell, *The Origins of Behaviorism:*

American Psychology, 1870-1920 (New York: New York University Press, 1985).

[53] Martin E. Marty, *The Modern Schism: Three Paths to the Secular* (New York: Harper & Row, 1969), p. 11; Martin E. Marty, "The Sacred and Secular in American History," in *Transforming Faith: The Sacred and Secular in Modern American History*, ed. M. L. Bradbury and James B. Gilbert (New York: Greenwood Press, 1989), p. 7.

I am not entirely unsympathetic to the view associated with Will Herberg and others that in a pluralistic society such as the United States, religion can be an important source of self-identification. See, for example, Michael Hout and Andrew M. Greeley, "The Center Doesn't Hold: Church Attendance in the United States, 1940-1984," *American Sociological Review*, 52 (1987): 341-342. On the other hand, insofar as this is the case, individuals will presumably carry those "selves" into other cultural spaces. Accordingly, it would seem to be incumbent upon supporters of this position to show the extent to which belief in the divine exercises authority over peoples' cognitive, economic, and social lives.

Crafts of Place: A Response to Jon Roberts

Elizabeth McKeown

Let us take our Introit from Clifford Geertz: "Like sailing, politics and poetry, law and ethnography [and we might add history] are crafts of place: they work by the light of local knowledge."[1] We might even universalize Geertz's observation: all knowledge is, at least initially, local knowledge. On that premise, it is appropriate to note that where I come from, God-talk is ubiquitous. On the airwaves and in the media, at my front door and *notably* in my workplace, the world is charged with the grammar of God. It shakes out like pollen in a Washington springtime.

Just this past weekend (May 1996), for instance, Georgetown University held its annual commencement. The honored speaker was Yale's Catholic philosopher, Louis Dupré. As we sat at attention on the platform behind him, among all of our colleagues from the social and physical sciences, languages and humanities, Dupré singled out the mere teachers of theology. Ours, it seems, is a burden larger than most academics carry. We must not only teach about God, read about God, and write about God; we must also actively foster the Catholic sacramental life on campus, infuse liturgies with renewed God-sense, and bring God to the public policy table. Dupré's earnest injunctions reminded us one more time that God is everywhere. As the pollen of this God-talk drifted to the back of the platform where I sat, I began to sneeze violently.

Newly aware of the fact that God-talk has paid the mortgage and given the children a college education, I nevertheless found it a welcome relief to turn to Professor Roberts's paper. Roberts brings word that somewhere out there, there is an American intellectual community that does not like to talk about God. The news was an antihistamine. I stopped sneezing and had a fine time reviewing his argument.

There has been, Robert argues, a relative decline in the extent to which cultural spaces are occupied by God-talk. This led me to check his own local spaces. These include history departments at Harvard and the University of Wisconsin, and a serious scholarly interest in the reactions of nineteenth-century American Protestant thinkers to Darwin and to the "transmutation hypothesis." In a 1988 volume that won the Brewer Essay Prize of the American Society of Church History, Roberts concludes that "for well over a century Christian theology has played a rather inconsequential role in shaping the direction, dynamics and pattern of American intellectual life."[2] Moreover, he suggests in that study that those Protestant thinkers could be faulted for the outcome he perceives. Describing his work as "admittedly an oblique approach to the problem of secularization," he argues that those Protestants were in some sense responsible for "the glorification of the scientific investigation of the natural world" and that their responses to Darwin shed "a good deal of light on the process by which the currency of Christian theology became devalued in the intellectual life of the West."[3]

Early on in their confrontation with [Darwinian] science, Protestant thinkers, according to Roberts, made an unfortunate choice to rely on what we might term "cosmological" or "design arguments" for the existence of God instead of a more Anselmian ontological reflection. In this nineteenth-century version, American Protestant apologists directed their attention to "the relationship between the Creator and creation grounded on the discoveries disclosed by science concerning the structure and behavior of phenomena." Although he acknowledges that "it is unlikely that any tactic religious thinkers could have employed would have prevented the elimination of theological discourse from scientific analysis,"[4] Roberts believes that this was a fateful decision which "greatly contributed to the transfer of cultural authority and prestige from theology to science, the impoverishment of the religious vision of the world, and the desacralization of nature."[5]

Roberts's analysis in the present paper rests on these earlier conclusions. It is an extension of that argument from "science" to "society" and from the nineteenth-century seminary location of the Darwinian controversy to the twentieth-century secular academy. The argument entails a functional notion of secularization. He uses the term to underscore his conviction there has been "a decline in the relevance of the transcendent and divine in integrating and legitimating life within modern culture" (p. 187 above). Nature and society are read as dimensions or "cultural spaces" in which the researcher attempts to measure this decline. Roberts does not turn his attention to falling attendance in mainline churches nor to an estimate of the popularity of first-year theology courses called "The Problem of God." Instead, he suggests that it is possible to evaluate "cultural spaces" for the presence and absence of "God-talk"—or for the location and pervasiveness of religious discourse in "public" life.

He reviews his conclusions about the absence of God-talk in discussions among nineteenth-century American intellectuals, first in the natural world and then in the moral and social world. The lesson is the same. Americans were discovering non-theological ways of explaining moral nature as well as the physical world. Natural law, Scottish Common Sense and the evolution of morals all appear at the point in the analysis to mark the mid-nineteenth-century sense of human agency, while paradoxically enough, the growing complexity of urban industrial society served to temper an older Jacksonian sense of the importance of the individual. References to God's role in all of this, however, became according to Roberts "increasingly uncommon."

Men in the new disciplines of social science seem to have been especially reluctant to talk about God. Roberts suggests that social scientists "fought doggedly during the twentieth century to attain the status that they believed had been accorded to the natural sciences" (p. 198 above), and that as a result, "most practitioners made a concerted effort to avoid making normative judgments that could be construed as religious in nature." Increasingly, he concludes, "public dialogue about society was dominated by the voices of those intent on avoiding the discussion of the transcendent in their discussion of the dynamics of the social order" (p. 198 above). For the rest of us, Roberts suggests that the God-talk that did appear was privatized, that public spaces were desacralized and that religion was, at best, "relocated."

Aware that his is not the only location from which to take the measure of God-talk, Roberts acknowledges that there are indeed "subcultures of conservatives, liberals, and Neoscholastics who continue to posit theological interpretations of nature . . . " (p. 192 above) and that it is also "perfectly reasonable to assume that some Americans have retained a lively sense of the beauty and theological significance of the natural world." But he concludes that, while this pattern may not be irreversible, "even the most cursory analysis of public discourse since 1900 will suggest that fewer and fewer members of the American intellectual community, at least, have continued to call attention to the link between nature and nature's God" (p. 192-193 above).

Roberts returns in his conclusion to the present paper to the suggestion with which he ended his book, namely that theologians need to do a better job. "I suspect," he says, "that before a significant change occurs in the allegiance of the American intellectual community to the kind of scientific world view that has largely eliminated God-talk from many cultural spaces, a radically different way of religiously envisioning the data of human experience will need to occur." He suggests that such an event would "involve an intellectual revolution of epic proportions" (p. 199 above).

If the hammerlock of secularization and scientific positivism is as strong as Professor Roberts suggests, a revolution may not be enough. On the other hand, we have to contend with the possibility that science and social science, like sailing and gardening, are "crafts of place." It is easier to see how sociology and psychology and anthropology may "work by the light of local knowledge." Social science, as Geertz reminds us, has not produced "the triumph of prediction control, and testability that had for so long been promised in his name."[6] But we also know that even the positive assurances of natural science are being tested by a growing conviction that its answers may be provisional and indeed "local."

It may soon be the case that God will be the only non-local talk in town. Then our interest in God-talk will depend entirely on whether we still feel that ancient longing for something finally universal. Jon Roberts has issued a welcome invitation to keep on talking.

Notes

[1] Clifford Geertz, *Local Knowledge* (New York: Basic Books, 1984), p. 167.

[2] *Darwin and the Divine in America: Protestant Intellectuals and Organic Evolution* (Madison: University of Wisconsin Press, 1988), p. 241.

[3] Ibid.

[4] Ibid.

[5] Ibid., p. xvi.

[6] Geertz, *Local Knowledge*, p. 3.

Tribal Encounters:
Catholic Approaches to Cultural Anthropology

Elizabeth McKeown

At the turn of the century, Catholics regarded cultural anthropology with deep suspicion. It was a "dangerous" science, one participant recalled. "A Catholic who went in for it was almost suspected of heresy." Anthropology promoted evolution, rejected Genesis, and "embraced a litter of theories that derived religion from superstition, the family from promiscuity, the state from anarchy, property from communism and morality from taboo." It was best "avoided or damned."[1] This estimate no doubt accurately reflects the popular temper of the period, and yet the evidence indicates that some Catholics were deeply involved in the creation of the discipline. Missionaries acted as ethnographers, producing extensive accounts of native cultures of Oceania, Africa, and the Americas, and forceful Catholic voices were present in the construction of the civilization and savagery that formed the nineteenth-century basis of the discipline.[2] At the end of the century, a group of European Catholics began to systematically develop ethnological resources in order to improve the Catholic position in the discipline.

This campaign, which involved ethnological training, intensive field work, and scholarly publication, was led by members of the missionary Society of the Divine Word (SVD). Founded in Holland in 1876, the order began to incorporate ethnology in its seminary program under the leadership of Austrian linguist Wilhelm Schmidt (1868-1954). At St. Gabriel's Seminary in Moedling, Austria and at the University of Vienna, Schmidt and his colleagues developed a notable voice in twentieth-century ethnology. The ethnography of SVD missionaries became the basis for the journal *Anthropos* (Vienna, 1906-   ) and for Schmidt's own *summa*, the twelve-volume *Der Ursprung der*

Gottesidee (1912-1954). Their prodigious labors and the quality of their field work gained the respect of other ethnologists even as the scope of their ambitions—a world-wide synthesis of cultural history— gave rise to persistent criticism.

The ethnological program of the *Wienerschule* was designed to challenge the positivism of nineteenth-century science. Arguing that there could be no real contradiction between science and faith—"truth cannot contradict truth"—Schmidt directed the *Anthropos* program according to conclusions established by Catholic theological and so- cial teaching. He and his colleagues were especially interested in dem- onstrating the existence of monotheism, mental acuity, free will, and monogamy in contemporary tribal cultures. Patriarchal forms of fam- ily organization and evidence of private property were also marqueed in their findings. Schmidt unabashedly bent scholarship to apologetic ends. His scientific program was driven by biblical and theological understandings that were carefully insulated from intellectual chal- lenge, and his views of patriarchy, private property, and gender were stock items in the arsenal of Catholic anti-modernism.

There was system and science in their apologetics, however. Two methodological assumptions governed *Wienerschule* interpretations of ethnological evidence. First, contemporary tribal cultures were all read as fossils or "survivals" from earlier cultural strata. Second, *Wienerschule* adherents assumed that there was a direct correlation between material simplicity and tribal age. Simpler contemporary tribes were "older"; the most rudimentary among them represented the most ancient human groups. Vienna ethnography therefore put a premium on the investigation of the most materially primitive existing cultures. "Primitive man" offered evidence of the truth of Catholic doctrine. If the "oldest" cultures gave evidence of monotheism, free will, and monogamy, then, according to Vienna logic, similar beliefs and prac- tices must have existed at the origins of human culture. The *Wienerschule* worked diligently to link the Pygmies to Adam and to identify moral monotheism in Tierra del Fuego, where Darwin had seen only cannibals.[3]

At the heart of the Vienna program lay a resistance to the unilinear evolutionary assumptions of nineteenth-century science. Catholics insisted that the study of cultural origins and development must op- pose the recipe of uniform evolutionary progress in the history of hu- man development. They believed that the ethnological evidence im- plied losses as well as gains. To oppose the evolutionary paradigm,

Schmidt and his colleagues promoted a theory of cultural diffusion.[4] They argued that cultural development was properly understood as the result of a dispersion of elements from three primeval *Kulturkreise* or "culture circles." These source-cultures were distinguished according to their economic characteristics: horticulture, hunting, and herding. The spreading out or diffusion of these simple *Kreise* and their subsequent interactions over time accounted for the rise of historical cultures. The Vienna school adherents were determined to apply their culture-historical method on a world-wide scale—to account for all human cultural developments under the rubric of culture contact in order to defeat the determinist "stages" of cultural progress that characterized theories of unilinear evolution. Although other historically minded ethnologists investigated geographical "trait distributions" and shared an interest in charting the spread of cultures from local centers, the universal ambition of Schmidt's program won few supporters in the discipline.[5]

The doctrinal assumptions of *Kulturkreislehre* also aroused opposition. Jesuit paleontologist Teilhard de Chardin strongly rejected Schmidt's monogenism and insisted that there was "no acceptable place for Adam" in the new sciences. In Teilhard's assessment, Schmidt's willingness to subordinate the paleontological and ethnological evidence to his theological convictions gave rise, not to the simple god-fearing family man of the *Wienerschule*, but to a monster. The Jesuit insisted that "when man has newly arrived at reflection, no movement is more instinctive to him than to breathe life into and to anthropomorphize . . . *the Other* whose existence, influence and menace he finds all around him." The Jesuit pointedly noted that this process of imagining the Other occurred naturally and without the need to rely on a theory of divine revelation—"in spite of anything urged by Father W. Schmidt and his followers."[6]

Although *Wienerschule* anti-modernism drew a much more positive response in the United States, especially among the writers of Catholic college textbooks, the small band of American Catholics in anthropology generally dissociated themselves from the universalizing sweep of *Kulturkreislehre* and cautioned against the apologetical use of their science. Schmidt's most consistent American Catholic critic was John Montgomery Cooper (1881-1948). Cooper gave serious and extended attention to Schmidt's ideas and worked hard to test them in his own field studies. Although he found evidence of belief in high gods, for instance, in Algonquian culture, Cooper remained convinced that the reach of Schmidt's claims made them scientifically insupportable and that Schmidt's apologetic use of ethnology posed serious risks to the defense of the faith.[7]

The Viennese influence was apparent nevertheless in the development of anthropological scholarship among Catholics in the United States. In the 1920s, Catholic University of America supported John Cooper's efforts to found the Catholic Anthropological Conference and publish the journal *Primitive Man*. Cooper also launched a monograph series designed to encourage the production of ethnography among Catholic missionaries. In 1934, he became the founder of the first American Catholic department of anthropology at Catholic University of America. Boston College began a graduate program and monograph series in the 1930s under the Jesuit Joseph J. Williams, who specialized in the religions of Africa and the Caribbean, and the Jesuits at St. Louis University also took up the academic study of anthropology.[8]

Some of the American Catholic resistance to Schmidt's theoretical claims was inspired by the work of another European-born scholar. The brilliant German Jewish émigré Franz Boas (1858-1942) settled in the United States at the end of the nineteenth century and concentrated his efforts on coastal tribes in western Canada and the United States. Boas recognized that mono-evolutionary assumptions were inappropriate for ethnological work and began to systematically challenge the dominant paradigm of Victorian anthropology. In its place, he championed closely focused, on-site fieldwork in local cultural areas and became a leading advocate of cultural particularism in the interpretation of field data.[9] Boas taught these ideas to an exceptional cadre of students at Columbia University, most of whom distinguished themselves by their fieldwork among the native cultures of the Americas. These Boasians dominated American cultural anthropology for the first half of the century. Their scholarship reflected the non-determinist, anti-racist tenor of Boas's outlook, and carried forward his sympathy for cultural "history" against the functionalism of the rising "science" of British social anthropology. Catholic ethnologists embraced the Boasian resistance to theory and welcomed the emphasis on disciplined observation and interpretative modesty.

Catholic appreciation for the Boasians extended beyond professional considerations of method. Apologists as well as anthropologists relished the Boasian attack on the nineteenth-century patriarch of American cultural anthropology, Lewis Henry Morgan (1818-1881).

Morgan's ethnography began with his account of the Iroquois of western New York state. His *League of the Iroquois* (1851) led him to inaugurate the systematic study of kinship, an approach which was destined to become a central concern of modern cultural anthropology. Morgan had noticed the unusual kinship terms used by the Iroquois in his western New York neighborhood and was subsequently startled to discover that the Algonquian-speaking Ojibwa on the southern shores of Lake Superior also grouped relatives in a pattern similar to that of the Iroquois. This discovery led to a path-breaking comparative study of kinship systems, *Systems of Consanguinity and Affinity of the Human Family* (1871), in which Morgan identified similar patterns among native American, Hawaiian, and Dravidian peoples.[10]

In addition to his comparative studies, however, Morgan also embraced an evolutionary position on the development of human society. He made the startling and controversial claim that early human society was a promiscuous "primal horde," lacking any semblance of family life or private property. In Morgan's view, the human family had evolved "from a condition of promiscuous intercourse through various stages of group marriage to monogamy, at last realized in civilized societies." In fact, he argued, civilization emerged through the collateral development from sexual promiscuity to monogamy, and from communism to private property.

Morgan presented these claims in *Ancient Society* (1877), a volume that was destined to become a standard reference of nineteenth-century socialism.[11] Both Karl Marx and Frederick Engels embraced Morgan's conclusions, delighted in particular with the connection he drew between monogamy and private property. Engels subtitled his volume on *The Origin of the Family, Private Property and the State* (1884) *In the Light of the Researches of Lewis Henry Morgan.* The book was based on a reproduction of Morgan's work drawn from Marx's extensive notes and published after the latter's death. Engels called it "the fulfillment [sic] of a bequest" and claimed that Marx "had planned to present the results of Morgan's researches [because] Morgan rediscovered in America, in his own way, the materialist conception of history that had been discovered by Marx forty years ago."[12]

The Morgan-Marx-Engels account of the origin and development of marriage, family, and property brought heated reaction from American Catholic commentators, who were appalled by the evolutionary, socialist, and "free love" implications of the doctrines. Those same critics responded with delight when Boasian Robert H. Lowie of the University of California at Berkeley published a full-length refutation of Morgan's views. The Austrian-born Lowie was an uncompromising opponent of nineteenth-century British evolutionism. He dismissed what he termed Morgan's "vapid evolutionary metaphysics" and offered a point-by-point criticism of Morgan's claims.[13]

Lowie, as it happened, also followed the work of Wilhelm Schmidt and his collaborators. He read the *Wienerschule* ethnology, published his own work in *Anthropos* and reviewed Schmidt's work for American journals. Lowie's younger colleague Clyde Kluckhohn of Harvard also developed an ongoing interest in the work of the Viennese Catholic ethnologists. Kluckhohn attended Schmidt's classes at the University of Vienna in the early 1930s and wrote the introduction to the English edition of Schmidt's methodology.[14] Kluckhohn took the case to the American professional community in 1937 when he published a detailed and sympathetic assessment of *Kulturkreislehre* in the *American Anthropologist*. Conceding that Schmidt and his co-workers were "steeped in the dialectical subtleties of Thomas Aquinas and Albertus Magnus," Kluckhohn argued that "those underlying the metaphysics of the Roman Catholic Church are as intellectually respectable as any others in the present state of our knowledge of man and the universe."[15] He urged readers to recognize that the scientific worth of the Vienna contribution was not automatically negated by their interpretative principles, or by the fact that its members were priests.

The cordiality shown to the European Catholics by Lowie and Kluckhohn drew fire from critics who challenged Boasian leadership in American cultural anthropology. The new generation of cultural anthropologists included those who were drawn to Marxist social thought and championed a material cultural view of evolution. Among the most outspoken was the University of Michigan's Leslie A. White (1900-1975). Trained in the Boasian tradition at Columbia and Chicago, White established a reputation as the leading anti-Boasian champion of evolutionary determinism.[16]

White was especially keen to remove what he viewed as the contamination of religious dogma from the study of cultural origins, and to restore the place of evolutionary theory in cultural anthropology. A substantial element of this campaign involved White's efforts to rehabilitate the reputation of Lewis Henry Morgan. He literally retraced Morgan's fieldwork footsteps, denounced his critics, defended his reputation at professional gatherings, and published his journals, portions of which detailed Morgan's deep aversion to Roman Catholicism.[17] Although White acknowledged that Morgan's theory of the evolution of the family from the promiscuous horde to monogamy was "demonstrably false," he insisted that Morgan's work continued to hold "great significance" in the history of ethnological theory. His reasons for this claim did not rest on Morgan's contribution to kinship studies. Rather, White was delighted that Morgan had "made a clean break with Christian theology" and that he had explicitly rejected "the so-called Degradation Theory and the 'Mosaic cosmogony' of which it was a corollary."[18]

Furthermore, White believed that the Vienna school was the current source of theological contamination in ethnological circles and complained that the German Catholics and their Boasian colleagues were collaborating to discredit Morgan and to block the development of a true "science of culture" in the United States. Couching his attack in strongly nativist terms, White charged that the Boasians were reactionaries of "foreign stock" who lacked American traits that would allow them to see the value of progressive theories of culture. He cited the same alien and reactionary deficiencies in the Catholic priests with whom he accused Boasians of collaborating.[19]

White carried on the campaign to expose the "clerical connection" in American anthropology throughout his career. In the introduction to his valedictory collection of *Ethnological Essays*, he could not resist again putting what he called "the Question": "If the theory of evolution was so pervasive in science, if it was fundamental and fruitful in all other fields, why was it rejected in ethnology?" he wondered. "Why did anti-evolutionism flourish only in orthodox theology and American ethnology?"[20]

James Clifford has noted that the production of ethnography always entails a "self" and "other" and inevitably involves a process of "self-fashioning."[21] Schmidt's apology for Adam and White's description of the enemies of the "science of culture" neatly makes Clifford's point. Catholic doctrine fashioned a view of human origins that held that the human race was created by God in a single act according to God's divine plan and pleasure, and that every human was endowed with reason and free will. *Kulturkreislehre* marshaled ethnological evidence to support this view of the primordial unity of the race and of the rationality and moral capacity of all of its members. The ethnographic productions of Schmidt and his colleagues attempted to demonstrate scientifically that human beings shared a common identity shaped by both grace and sin and that human culture was the product of these God-given faculties.

Meanwhile, Leslie White became convinced that culture was a force independent of human control and indifferent to human interests. As his confidence in the revolutionary possibilities of his science faded, he offered a stoic admission: "I no longer think of culture as designed to serve the needs of man; culture goes its own way in accordance with laws of its own. Man lives within the embrace of cultural systems, and enjoys or suffers whatever they mete out to him."[22] However, White never relaxed his vigilance against the tribe of ethno-theological reactionaries who seemed to block the progress of his science. Their work became Leslie White's "other," just as the evolutionary determinisms of Darwin, Morgan, and Marx formed the foil for the *Wienerschule* program.[23]

Ironically, as White's pessimism deepened, Catholics began to embrace the idea of evolution. When Teilhard de Chardin first criticized Schmidt's monogenism in the 1920s, he was radically out of step with the views of most of his co-religionists, the vast majority of whom preferred Schmidt's apology for Adam. Four decades later, however, Teilhard's work became enormously popular, as Catholics began to bid goodbye to the older orthodoxy that drove Schmidt's ethnological construction of primitive man.[24] Enthusiasm for an evolutionary universe reflected a new cultural confidence among Catholics in Europe and North America, and the Omega point quickly displaced the primitive Adam as a compelling expression of human unity and purpose.

The period of evolutionary optimism among Catholic intellectuals was short-lived, however. The appearance of post-modernism in Western academic culture soon challenged both the claims of theology and those of cultural materialism. Clifford Geertz's insistence on the priority of "local knowledge" in human studies, for example, implicitly dismisses the universals of both Schmidt and Teilhard, along with the cultural materialism of Leslie White. In Geertz's view, cultural anthropology is a systematic practice of "interpretation" that cannot yield general theories. Arguably the leading voice among current American cultural anthropologists, Geertz's epistemological agnosticism and cultural particularism remind us that cultural anthropology continues to pose compelling challenges for Catholic theology, in what Terrence Tilley calls this "*post*-age."[25]

Notes

[1] John M. Cooper, "Anthropology and the Missions," *The Ecclesiastical Review* 75 (November 1926): 507-514, and F. Lynch, "Anthropology, Cultural," *New Catholic Encyclopedia* 3 (New York: McGraw-Hill, 1967): 597-605.

[2] Among the missionary ethnographies that receive regular citation in histories of anthropology is Joseph Lafitau, S.J., *Customs of American Savages Compared with Those of Earliest Times* (1724). For an extensive catalog of sources on missions, see Joseph Schmidlin, *Catholic Mission History* (Techny, Ill.: Mission Press, SVD, 1933) and Schmidlin, *Catholic Mission Theory* (Techny, Ill: Mission Press, SVD, 1931). George Stocking, Jr., *Victorian Anthropology* (New York: Free Press, 1987) has the best account of the nineteenth-century European origins of ethnology and cultural anthropology. The terms "anthropology" and "ethnology" are used interchangeably in this account. Marvin Harris, *The Rise of Anthropological Theory* (New York: Crowell, 1968) provides a reading of the role of Catholics like Bonald and de Maistre in the culture wars of the nineteenth century.

[3] At the end of the nineteenth century, Scottish theorist Andrew Lang challenged Edward Tylor's animist account of early religion with field data from Australia and Africa that indicated the presence of high gods in simple cultures: "It is a positive fact that among some of the lowest savages there exists, not a doctrinal and abstract Monotheism, but a belief in a moral, powerful, kindly, creative Being." Andrew Lang, *The Making of Religion* (London: Longmans, Green and Co., 1898), p. 254.

[4] For an historical account of evolution in cultural anthropology, see Stocking, *Victorian Anthropology*. Diffusionism appeared in reaction to evolution and was employed in England as well as in Germany. See George Stocking, *After Tylor* (Madison: University of Wisconsin Press, 1995) for discussion of British diffusionism. Schmidt acknowledges his methodological debt to the "Berlin School" led by Fritz Graebner (1877-1935) in Wilhelm Schmidt, *The Culture Historical Method of Ethnology: The Scientific Approach to the Racial Question*, trans. S. A. Sieber (New York: Fortuny's, 1939), pp. 12-31.

[5] His contemporary stature is evident from the fact that most of the leading anthropologists of the period felt it necessary to address his work. The American Paul Radin noted Schmidt's "admittedly great critical powers," but admitted that he was "deeply suspicious of [Schmidt's] treatment of the facts wherever they would seem to militate against the dogmas of the church." Paul Radin, *Primitive Religion: Its Nature and Origin* (New York: Dover Publications, 1957), p. 76. Bronislaw Malinowski dismissed Schmidt's "culture circles" as "lifeless and inorganic," and A. R. Radcliffe-Brown urged his own functionalist approach as the realistic alternative to "the conjectural history" of the diffusionists. See Bronislaw Malinowski, "Culture," *Encyclopedia of the Social Sciences*, 4 (1931): 624, and

Malinowski "Concepts and Methods of Anthropology," in *A Scientific Theory of Culture and Other Essays* (Chapel Hill: University of North Carolina Press, 1944), pp. 15-36. For an index to the views of both Malinowski and Radcliffe-Brown, see Clyde Kluckhohn, "Some Reflections on the Method and Theory of the Kulturkreislehre," *American Anthropologist* 38 (1936): 157-196.

⁶ See Pierre Teilhard de Chardin, S.J., "Note on Some Possible Historical Representations of Original Sin," in *Christianity and Evolution* (New York: Harcourt, 1971), pp. 45-55. (The note accompanying this undated essay indicates that it was written "before Easter 1922.") And Pierre Teilhard de Chardin, S.J., "The Christian Phenomenon," *Christianity and Evolution* (New York: Harcourt, 1971), pp. 199-208 (201). The latter essay was written in 1950, but Teilhard's views were already evident in 1920. See Teilhard de Chardin, "Fall, Redemption, and Geocentrism" (20 July, 1920), collected in *Christianity and Evolution*, pp. 36-44.

⁷ Cooper was forthright about his objections in correspondence with Schmidt. See, for example, John M. Cooper to Wilhelm Schmidt, March 27, 1923, and January 23, 1935, Cooper-Schmidt correspondence, Archives of the Catholic University of America, Washington D.C. For a review of Cooper's work, see Elizabeth McKeown, "From *Pascendi* to *Primitive Man*: The Apologetics and Anthropology of John Montgomery Cooper," *U.S. Catholic Historian* 13 (Winter 1995): 1-22.

⁸ See, for example, Albert Muntsch, S.J., *Evolution and Culture: Their Relation in Light of Modern Ethnology* (St. Louis: Herder, 1923); Muntsch and Henry S. Spalding, S.J., *Introductory Sociology* (New York: Heath, 1928), and Muntsch, *Cultural Anthropology* (Milwaukee: Bruce, 1934). Sociological borrowers include Eva J. Ross, *Social Origins* (New York: Sheed & Ward, 1936), and *Fundamental Sociology* (Milwaukee: Bruce Publishing Co., 1939); Sylvester A. Sieber and Franz H. Mueller, *The Social Life of Primitive Man* (St. Louis: Herder, 1941).

⁹ For a Catholic appreciation of Boas, see Joseph J. Williams, S.J., "Boas and American Ethnologists," *Thought* 11 (1936): 194-209.

¹⁰ See Fred Eggan, "Lewis H. Morgan in Kinship Perspective [1960]," in *Essays in the Science of Culture in Honor of Leslie A. White*, ed., Gertrude E. Dole and Robert L. Carneiro (New York: Crowell, 1960), pp. 179-201; and Fred Eggan, "Lewis Henry Morgan's Systems: A Reevaluation," in Priscilla Reining, ed., *Kinship Studies in the Morgan Centennial Year* (Washington: The Anthropological Society of Washington, 1971), pp. 1-16.

¹¹ Leslie A. White, "Introduction" to Lewis Henry Morgan, *Ancient Society* (Cambridge: Harvard University Press, 1964), pp. xvi-xvii. See Carl Resek, *Lewis Henry Morgan, American Scholar* (Chicago: University of Chicago, 1960) for a discussion of Morgan's "conversion" to evolution.

¹² Frederick Engels, "Preface to the First Edition," *The Origin of the Family, Private Property and the State*, subtitled *In the Light of the Researches of Lewis Henry Morgan* (Moscow: Foreign Languages Publishing House, 1884), p. 5. French anthropologist Claude Lévi-Strauss recognized Morgan's contribution by dedicating his *Elementary Structures of Kinship* (1958) to the American.

[13] Robert Lowie, *Primitive Society* (New York: Boni and Liveright, 1920). Lowie (1883-1957) was born in Vienna and raised in the German community in New York. He was a leading member of the first generation of Boas students.

[14] Clyde Kluckhohn, "Preface," in Wilhelm Schmidt, *The Culture Historical Method of Ethnology: The Scientific Approach to the Race Question* (New York: Fortuny's, 1939). Kluckhohn, who called Schmidt his "revered teacher," also reviewed Schmidt's position and its reception in English-speaking anthropological circles in "Some Reflections on the Method and Theory of the *Kulturkreislehre,*" *American Anthropologist* 38 (April-June, 1936): 157-196.

[15] Clyde Kluckhohn, "Reflections on the Method and Theory of the *Kulturkreislehre*," p. 173.

[16] For a concise critical description of White's views, see Edward Evans-Pritchard, *A History of Anthropological Thought* (London: Faber and Faber, 1981), pp. 202-204.

[17] For biographical information on White, see Harry Elmer Barnes "Foreword," in *Essays in the Science of Culture In Honor of Leslie A. White*, ed. Gertrude E. Dole and Robert L. Carneiro (1960). For a critical assessment of the Boasian influences in White's work, see Richard A. Barrett, "The Paradoxical Anthropology of Leslie White," *American Anthropologist* 91 (1989): 986-999. For comments on the Catholic church, see Leslie A. White, ed., "Lewis H. Morgan's European Journal," *The Rochester Historical Society Publications*, XVI (Rochester, 1937), pp. 221-390.

[18] White, "Introduction," *Ancient Society*, pp. xxviii-xxix.

[19] Leslie A. White, "Evolutionism and Anti-Evolutionism in American Ethnological Theory," in *Ethnological Essays*, Beth Dillingham and Robert L. Carneiro, eds. (Albuquerque: University of New Mexico Press, 1987), p. 98. See also White's remarks on Lowie's Jesuit supporters in Leslie A. White, "Evolution and Cultural Anthropology," *American Anthropologist* 49 (1947): 400-413. Robert Lowie defended Catholics and Boasians against the charge of anti-evolutionism. "No reputable scholar challenges either the demonstrable findings of prehistory or the economic truisms claimed by [Leslie] White, least of all the Austrian school whose writings are evidently on his Index librorum prohibitorum," Lowie concluded acidly. "It is unilinear evolution that the Austrians and the Boasians reject . . ." Robert Lowie, "Evolution in Cultural Anthropology: A Reply to Leslie White," in Cora Du Bois, ed., *Lowie's Selected Papers in Anthropology* (Berkeley: University of California Press, 1960), pp. 411-424. For the extended exchange between Lowie and White, see Robert H. Lowie, "Professor White and 'Anti-Evolutionist' Schools," *Southwestern Journal of Anthropology* 21 (1946): 240-241; and White's response in Leslie A. White, "Evolutionism in Cultural Anthropology: A Rejoinder," *American Anthropologist* 49 (1947): 400-413.

[20] White, *Ethnological Essays*, p. 13. For samples of White's accusations against the Catholic clergy and their sympathetic Boasian colleagues, see his *Ethnological Essays*, especially in chs. 2, 3, 5, 20, and 23. White's suspicions against Catholic scholars were inflamed by his personal experience with Catholic ecclesiastical authorities in the archdiocese of Detroit. When he introduced his

"naturalist" version of human origins and his evolutionary determinism in undergraduate classes at Michigan, Catholic students joined the rush to hear the new atheism, and local Catholic authorities reacted with great concern. In his obituary for White, Elman R. Service recalled that "the Catholic church in Ann Arbor singled out White for virulent attack, even pressuring state legislators for his dismissal." Elman R. Service, "Leslie Alvin White," *American Anthropologist* 78 (1976): 612-617.

[21] James Clifford, "Partial Truths," in James Clifford and George E. Marcus, eds., *Writing Culture: The Poetics and Politics of Ethnography* (Berkeley: University of California Press, 1986), p. 23.

[22] Leslie White, *The Concept of Culture Systems: A Key to Understanding Tribes and Nations* (New York: Columbia University Press, 1975), p. 159.

[23] The Vienna program continued after Schmidt's death in 1954. For a review of the program during the Darwin centennial year, see Josef Haekel, "Trends and Intellectual Interests in Current Austrian Ethnography," *American Anthropologist* 61 (1959): 865-874.

[24] See, for example, the discussion of Karl Rahner's changing views on monogenism and cultural evolution in Leo J. O'Donovan, S.J., "Evolution as a Systematic Concept in Recent Catholic Thought: A Study of Post-Teilhardian Moments in the Dialogue Between Christianity and the Evolutionary World View," Th.D. dissertation, Munster, 1971.

[25] See Terrence W. Tilley, *Postmodern Theologies: The Challenge of Religious Diversity* (New York: Orbis Books, 1995). For a selection of cultural materialist responses to post-modernism, see the recent *Festschrift* for Marvin Harris, *Science, Materialism and the Study of Culture*, Martin F. Murphy and Maxine L. Margolis, eds. (Gainesville: University Press of Florida, 1995).

Biblical Brinkmanship:
Francis Gigot and the *New York Review*

Patricia M. McDonald

Francis E. Gigot (1859-1920), a French-born one-time Sulpician and then priest of the Archdiocese of New York, has been judged the most "advanced" (Gannon), "distinguished" (Fogarty), and "accomplished" (Appleby) Catholic biblical scholar in the United States around the turn of the century.[1] His reputation rests largely on the texts he wrote for seminarians and on his contributions to the *Catholic Encyclopedia* (1907-14). His other great work, in many respects more interesting, consists of twenty-three articles in the *New York Review* (henceforth, *NYR*), the most scholarly American Catholic journal of its day. These have not been readily available because the Dunwoodie-based periodical lasted only three years (1905-8) before anti-modernist pressure shut it down and ensured for it a long spell in limbo. Although the *NYR* articles have recently attracted some historians,[2] they have not yet received from the biblical guild the study they merit. Nor will they here, although a start will be made. This paper offers a concise introduction to Gigot's *NYR* articles as a way of drawing attention to the erudition and fate of a Catholic scholar who, from 1885 until his death in 1920, was dedicated to teaching Scripture in the only places it could then be taught, seminaries, but who seized the opportunity offered by the *NYR* to reach a wider audience.

The *NYR*[3] was a bimonthly periodical aptly subtitled *A Journal of the Ancient Faith and Modern Thought*, founded and run by a highly talented and industrious group of priest faculty at St. Joseph's Seminary, Dunwoodie. It was, at least in theory, authorized by the then Archbishop of New York, John M. Farley, who evidently took years to realize that most of the wide array of American and European contributors fell on the "wrong" side of the barrier between orthodoxy and modernism that was taking shape at the time. Its primary aim, as expressed in the 25,000 announcement sheets (headed "Notice") circulated prior to the first issue,[4] was "To treat in a scholarly fashion, yet in a manner intelligible to the ordinary cultured mind, topics of interest bearing on Theology, Scripture. . . ." Gigot took up the task with energy and skill.

His twenty-three articles comprise five groups: six each on higher criticism, the synoptic gospels, and divorce; four on Old Testament books (two on Isaiah and one each on Job and Jonah); and one on Abraham. They display different aspects of Gigot's understanding of Scripture: how he saw the exegete's task and function, how he handled specific questions of introduction, his approach to Pentateuchal criticism, his detailed method of exegesis, and a more synthetic presentation of a morally and socially important issue.

Gigot's six *NYR* articles on higher criticism[5] provide a moderate and very balanced viewpoint to an audience that he presumes will be (at best) hesitant about it. Like many of his peers, he is impressed by "scientific" theories and convinced that mere appeals to authority are insufficient, even for those who, like himself, are determined to remain within the tradition. So he insists that, far from threatening the Bible's position as God's inspired word, such methods ensure that the believing scholar read it with the utmost care. This view is tenable because Gigot excludes questions of introduction from "the sacred deposit of Revelation."[6]

By our standards, Gigot is somewhat naive, politically and methodologically. His lack of political acumen soon became apparent with the early decrees of the Biblical Commission and the antimodernist documents of 1907. Methodologically, though, it took almost fifty years (to 1943) for Catholic exegetes to reach Gigot's position of publicly accepting higher criticism without fearing its rationalist and antitraditional baggage, and yet another fifty (until 1993, with the Biblical Commission's "The Interpretation of the Bible in the Church") for them to move beyond near total reliance on the historico-critical method that Gigot espoused. He probably contributed to the first of these stages through the influence of his books on such key figures as the Sulpician biblical scholars Edward Arbez and Wendell Stephen ("Babe") Reilly,[7] but that would be another paper.

The Authorship of Isaiah 40-66

Models of order and clarity, like all his work, Gigot's two articles on the authorship of Isaiah 40-66[8] offer, respectively, arguments for and against the traditional ascription of the whole book to Isaiah of Jerusalem. The first gives five different sorts of argument for unity of authorship. Only one of these (various kinds of external evidence) stands uncriticized; Gigot follows each of the others with cogent reasons for its unreliability and refers to the work of others sharing his view.

The second article is about why the Book of Isaiah is thought to have had multiple authors, Gigot's own position. He all but presumes his conclusion in the first paragraph: chapters 36-39 "for some time marked the close of the then existing book of Isaiah" (277). Gigot presents strong internal evidence, characteristics of language and style, and theological ideas that support the separate authorship of chapters 40-66, before summarizing his findings. He here quotes much more of the biblical text than before and refers more extensively to other authorities. The chief of these is Oxford's Regius Professor of Divinity, S. R. Driver, whose position on the authorship of Deuteronomy, Gigot will elegantly refute in 1909. He also cites with approval "Father Corluy, S.J." and concludes by quoting cardinals Newman and Meignan to show that the matter "is not one settled by the authority of the church" (296). That was no longer exactly the case from June 1908, when the Biblical Commission decided that there was insufficient evidence for multiple authorship of the Book of Isaiah.[9]

On the Historicity of Jonah

Also included in the first volume of the *NYR* was Gigot's article on Jonah and the one on Job.[10] The subtitle of the former, "Arguments For and Against Its Historical Character," indicates its structure and contents, except that, in deference to his mostly Catholic readers, Gigot wisely starts by summarizing the story of Jonah. There follow, without comment, five arguments in favor of its historicity;[11] the refutation of each comes next, clearly argued and with some supporting documentation. Gigot then produces five different arguments, those often given against the book's historicity. He offers two sub-options that go with this position: either to regard the work as somehow based in the

Jewish (presumably historical) tradition, or to take it as a parabolic or allegorical invention of didactic character. He then gives his own view, which combines the two options. Thus, Jonah may be a didactic allegory but of "which the materials of the narrative were, at least substantially, supplied by the tradition."[12] One may wonder if he wants to have his cake and eat it, but he has certainly delivered on his title.

Despite his enthusiasm for "science" and rational enquiry, Gigot remains faithful to the tradition in which he stands and insists that such a position is possible. In this piece on Jonah and in the second Isaiah article, he accepts that some biblical critics are motivated by a refusal to believe in the possibility of prophecy (294) or miracles and the supernatural (424). From each of these positions, the priest firmly dissociates himself both here and elsewhere, but always without prejudice to the historico-critical method itself.[13]

On the Book of Job

At the start of the Jonah article, Gigot indicates how he understands the Book of Job, when he asserts that "critics have disproved the full historical character of the book," and quotes the conservative Vigouroux to the effect that it "is generally regarded in the present day as a kind of drama" (411). Despite the three-page summary with which it starts, this is a more ambitious article to present to the intelligent non-specialist targeted by the *New York Review*. For, having easily established the "highly poetical" nature of Job, Gigot must then deal, first, with the text's integrity and thus with how the Old Testament was transmitted, then with how the text of Job reached its present form. In both parts of this discussion, he presents and assesses the various options offered by the main scholars over the years. He is quite at ease with ambiguity where the evidence is inconclusive. Thus, like contemporary scholars interpreting Job for a general audience,[14] Gigot points out that neither the received Hebrew text nor the Greek is to be relied on, and that, although Elihu's speeches (chapters 32-37) were probably not in the original work, it is more difficult to reach a conclusion about various other parts that have been proposed as secondary. Next, Gigot notes that all parts of the present text "refer to one great subject . . . the relation of suffering to sin" (590), and briefly shows the inadequacy of interpretations that do not take this into account.

He then moves on to present and examine arguments about the

historicity of Job: the minority view (with some support from Jewish tradition) that denies any basis in history, the reluctance of "most contemporary critics and interpreters" to accept either this view or its opposite, and Gigot's own conjecture that a traditional story was worked up into the high poetry of the present text, a view equivalent to his conclusion on Jonah. None of the prevalent suggestions about authorship satisfies him (594) and, although it was not written "till at least the closing period of the monarchy" (595), greater precision in dating cannot be reached. Finally, Gigot summarizes the issues that were unsettled and those on which there was general agreement. He concludes with the wry observation that these results should vindicate biblical scholars from charges of being too hasty in accepting "views which go, or seem to go, against dogmatic, or at least, traditional, positions" (506).

In this article Gigot presents and evaluates a range of views on a popular topic of his day. He applies to a whole book the method he wrote about more generally in his six articles on higher criticism. Of course, such views on Job and Jonah would soon prove to be out of line with the June 23, 1905 decree of the Biblical Commission, "Concerning the Narratives in the Historical Books Which Have Only the Appearance of Being Historical."

The Figure of Abraham

The article "Abraham: A Historical Study"[15] throws a different light on Gigot's understanding of the Old Testament. His concern is to establish what might be known of Abraham as an historical figure, by locating him in his historical, geographical, and social context. So Gigot's summary of the story of Abraham in Genesis is well-laced with such details. Next, he notes the other Abrahamic traditions in the Bible, in extra-biblical Jewish texts, and Islamic writings,[16] before going on to consider the modern critical approach.

In this connection, Gigot deals first with the sources of Genesis 11:26-25:10. He accepts that the stories were compiled from three earlier sources which, he says, "are usually called the Judean, the Ephraimite, and the Priestly narratives" and "are commonly denoted by their respective letters: J., E., P." (46).[17] This origin "accounts best for most of the difficulties and discrepancies which may be noticed in the present narrative" (ibid.). Gigot concludes his article by noting that critical scholarship cannot ground a view of Abraham as "a pure mythical creation, or as an impersonation of a Semitic tribe." In other words, Genesis presents Abraham as a historically credible religious figure, "even apart from the inspired character of the narrative" (47). Three further arguments of modern scholars are then offered for taking the Genesis account as containing "a substantially correct picture of [Abraham's] career": one from the history of religions, a second from Abraham's relatively modest territorial claims in Genesis, and the third (less convincingly) about the relative positions of Abraham and Moses in Israelite tradition. Gigot admits that the sources "contain much of the legendary and fictitious," but claims that the very diversity of the documentary sources in Genesis shows that the tradition has been faithfully transmitted (47-48).

The Abraham article is not essentially different from the other Old Testament pieces in the *NYR*. Gigot is still providing readers access to modern resources to help them make more sense of the biblical text while avoiding rationalistic excesses. The thesis of this article is, by its nature, more conservative than those of the others, and nearly all the footnotes refer to the biblical text, rather than to works of modern scholars.[18] This is, perhaps, simply a different expression of Gigot's all-pervading respect for the scriptural text.

Unfortunately, the Biblical Commission's June 27, 1906 decree "On the Mosaic Authorship of the Pentateuch" more or less coincided with the appearance of Gigot's Abraham article. This decree rejected the possibility of sources that postdated Moses. The priest would not be free to publish more on these lines. In particular, there was no future for the series of articles on Genesis that Herman Heuser had wanted him to write for the *Ecclesiastical Review*.[19] By 1915, in the published version of his lecture organized by the Catholic Students' Organization Committee of the University of Pennsylvania, Gigot had turned full circle and was now arguing strenuously in favor of Mosaic authorship and showing the inadequacy of higher criticism as commonly practiced then.

The Synoptic Gospels

That change, however, was still in the future in mid-1905, when the first of the series "Studies on the Synoptic Gospels" I-VI was published. Each was subtitled "A[20] Literary Analysis of [the relevant biblical texts]."[21] There are four in volume 1 (1905-6) and one in each of volumes 2 and 3: "I. The Preparatory Ministry of John the Baptist:

Matt 3:1-12; Mark 1:1-8; Luke 3:1-20"; "II. The Baptism of Jesus: Matt 3:13-17; Mark 1:9-11; Luke 3:21-23"; "III. The Temptation of Jesus: Matt 4:1-11; Mark 1:12-13; Luke 4:1-13"; "IV. The Early Preaching of Jesus in Galilee: Matt 4:12-17; Mark 1:14,15; Luke 4:14,15"; "V. The Call of the First Disciples: Matt 4:18-22; Mark 1:16-20; Luke 5:1-11"; "VI. Jesus 'taught as one having authority': Matt 7:28b, 29 (G. has 8 for the chapter); Mark 1:21-22; Luke 4:31-32."

Related to these six is another in the *Ecclesiastical Review* 32 (1905) 225-32: "Jesus' First Circuit of Galilee: An Account of the Differences between Mark 1:35-39 and Luke 4:42-44." It was published in March 1905, just three months before the first issue of the *NYR*, but its subject matter belongs after that of the sixth article. These facts, and the concentration of the first four articles in volume one of the *NYR*, suggests that Gigot had already completed these papers. One might, indeed, conjecture that they were part of the preparation for his projected *Special Introduction to the New Testament*.

The series on the synoptics shows a very careful scholar presenting, in a way comprehensible to non-specialists, an intelligent and perceptive reading of the gospels. So he is once more fulfilling the first of the "objects in view" announced by the *NYR*'s editors.[22] To help the reader follow his argument easily, Gigot usually gives at the end of each article "a direct translation of [the biblical text] from the original Greek," arranged in three parallel columns.[23] He does not use the Douay version familiar to his readers;[24] his own version differs frequently in wording and the choice of variant readings. Gigot cites copiously from the relevant biblical books and makes judicious use of Greek (mostly in footnotes) and, more rarely, Hebrew. (In the original fonts, there is a steady decline in the use of diacritical marks from vol. 1 to vol. 3.) When using the work of others, he usually assesses it and gives his own position, although not always when the view is a progressive one that he might well entertain.[25]

From the start, it is clear that Gigot's focus is the gospel text, understood in its New Testament and broader biblical context. In the first paragraph he implicitly presents himself as "one who studies inductively the origin and method of composition of the Synoptic Gospels" (89). The six pieces are highly systematic, written in a similar pattern that is marked out with headings: Mark, then Matthew as dependent on Mark, followed by Luke as dependent on them both.

In the first article, Gigot presents good reasons for holding that

Mark contains traditions that are more "primitive" than the others; in this, he aligns himself with "nearly all contemporary scholars" (90). Throughout, his characteristic adjectives for Mark's work are "primitive" and "graphic."[26] Although Gigot frequently presents as "primitive" things that would not necessarily be so regarded today, he argues convincingly for Markan priority. Unsurprisingly, he has no sense of Mark as a theologian in his own right:[27] for this, he would probably have to have read and digested for his audience William Wrede's 1901 book, *Das Messiasgeheimnis in den Evangelien* (*The Messianic Secret in the Gospels*). There is no evidence that Gigot knew Wrede's work, though perhaps he did and for good reasons regarded it as too radical for these articles.[28]

On the other hand, although Gigot thinks that "Mark's narrative is distinctly objective, simply stating facts" ("Studies" II, 224), he has a clear and nuanced sense of the other two evangelists as modifying Mark's work for their own different theological purposes. Matthew, in his aim, "is apologetical, adapting Mark's primitive account to the circumstances and needs of his readers" (ibid.); an example of this is Matthew's concern not to take over from Mark's text any suspicion that Jesus, in submitting to John's baptism, was sinful and, indeed, positively to present Jesus as "conform[ing] to this as to all other divine ordinances" (ibid.). Similarly, Matthew expands Mark's account of Jesus' temptation "to show that such an event was not derogatory to His messianic character" ("Studies" III, 354). Gigot notes that Matthew also has to modify these early Markan passages to make them connect with his infancy narrative and his expanded temptations story. Luke does the same, and also has his own features of style, to which Gigot draws frequent attention.[29] He further notes that Luke alone presents Jesus as praying during the baptism scene, mentions the "bodily" descent of the "Holy" Spirit, and avoids using John's name during the baptism ("Studies" II, 226 and 229). Although Gigot's treatment of these passages does not add up to full-blown redaction criticism, that is where it is moving.[30]

By far the must puzzling aspect of Gigot's treatment of the synoptics is his claim that Luke depended on Matthew as well as on Mark. He "establishes" this dependency, insofar as he does in the first article, on the Baptist's ministry. The evidence he offers for it is never forced but is very meager, compared with that supporting Luke's dependence on Mark. It consists of three elements: the phrase in Matt 3:5c and Luke

3:3, "all the region about the Jordan" (Matthew has *hē perichōros tou Iordanou*, Luke the accusative, *tēn perichōron tou Iordanou*; Mark has no equivalent); Luke's agreement with Matthew in omitting Malachi's words from the Markan quotation in which a quotation from Malachi is added to one from Isaiah (Matt 3:3; Luke 3:4; cf. Mark 1:2-3); and the Baptist's preaching to the "offspring of vipers" (Matt 3:7-10; Luke 3:7-9). The first, the use of the same geographical phrase (with the difference in case) may be coincidence, although one cannot prove this, since the expression is not attested elsewhere. Gigot's second example is likely to be a deliberate change on the part of both evangelists, to avoid attributing to Isaiah the words of Malachi.[31] In his 1987 edition of Q, John Kloppenborg classifies this passage (Luke 3:2-4) as one "for which an origin in Q seems unlikely."[32] Gigot's third text suggesting that Luke used Matthew, John the Baptist's preaching, certainly demonstrates literary connectedness of Matthew and Luke, but the Sulpician presents no argument at all for his presumption that Luke used Matthew and not vice-versa.[33] Yet the fifth of his "General Conclusions" at the end of this first article reads:

> The literary dependence here of Mt. on Mk., and of Lk. on them both, is similar to that which an attentive examination of our first three Gospels discloses throughout their respective narratives of Our Lord's public life. (100)

In the second article, arguments for Luke's dependence on Matthew are similarly weak: they are that both evangelists use (different forms of) an aorist passive participle of *baptizein* (Luke 2:21 and Matt 3:16a) and change Mark's *schizein* to (again, different forms of) *anoigein*, describing the opening of the heavens ("Studies" II, 228-29). By the time Gigot comes to his third article, the temptation narrative, with its three-fold extension in Matthew and Luke, he simply presumes Lukan dependence on Matthew ("Studies" III, 354-67), and continues to do so in the remaining articles.

Gigot's position here is difficult to account for. He does not refer to the hypothetical Aramaic Matthew and, indeed, his arguments from the Greek text of the gospels count against this as his presupposition. He does know about what we would now call Q: this is clearly what he refers to in a note relating to Matthew 3:7-10 and 3:12 in the first of the articles.[34] He again alludes to this material (and, oddly, to Matt 3:14-15) at the end of article three:

As regards the special source to which we should refer the three onsets [sic] inserted by St. Matthew into Mk's narrative of the temptation, only this much can now be stated. In form (that of a dialogue) and purpose (apologetics against the Jews), they resemble Mt's insertions into Mk's narratives of the Preparatory ministry of John (Mt. iii, 7-10), and of Our Lord's baptism (Mt. iii, 14-15), which we have already noticed in our preceding Studies. So that these three additions of St. Matthew may well be referred to one and the same source. What that precise source was will be examined later.[35]

The trouble is that he did not examine it later,[36] his projected New Testament book never materialized,[37] and I have not yet found evidence of what he taught on the synoptics at Dunwoodie.[38] Gigot's long and lucid *Catholic Encyclopedia* article, "Synoptics," was written after the Biblical Commission's decree of June 19, 1911, when he could no longer hold any view that did not posit the priority of "a Gospel substantially identical with our present Greek Gospel According to St. Matthew."[39]

So Gigot knew about a non-Markan special source of Matthew and Luke. That he also knew of the documentary hypothesis is evident from his review of a book by E. Jacquier in the first volume of the *NYR*.[40] He notes that Jacquier treats "the Synoptic Problem" in his third and fourth chapters; the reviewer then observes that "[t]he Documentary hypothesis, under its various forms, takes up much of [Jacquier's] attention (pp. 313-354), yet fails to satisfy him."[41] It is strange, therefore, that the rather cryptic paragraph at the end of "Studies" III and the footnote quoted in n. 34 are Gigot's only clear references to what we would call Q. Despite his promise, he does not return to consider "what that precise source" may be, presumably because the texts considered in articles four through six contain no Q material. After that, the *Review* was discontinued and, despite another promise of "forthcoming studies" given in the final article,[42] Gigot produced no more work of this kind, which is not surprising, given the decrees emanating from the Biblical Commission between 1905 and 1915.

It seems, then, that in 1905 Gigot knew of a sayings source but thought that Luke had access to it only through Matthew's gospel, even though his arguments for that are so weak. I am at a loss to understand why he would insist on this. It is true that Adolf Schlatter (1852-1938) regarded Luke as dependent on Matthew,[43] and that Gigot lists Schlatter's *Einleitung in die Bibel* of 1890 among the "Protestant Works on *General* Introduction" (Gigot's emphasis) in his own *General Introduction to the Study of the Holy Scriptures* (21), but he never refers to Schlatter thereafter in the book, does not list him in the impressive-looking index, and makes no reference to him in connection with the synoptic gospels.

One component of Gigot's position may be the church's long-standing presumption of Matthean priority: perhaps, having rejected this, Gigot wished to leave Matthew some dignity! His evidence and conclusions are, however, unexpected in a writer who is otherwise so careful in the deductions he makes from the biblical text.[44] Furthermore, despite the repetition of this view up to the end of "Studies" V (361), the final article does not explicitly state such dependence: Mark "was written first and utilized by the other two Synoptics"; "the order between the first three Evangelists is (1) Mark; (2) Matthew; and (3) Luke" ("Studies" VI, 200).[45]

These six articles, then, convey very clearly Gigot's respect for the text, his careful attention to its details, and his attempts at accounting for differences among the synoptic gospels. Finally, he repeatedly and emphatically shows a concern to present Matthew and Luke as being deeply in harmony with the "primitive" tradition as represented by Mark. All the pieces state this as their final sentence (nos. I, V, and VI) or elsewhere on their last page.[46]

Divorce in the New Testament

Gigot's *NYR* articles on divorce in the New Testament[47] are in some respects different from the others. This is partly because of the topic: it would be imperative that New Testament "findings" of any priest teaching Scripture in Archbishop Farley's seminary be in line with official Catholic teaching on the indissolubility of marriage. Gigot may have had particular reason for stressing his commitment to that teaching. For in 1906 he had belonged to the archdiocese for less than a year and, as a Scripture scholar who had long used higher criticism, was inevitably at the storm center of the modernist crisis. As we have seen, all his *NYR* articles considered so far could be taken as not meeting the standards of the relevant Biblical Commission decrees.[48] Prudence was in order. Indeed, Gigot was so prudent in his six articles about divorce that he was later able to add an introduction, complete the section on Matthew 19:3-9,[49] include two appendices and three indices, and, "with but slight modifications,"[50] publish the whole thing in 1912 with a most fulsome dedication to his archbishop, who had been made a cardinal the previous year.[51] None of his other *NYR* articles would have served that purpose.

There is, however, another reason why Gigot might have wished to state Catholic teaching very clearly and to show that prohibition of divorce was entailed by the best understanding of the biblical text. Early in 1906, a committee had been set up in Washington to explore the possibility of uniform divorce laws throughout the country. A convention was then held in Philadelphia, "the first Conference of the States outside of Congress," the *New York Times* termed it.[52] By November, this National Congress on Uniform Divorce Laws had agreed to a bill to send to the various state lawmakers, its way being eased by the continuing activity of the original committee.[53] The first of Gigot's "divorce" articles was in the January-February 1907 issue of the *NYR*, along with comments in the journal's "Notes" (528) linking it to the outcome of the Philadelphia convention the previous November. This series on divorce has, therefore, a double thrust: to reassure Farley that higher criticism could be used in the service of traditional teaching, and to contribute to the Catholic apologetic addressing a nation that was, generally, prepared to tolerate divorce even while disapproving of it.[54]

How different from the others are these articles? In many respects, not at all. Gigot still deliberately uses higher criticism from within the tradition. He continues to give plentiful biblical text in his own translation and in two cases he includes the full Greek text;[55] he refers to Greek and Hebrew words when appropriate. The scholar takes full account of the circumstances in which the gospels were written; presumes the priority of Mark and its "primitive" nature and that Luke used Matthew in addition to Mark.[56] He finds the gospels as well as Paul to be in close conformity with one another;[57] treats the gospel text meticulously; cites modern sources to back up his positions (especially, in these articles, when Protestant authors support the Catholic view);[58] and presents his conclusions clearly.

What is different is the presence of some language that was not used in his other articles. Thus, "the Roman Catholic Church" appears in the first sentences and the last paragraphs of articles one and two, in the last paragraph of the third, and on the first and (without "Roman") last pages of the fifth.[59] In the other series he occasionally refers to his co-religionists as "Catholics," and speaks of "the Catholic faith" and

"Catholic belief," but uses the word "Church" very rarely, and never with either "Roman" or "Catholic" qualifying it, even when he is explaining why higher criticism is not to be feared. Likewise, Scripture is designated "sacred records" only in the first divorce article and in the one about Abraham. The series on divorce is also characterized by law-related language (appropriately enough) and by claims to impartiality that are, in places, repeated with such frequency as to raise suspicions,[60] especially as they are not found in his other articles.

Gigot is obviously sensitive to the minority status of the Catholic position. For example, he insists that divorce "remains wrong in the eyes of conscience and religion which rightly view it as opposed to the divine will, although it be treated as valid by a law which tolerates and regularizes it as a necessary evil":[61] the United States of his day was about to put in place just such legislation. Again, Gigot's view that "[h]umanly speaking, it was a bold thing on Our Lord's part thus to stand alone denouncing divorce as intrinsically evil" could be taken as an encouragement to his fellow-Catholics to be similarly bold.[62]

We cannot here give detailed comment on the exegesis of the six articles, which is complex, controverted, and, as Gigot himself admitted, incomplete.[63] His assumption that Luke used Matthew confuses matters somewhat. It is also surprising that he does not notice that translating a wife's *porneia* as "fornication" in the Matthean exceptive clauses in 5:32 and 19:9 (as in the Vulgate)[64] makes it essentially the same as her ex-husband's act of *moichan*, which is surely problematic and why many modern commentators think that the phrase refers not to a moral lapse but to a legal irregularity.[65] There are no surprises in his treatment of 1 Corinthians 7 and Ephesians 5 ("the genuineness of which [epistle], though sharply questioned, is not disproved"),[66] either in the third article or in the fourth, where he deals with the so-called "Pauline privilege." In the latter case, one wonders where his source[67] found the alleged Jewish legislation that he writes about so confidently, especially when recent commentators such as Hans Conzelmann appear ignorant of it.[68]

In article five Gigot works hard to show that in the antithesis about divorce in Matthew 5:31-32, the "fornication" exception relates to the proper interpretation of Deuteronomy 24:1-4 and results in absolute prohibition of divorce by Matthew. Gigot really does not deal adequately with the relevant aspects of the Greek text, either here or in the final article, an investigation of Matthew 19:3-9 that repeats much of the previous argumentation. He notes that Moses tried to make divorce as difficult as possible,[69] since he could not forbid it altogether and concludes (correctly) that Matthew's Jesus regards marriage as indissoluble.

There is much of interest in these six articles but the topic is too complex and the stakes too high for Gigot to have written pieces that read well today. In this sense, they are very different from his other seventeen *NYR* offerings.

Gigot after the *New York Review*

Gigot did not cease to write with the *NYR*'s demise in 1908. Most notably, between 1907 and 1914 he contributed sixty-two articles on a wide variety of topics to the *Catholic Encyclopedia*.[70] In addition to the 1912 book on divorce, he published two articles in the *Irish Theological Quarterly*, the first defending the Mosaic authorship of Deuteronomy[71] and the other, in two parts, written to show that the virginal conception was "a historical fact in the eyes of Saint Luke" and proof of the Church's "faithfulness to her Divine mission of preserving 'the faith once delivered to the saints' (Jude, verse 3)."[72] In these articles, Gigot has not abandoned the practice of higher criticism but now uses it to defend the tradition from what he regards (not without reason) as the excesses of its rationalistic practitioners. His reactionary response goes even further in a 1915 pamphlet, where he argues (against his earlier position) for Moses as author of the Pentateuch; this makes sad reading, as does his aptly named *A Primer of Old Testament History* (New York: Paulist, 1919), which is nowhere near as detailed as his *Outlines of Jewish History from Abraham to Our Lord*, written for seminarians at St. John's, Brighton, in 1897.

Gigot's final works, three "volumes" in the Westminster Version of the Scriptures,[73] are short and, for the most part, highly circumspect, with only the occasional reminder, especially in some of the notes, of the fine scholar who paid such a high price for remaining faithful to his vocation as a seminary professor of Scripture.[74] Scholarship on a par with his *NYR* corpus would not be seen again, at least in public, until after *Divino Afflante Spiritu* in 1943.

Notes

[1] On the period as a whole, see Michael V. Gannon, "Before and After Modernism: The Intellectual Isolation of the Modern Priest," in John Tracy Ellis,

ed., *The Catholic Priest in the United States* (Collegeville, MN: St. John's University Press, 1971), pp. 293-383. On Gigot's life, see Michael DeVito, *The New York Review (1905-1908)* (United States Catholic Historical Society Monograph Series XXXIV; New York: United States Historical Society, 1977), pp. 33-35 and the references there; for Gigot's Sulpician background and his transfer (along with Dunwoodie seminary and four confrères) to the Archdiocese of New York, see Christopher J. Kauffman, *Tradition and Transformation in Catholic Culture: The Priests of Saint Sulpice in the United States from 1791 to the Present* (New York: Macmillan, 1988), pp. 153-223. On Gigot's Dunwoodie years, see Arthur J. Scanlan, *St. Joseph's Seminary, Dunwoodie, New York, 1896-1921* (The United States Catholic Historical Society Monograph series VII; New York: The United States Catholic Historical Society, 1922), pp. 108-158; Thomas J. Shelley, *Dunwoodie: The History of St. Joseph's Seminary, Yonkers, New York* (Westminster, MD: Christian Classics, Inc., 1993), pp. 92-171; R. Scott Appleby, *"Church and Age Unite!": The Modernist Impulse in American Catholicism* (Notre Dame, IN: University of Notre Dame Press, 1992), pp. 91-116. For Gigot's place in American biblical scholarship, see Gerald P. Fogarty, *American Catholic Biblical Scholarship. A History from the Early Republic until Vatican II* (San Francisco: Harper & Row, 1989), pp. 120-139. See Bernard J. Noone, *A Critical Analysis of the American Catholic Response to Higher Criticism as Reflected in Selected Catholic Periodicals—1870 to 1908* (Ann Arbor, Mich.: University Microfilms, 1976), pp. 322-409, for a detailed study of Gigot's positions on Pentateuchal criticism and inspiration. Noone's bibliography of Gigot's works is the most complete to date, although lacking some items.

[2] DeVito (*Review*, pp. 90-97), Noone (*Analysis*, pp. 335-339), and Appleby (*Church*, pp. 134-142) have considered the series on higher criticism.

[3] The most complete study of the *NYR* is still DeVito's; see also all the above references except Scanlan.

[4] DeVito, *Review*, pp. 47-49 and Appendix A. Also printed at the end of the first issue: *NYR* 1 (June-July 1905):132.

[5] *NYR* 1 (1905-1906): 724-727; *NYR* 2 (1906-7): 66-69; 158-161; 302-305; 442-451; 585-589. The articles develop aspects of Gigot's book, *Biblical Lectures: Ten Popular Essays on General Aspects of Sacred Scripture* (Baltimore: Joseph Murphy and Company, 1901). See Noone, *Analysis*, pp. 335-339.

[6] "Higher Criticism" V, p. 442.

[7] Gigot also lived with them at St. Austin's in Washington, D.C. in 1901-1902 but found life difficult there. On March 7, 1903 he tells James Driscoll that the house needs "a clean sweeping" (Record Group 10, Box 9, Sulpician Archives in Baltimore, henceforth SAB).

[8] "The Authorship of Isaias, XL-LXVI. I. Arguments in Favor of the Traditional View," *NYR* 1 (Aug-Sept 1905): 153-168; "II. Arguments Against the Isaianic Authorship," ibid. (Oct-Nov 1905): 277-296.

[9] See, e.g., *New Jerome Biblical Commentary*, 72.27.iii.

[10] "The Book of Jonas. Arguments For and Against Its Historical Character," *NYR* 1 (Dec 1905-Jan 1906): 411-424; "Leading Problems Concerning the Book of Job. A Brief Exposition and Discussion," ibid. (Feb-March 1906): 579-596.

[11] They are arguments from the book's place in the Jewish canon, its historical and geographical verisimilitude, its psychological plausibility, the testimony of later Jewish tradition, and that of Jesus in the gospels.

[12] "Jonas," pp. 423-424.

[13] For example, reviewing a book about prophecy, Gigot regards as "rather naturalistic" the author's view of the prophet's call (*NYR* 1 [Dec 1905-Jan 1906]: 523).

[14] See, e.g., the *New Jerome Biblical Commentary.*

[15] *NYR* 2 (July-August 1906): 37-48.

[16] Gigot does not reference his Jewish and Islamic sources; he assesses their historical worth realistically but not delicately!

[17] Gigot's terminology about J and E is inconsistent. In his *Special Introduction to the Study of the Old Testament. Part I: The Historical Books* (New York: Benziger Brothers, 1901), he says that "nearly all contemporary Critics" refer to them as "the Jehovistic or Judaic (J), [and] the Elohistic or Ephraimitic (E)" (p. 46, n. 1). It is unclear why the *NYR* article takes J as "Judean." In his 1915 talk, *The Message of Moses and Higher Criticism* (New York: Benziger, 1915), p. 14, n. 7, Gigot says that "J and E (i.e., the two prophetical narratives) are ascribed by many Critics to prophets of Juda and Ephraim respectively": no mention of the Yahwist or Elohist. Noone (*Analysis*, pp. 331-76) does not address this problem.

[18] Only three references are to modern scholars; the Jonah article, of comparable length, has about thirty-five.

[19] See Gigot's February 4, 1905 letter to the Sulpician vicar-general, Edward Dyer and Dyer's request later that month that Francis L. M. Dumont censor the articles, which Dyer says will be on the Pentateuch (Record Group 10, Boxes 10 and 16, SAB).

[20] The titles of nos. II, IV, and VI lack the indefinite article. See *NYR* 1 (June-July 1905): 89-102; (Aug-Sept 1905): 217-231; (Oct-Nov 1905): 346-367; (Feb-March 1906): 640-657; *NYR* 2 (Nov-Dec 1906): 335-361 and 363-364; *NYR* 3 (Sept-Oct 1907): 181-203.

[21] The titles of articles I and III list the gospels in the order: Matthew, Mark, Luke; Matthew follows Mark in the others.

[22] See above, n. 4 and related text.

[23] "Studies" I, p. 89. Gigot does this for nos. I, IV, V, and VI and says that he does so for II, but the Dominican House copy of *NYR* that I used lacks it. "Studies" III gives the text passim, as Gigot refers to its various parts.

[24] So Gigot does not use or refer to his colleague Bruneau's *Harmony of the Gospels* (New York: The Cathedral Library Association, 1898), a synopsis based on the Douay text.

[25] He cites without comment the view of "Fr. V. Rose, O. P." that Jesus' temptations were not historical but in his imagination only ("Studies" III, p. 346, n. 1).

[26] "Primitive" is used of Mark's gospel eight times on pp. 218-19 of "Studies" II.

[27] Lagrange's 1910 commentary presents Mark as not a mere editor of traditions, although this causes tension with his view of Mark as historically reliable:

see Nadia M. Lahutsky, "Paris and Jerusalem: Alfred Loisy and Père Lagrange on the Gospel of Mark," *Catholic Biblical Quarterly* 52 (1990): 444-466, 449.

[28] What one needs here is Gigot's *Special Introduction to the New Testament*, announced as "In Preparation" in his *General Introduction to the Study of the Holy Scriptures* (New York: Benziger, 1900) and, at the end of the Preface to Part II of Gigot's 1906 *Special Introduction*, specified as a two-volume work; it never appeared.

[29] See also the account of Luke's tendencies in "Studies" IV, pp. 652-653, on Luke 4:14-15. Gigot comments on Matthew's and Mark's styles, too; for the latter, see ibid., pp. 641-643.

[30] At the end of "Studies" IV (p. 657), Gigot notes that he can now conclude further "that in beginning their respective narrative of the public ministry itself, our first three evangelists have actually preserved their respective methods of composition." Article six even uses "redaction" to denote Matthew's and Luke's work (pp. 186 and 193; 199), although not in the later technical sense, of course.

[31] Matthew and Luke probably got this quotation from Mark, since, as Gigot notes, they all have "make straight his paths" instead of the Septuagint's ". . . the paths of our God" ("Studies" I, pp. 91, 97). See, e.g., Joseph A. Fitzmyer, *The Gospel According to Luke, Vol. 1* (Garden City, New York: Doubleday, 1981), p. 452.

[32] John S. Kloppenborg, *Q Parallels: Synopsis, Critical Notes, and Concordance* (Sonoma, CA: Polebridge, 1987), pp. xxiii and 4.

[33] Nowadays, Luke 3:7-9 is regarded as vintage Q; see, e.g., Kloppenborg, *Parallels*, p. 8.

[34] "As regards the source from which Mt's additions (iii, pp. 7-10; iii, p. 12) are derived, nothing can be defined with certainty. Their tone resembles that of many other additions found in our first gospel, so that the question of their probable origin may be more easily studied later on" ("Studies" I, p. 95 n. 1).

[35] "Studies" III, p. 367,

[36] Gigot similarly does not deliver on the promise of his fifth article: "The question of the probable source utilized by Luke [in 5:1-11] will be studied later on" ("Studies" V, p. 350, n. 1).

[37] He had promised in his *General Introduction*, "The questions connected with the Origin, Date, Authorship, etc., of the Gospels . . . will be dealt with in our forthcoming volume on *Introduction to the New Testament*" (p. 90, n. 1).

[38] Shelley (*Dunwoodie*, p. 151) writes that in 1906 Gigot "introduced a weekly seminar on the study of the synoptic Gospels." In conversation, Shelley described his source as "a logbook kept by a seminarian," the Regulator's Book, which DeVito (*Review*, p. 34, n. 46) calls the *Regulator's Diary*.

[39] *The Catholic Encyclopedia*, vol. XIV (New York: The Encyclopedia Press, 1914), pp. 389-394, 394.

[40] Gigot reviewed *Histoire des Livres du Nouveau Testament. Tome second*, by E. Jacquier (Paris: Lecoffre, 1905), in *NYR* 1 (Aug-Sept 1905): 247-249.

[41] Ibid., p. 248.

[42] "Studies" VI, p. 192.

[43] See W. G. Kümmel, *Introduction to the New Testament* (Revised Edition;

Nashville: Abingdon, 1973), p. 64, n. 48, who lists twelve holders of this odd position, none (apart from Schlatter) with any obvious connection to Gigot.

⁴⁴ Although its format is like that of the *NYR* articles, Gigot's 1905 *Ecclesiastical Review* article ("First Circuit"; see above, in text) lacks a section on Matthew and so casts no light here.

⁴⁵ Gigot holds to Luke's dependence on Matthew even in the *1912 Encyclopedia* article. His third difficulty with the "Two Document theory" is "its common but very improbable denial of St. Luke's dependence on both St. Matthew and St. Luke" (p. 393); he must mean "Luke's dependence on both Matthew and *Mark*," but again offers no supporting argument.

⁴⁶ The first concludes by noting the "wonderful agreement in regard to the substance of these three narratives, and none of the differences amounts to what might be called a contradiction" and the second refers to "their harmony ("Studies" I, p. 100; II, p. 231). See also "Studies" III, p. 367; IV, 657; V, p. 361; VI, p. 200.

⁴⁷ "Divorce in the New Testament: An Exegetical Study" I, *NYR* 2 (Jan-Feb 1907): 479-494; II (March-April 1907): 610-622; III (May-June 1907): 749-760; IV, *NYR* 3 (July-Aug 1907): 56-68; V (Jan-Feb and March-April 1908): 545-560; VI (May-June 1908): 704-721.

⁴⁸ On the (non-)Mosaic authorship of the Pentateuch see additionally "Higher Criticism" V, p. 449.

⁴⁹ Article six was intended to cover Matthew 19:3-12 (see "Divorce" VI, pp. 706-707, the journal's last issue); detailed coverage stops after verse 9, without explanation. For his book, Gigot divided article VI and expanded it towards the end; that became chapters VII and VIII. He then added a chapter dealing with verses 10-12, about celibacy.

⁵⁰ Author's preface to Gigot's book, *Christ's Teaching Concerning Divorce in the New Testament: An Exegetical Study* (New York: Benziger, 1912), p. 6. The modifications were "mostly entailed by the adaptation of their text to the form which has been adopted for the remaining chapters of the work" (ibid.).

⁵¹ See Scanlan, *Dunwoodie*, p. 122. Gigot's dedication reads: *"Eminentissimo Sanctae Romanae Ecclesiae Cardinali Joanni M. Farley, D.D., Hoc Volumen Gratissimo Piissimoque Animo Inscribitur Ab Auctore."*

⁵² *Times* editorial, February 21, 1906, p. 8, col. 2. It credits the Pennsylvania State Legislature and remarks, "If the convention shall succeed in arriving at a common denominator, without doubt it will have deserved very well of the whole country."

⁵³ For details, see the *Times* of February 21, 1906, p. 8, col. 2; April 11, p. 11, col. 1; April 12, p. 8, col. 4; October 24, p. 9, col. 3; October 25, p. 8, col. 2; November 14, p. 5,col. 3; November 15, p. 7, col. 2 and p. 8, col. 2.

⁵⁴ See the *Times* editorial of November 15, 1906, p. 8, col. 2.

⁵⁵ "Divorce" I, p. 480; II, pp. 610-611, n. 1. The Greek text for articles II and III is on pp. 622-623 and 750 of *NYR* 2.

⁵⁶ On Mark, see, e.g., "Divorce" I, pp. 481, 489, 490 n. 18. For Luke's "use of Matthew," see II, pp. 615-617.

⁵⁷ E.g., ibid., p. 619 and (including Paul), "Divorce" III, p. 749.

⁵⁸ See, e.g., ibid., pp. 754-755 and 760; "Divorce," IV, p. 68.

[59] "Divorce" I, pp. 479 and 494; II, pp. 610 and 622; III, p. 760; V, pp. 545 and 560. The fourth and sixth *NYR* articles lack such a reference, but Gigot added one to the latter in its 1912 version, as the last words of the book's eighth chapter, on p. 240.

[60] See especially Gigot's treatment of 1 Cor 7:10-11: "Divorce" III, pp. 649, 652, referring to impartiality; pp. 650 and 653 ("unbiassed"); p. 652 ("without dogmatic preoccupation"). Page 654 includes "thoroughly objective," "reads nothing else into" the words of St. Paul than "their natural sense," "every unbiassed mind," and "impartially examined." Similarly, VI, p. 708 (although not the first "impartial" here), pp. 709-711, and 715.

[61] "Divorce" I, p. 148.

[62] Ibid., pp. 488-489. See also, e.g., p. 491: Jesus, in addressing the Pharisees in Mark 10:2-9, "was speaking in public, that is under a circumstance when one usually sets forth with considerable reserve a position of his that goes against a universally received opinion of the day."

[63] "Divorce" V, p. 557, n. 15.

[64] See "Divorce" VI, pp. 706-707 and n. 4.

[65] See "Divorce" II, pp. 615-619.

[66] "Divorce" III, pp. 758-759.

[67] He cites A. Edersheim, *Jewish Life in the Days of Christ*, 158 ("Divorce" IV, p. 62, n. 4.); it was published in Boston by Ira Bradley and Co. in 1876 (VI, p. 713, n. 8).

[68] Hans Conzelmann, *1 Corinthians: A Commentary on the First Epistle to the Corinthians* (Hermeneia; Philadelphia: Fortress Press, 1975).

[69] He is, perhaps, trying too hard: "Moses had manifestly meant to make the giving of that bill particularly onerous on the dismissing husband, in saying that such a one should write the bill of divorce, *deliver* it into the hand of his repudiated wife, and then only, put her away" ("Divorce" VI, pp. 719-720). Onerous?

[70] See *The Catholic Encyclopedia and its Makers* (New York: The Encyclopedia Press, 1917), p. 65. In the *Index Volume* his only article referenced is "Biblical Introduction."

[71] "The Mosaic Authorship of Deuteronomy" (*Irish Theological Quarterly* 4 [1909]: 411-426); at the end, he refers to "our next paper" about the other two laws in Exodus 21-23 and Deuteronomy 15, but it did not appear.

[72] "The Virgin Birth in St. Luke's Gospel: The Genuineness of Luke 1:34-35," *Irish Theological Quarterly* 8 (1913): 123-143; "The Virgin Birth in St. Luke's Gospel. II," ibid., pp. 412-434. The two quotations are from pp. 143 and 434, respectively.

[73] A translation from the Greek under the auspices of the English hierarchy, edited by Jesuits Cuthbert Lattey and Joseph Keating, and published in London by Longmans, Green and Company. Gigot's contributions appeared in 1915 (*The Apocalypse of Saint John*, Part III of Volume IV of the series) and (posthumously) in 1924 (where Gigot was responsible for the Pastoral and Johannine Epistles in Part II of Volume IV, *The Pastoral and Catholic Epistles*). In each case, a brief (and very safe) introduction is followed by short but scholarly notes accompanying Gigot's translation. Surprisingly, a note about the Johannine comma (1 John 5:7-

8), supposedly written by Gigot, is followed by reference to a conference in Cambridge (England) in 1921, the year after his death! The copy of the 1924 volume originally in St. Beuno's School Library (now in Heythrop Library, University of London) contains a loose half-sheet with a "Prefatory Note" indicating that Gigot had died before the book was published.

[74] In the separately printed 1915 version of the *Apocalypse*, Gigot writes on Rev 21:1: "The 'new heaven and new earth' have a symbolic force and, doubtless, like so much else in the Apocalypse, are not intended to be taken literally." By contrast, in an edition of 1931, the passage now reads: "The 'new heaven and new earth' are so definitely promised in these passages, that it appears safer to take them literally." Obviously, even the 1915 Gigot was too much for a later editor, although this is the only alteration of its type.

College Theology in Historical Perspective

Patrick W. Carey

The discipline of college theology is badly in need of historical examination and analysis. What I present here is a brief and tentative historical overview of the aims of college theology.[1]

At the beginning of the twentieth century, the idea of a theology course designed specifically for college students was entirely new—having no historical precedents either in European or American Catholic higher education. And, there were only a few American Catholic pioneers, as far as I know, who saw that undergraduate theology must be different from catechesis as well as from seminary or university theology.

College theology emerged very slowly in the twentieth century; in fact, more slowly than any other college discipline. At the beginning of the twentieth century there were no departments of religion or theology, no full-time teachers who were specifically and exclusively assigned to teach religion, no budgets, no credit-hour courses, and no definition of how theology or religion fit into the academic curriculum. College theology, moreover, was the last of the college disciplines to develop its own national professional organization (the Society of Catholic College Teachers of Sacred Doctrine which was established in 1954, predecessor of the College Theology Society).

By the 1920s most Catholic colleges had separated high school students from the collegiate program, adopted the American departmental system of college education, and instituted the credit-hour system as a means of measuring qualifications for graduation. By the 1930s some colleges began to organize departments of religion or theology, but still there were no full-time teachers of religion in most places and there were no university or college programs devoted to the education of college teachers of religion. Between the late 1930s and the late 1950s the discipline emerged in most colleges with organized departments, credit-hour courses required for graduation, some full-time teachers, and one or two graduate programs for the explicit teaching of theology for college teachers. The teachers, too, until the 1940s, were almost always seminary-trained priests, and after the 1940s a number of women religious. The emergence of non-religious laity as teachers was primarily, although not exclusively, a post-1960s phenomenon. It was a hard-won battle to define the discipline, to relate it to other disciplines, to get it accredited, to obtain full-time teachers, and to establish the infrastructure (i.e., graduate schools) that would train future teachers.

Defining the discipline became a major problem during the twentieth century. National leaders disagreed among themselves on its nature and function. In defining the aims of the discipline they generally tried to solve specific problems and in responding to one problem they tended to create others.

In what follows I outline the struggles to define the aims of the discipline as it emerged into its present forms and I argue that the conflicting definitions of the aims must be brought into some kind of historical synthesis in the present if we are to develop an adequate approach to the discipline. Some of the defined aims of the discipline, just as some of the problems the aims were intended to solve, were time conditioned, but others are perennially significant and need in some cases to be retrieved to make the discipline true to its own integrity and to the needs of the students.

Emergence of College Theology as a Discipline, 1900-1939: Shields, Cooper, and Russell at the Catholic University

College theology first emerged as a self-conscious discipline at the Catholic University of America. By a self-conscious discipline I mean an explicit attempt to separate religious instruction at the college level from religious instruction in catechetical and seminary programs—in other words, the realization that college students had specific needs that neither the catechism nor the seminary theological manuals could address appropriately. The father of the discipline in this regard was John Montgomery Cooper (1881-1949), a priest of the diocese of Washington, D.C., a faculty member at the Catholic University of America, and the founder of the department of religion for undergraduates at the Catholic University.[2] To understand Cooper's perspective on college theology it is necessary to examine something of the intellectual context at the Catholic University, the innovative leader in Catholic higher education for the first half of the twentieth century.[3]

To understand Cooper's definitions of the aims of college theology one needs to understand what Edward Aloysius Pace (1861-1938) and especially Thomas Edward Shields (1862-1921) were trying to do at the Catholic University during the progressive era of American history. Cooper was a direct intellectual descendant of these two priest-professors. Both men were progressives; both were influenced by the inductive scientific method; both had studied the new science of empirical psychology after their seminary and theological education—Pace under Wilhelm Wundt at Leipzig, and Shields at the new graduate school of Johns Hopkins University (where John Dewey and numerous other leaders of progressive education had studied in the late nineteenth century).

From 1902 until 1921, Shields and Pace established a School of Education at the Catholic University, a College for Sisters teaching in the Catholic schools, and, more important for our purposes, developed a rationale for religious education at the primary and secondary levels of education that had implications for college theology as well. Shields's view of religious education is particularly important because Cooper considered Shields's philosophy to be a creative and justified alternative to the current forms of religious education (i.e., those based upon the *Baltimore Catechism*).[4]

Shields represents a continuing influence of Americanist and quasi-modernist ideas in the post-*Pascendi* period—demonstrating, to some extent, that *Testem Benevolentiae* and *Pascendi* did not universally stamp out the Americanist and modernist tendencies as many historians have argued. Shields and some of his successors at the Catholic University had a progressive-era confidence in empirical science and scientific method and he was very much in dialogue with modern psychology and progressive education.

Hired to teach biology at the Catholic University, Shields's interest soon turned to the problems of education and the philosophy of education. Like some other progressive-era representatives (such as John Dewey), Shields tried to create a synthesis between the findings of empirical psychology and a philosophy of education. Unlike the secular progressives, however, he brought the methods of the progressive education movement into communion with his Catholic understanding of human nature and destiny.

According to Shields, the discoveries of modern science, particularly in biology and psychology, brought to light the pedagogical principles of Jesus as revealed in the Gospels and as applied by the church in her liturgical and educational activities for 2000 years. The new discoveries in psychology and biology brought to light the laws that governed the mind and its development, laws that would help Catholics recover their own tradition in teaching.

Modern psychologists, he argued, had uncovered what the church had known instinctively but had failed to put into practice in the classrooms and in the teaching of the catechism since the Protestant Reformation. Psychology had pointed out that

> a conscious content strictly confined to the intellect lacks vitality and power of achievement. Every impression tends by its very nature to flow out in expression, and the intellectual content that is isolated from effective consciousness will be found lacking in dynamo-genetic content because it has failed to become structural in the mind and remains external thereto. From the evidence in this field, we may safely formulate as a fundamental educative principle: the presence in consciousness of appropriate feeling is indispensable to mental assimilation.[5]

Modern biology and the doctrine of evolution, Shields held, had also given the method of correlation in teaching a new meaning. Correlation demanded that "each new thought element be related to the previous content of the mind not along structural lines alone, but in a relationship of reciprocal activity." According to empirical evidence, the mind was developed "by each new truth that functions in it, whereas those truths that are not functional, however valuable they may be to the adult, impede development and menace the health of the child's mind."[6] Correlation meant that the teachers should try to accomplish three things in religious education: (1) integrate what was taught with the pupil's need, capacity, and stage of development; (2) do so in such a way that what was taught interlocked with what the pupil already knew, felt, and sensed; like Jesus, the teacher must use the concrete (e.g., parables, stories, action lessons) to communicate to the whole person; (3) couple what the pupil was learning in other subjects with what the pupil was learning in religion. To be taught effectively, religion "must be interwoven with every item of knowledge presented to the child and it must be the animating principle of every precept which he is taught to obey."[7]

Modern psychology also emphasized that learning was an organic communal activity, one not confined to the classroom. In practice, the church, too, had accentuated the same organic approach to learning, but it had not done so self-consciously in the past. Shields was trying to make Catholics self-consciously aware of the multiple avenues to learning that were an inherent part of the church's past practices—practices, he believed, that had been forgotten in the church's present educational arrangements. The church's teaching had been organic, teaching formally through her councils and dogmatic definitions, but also through the lives and example of the saints, art and music, liturgical forms and sacraments, and through her schools.[8]

For modern psychology as for the church, moreover, learning was a holistic experience. The church appealed to the

> whole man: his intellect, his will, his emotions, his senses, his imagination, his aesthetic sensibilities, his memory, his muscles, and his powers of expression. She neglects nothing in him: she lifts up his whole being and strengthens and cultivates all his faculties in their interdependence.[9]

And this approach was also democratic; it appealed to all, the young and the old, rich and poor, learned and unlearned. The church, too, knew instinctively that human beings learn not just by listening but also by doing. The whole person, mind and body, became involved in the learning process. This was particularly evident in the liturgical drama when one became a living, moving part of it by song and prayer, by genuflection and posture, entering into the liturgical action, which "in its totality, shows forth the divine constitution of human society by which man is made to cooperate with his fellow-man in fulfilling the destiny of the individual and of society."[10]

Shields's approach to the teaching of religion was functional and practical. Religious educators had to make "the saving truths of religion functional in the minds and hearts of the pupils." The "only legitimate criteria of the truths" to be presented to the mind were the "need and capacity of the developing mind." Even Christ did not present his followers with the mysteries of his kingdom in abstract formulations that could be committed to memory.[11] For Christ, according to Shields, truth was of its very nature functional and practical.[12] The aim in teaching religion, therefore, must be to affect the whole person and to move the person, according to the person's capacity, to Christian living and virtue. This moral and functional aim of education would be the hallmark of undergraduate education at the Catholic University for almost fifty years.

Shields faced two major problems in advocating and implementing his new methods and approaches to religious education. One problem was opposition from some Catholics like the San Francisco priest and educator Peter Yorke who found Shields's departure from the method of recitation and memory, used in so much public and Catholic education, to be "nothing less than revolutionary."[13] Shields did indeed reject the exclusive use of memory because he believed that that method of education could lead to "mental parasitism," which was unfavorable to initiative and self-reliance. He believed the opposition his approach generated in Catholics was due to the fact that many Catholics were unfamiliar with the laws of biology and with the recent discoveries in developmental psychology—an ignorance that translated itself into a suspicion of the unknown, the unfamiliar, and the modern. Changing current Catholic practices, moreover, threatened the Catholic educators' routines.

The second problem stemmed from the contemporary secular progressive educators (people like G. Stanley Hall and John Dewey) who used the new scientific discoveries to develop naturalistic or materialistic philosophies of education. Differing radically from the modern educators in his view of human nature and destiny, he could not accept, for example, Dewey's view that "apart from participation in social life, the school has no moral end nor aim."[14] The ultimate aim of education, democratic as it had to be, could not be simply training for good citizenship or for the betterment of a democratic society. Beyond these aims, which were good in themselves, the ultimate value and aim of education was the development of moral virtue and Christian character, and the salvation of the human being's soul.

Shields set the stage for the development of college theology during the first fifty years of the twentieth century at the Catholic University. His principles and methods of religious education, geared toward primary education in particular, were part of the background for the development of a philosophy of undergraduate theological education. Like many progressives, he believed that religious education or theological education had to be organic, holistic, functional, and ultimately aimed at the development of Christian character. To some extent his views of education were non-scholastic and anti-intellectualistic (not anti-scientific).

John Montgomery Cooper followed in Shields's progressive path by developing a philosophy of undergraduate theology at the Catholic University from 1909 until his death in 1949. At the beginning of his career as a part-time teacher at the Catholic University, Cooper tried to use watered-down seminary manuals to teach theology to undergraduates. This approach, he soon discovered, did not work because it was dry, intellectualistic, and did not meet the students' questions, their needs, or their capacities.

His experience in the classroom led him to create a new, self-conscious alternative to the scholastic form of theological education.[15] The new undergraduate discipline he called religion, rather than theology, in order to distinguish clearly what he was doing at the college level from what was done in the seminaries and in contemporary catechesis. Theology for him meant the post-Vatican I manual theology that was taught in the seminaries and that had become institutionalized in the *Baltimore Catechism*. The theology of the Latin manuals was individualistic, intellectualistic, and separated from the devotional and liturgical life of the church. Manual theology, moreover, was intended for priests. Written in Latin, the manuals themselves were meant for general situations in the universal church; they were not applicable (particularly in moral theology) for the specific conditions in the United States and thus were irrelevant to students' lives. Theology, furthermore, had become so compartmentalized (into dogmatic, moral, ascetical, and mystical) since the scholastic era that it no longer functioned as the life-giving discipline it had been during the age of the fathers. Scholastic moral and dogmatic theology in particular had become strictly a technical intellectual discipline. Its "dominant spirit is not parenetic or devotional, but didactic, dialectic, apologetic, speculative."[16] The discipline he called religion was "a revival of theology's better, pre-manual days."[17]

College religion was an academic discipline, in other words, "the science or discipline whose subject matter is drawn from the entire range of Catholic teaching." It tried to integrate, in a way the manuals did not, the church's devotional and liturgical life with doctrinal teachings in such a way that the student could see the implications for loving God and neighbor, the ultimate aim of all Christian education according to Augustine and many of the other church fathers. In a word, religion was a "life-oriented theology."[18] The goal of a religion course was not predominantly intellectualistic. Its purpose was indeed to inform, but also to appeal to the senses, stir the imagination, warm the heart, and educate by focusing upon the students' emotional and psychological needs and capacities.

Cooper was more Augustinian than neo-scholastic in his approach to college theology. For him the "attainment of truth is preliminary to and preparatory for the attainment of love."[19] Love should be the supreme and crowning achievement of Catholic education. In aiming to achieve this goal religion should appeal to the students' individual needs and capacities but it must also prepare students for the social dimensions of their life in the world. For him love of God and neighbor was social.

The religion course was student-oriented—focused upon character development and correlated with students' experiences—but he noted that it should also be integrally related with other subjects in the college curriculum. Most college religion courses, he asserted, were divorced from other disciplines. He pleaded that they be integrated in particular with the social sciences (especially psychology and sociology). The problem (still with us I might add) was that very little was being done to correlate what students were learning in one discipline with what they were learning in another. The task of correlation and integration, however, was difficult, arduous, and indeed baffling especially under the departmentalized system of college education. Students, however, needed to correlate what they learned in religion with what they learned in the social sciences in order to understand themselves and their society. The new social sciences, he asserted, could indeed help students to understand what it meant concretely to love God, self, and neighbor in the modern world.[20]

The religion course could not do everything that a seminary or graduate course in theology might attempt to do. There was only so much time in the curriculum for religion.[21] A college religion course, therefore, had to be an integrated program that focused on essentials.

Cooper organized the religion course content around what he considered the essentials of religion: code, creed, and cult—in that order. An integrated college curriculum in religion should be organized in such a way that students are first presented with the ideal moral life, then the motives for accepting it, and finally the means for living it. Thus, the college courses should deal with morality, Christian dogmas (i.e., motives), and the sacraments and liturgy (i.e., means) as the essentials of the Christian and Catholic tradition. The final year of college religion then should be given over to what Cooper called life-problems (i.e., the religious and moral dimensions, for example, of marriage, poverty, a living wage, leisure and play, international justice, and racism in American society).

Religion for him was primarily moral and, therefore, most of the college curriculum should be focused on the moral issues of the day. The study of Christian dogmas supplied students with the motivation they needed to live morally. In order to become meaningful and motivating forces for undergraduates the Christian dogmas needed to be studied in their dynamic and functional aspects. For Cooper "we may have a functional theology as we have a functional psychology." It was more important to know what dogmas do than what they are. Divine revelation "utilizes and builds upon human instinctive driving forces" and so should the teacher in using the church's dogmas. "Dogmas furnish a motive power, a driving force, a dynamic motivation, which impels us to live up faithfully to our Catholic ideal of life." For Cooper "it is not always the intellectual precision of thought so much as the vivid and vital effective grasp of the nuclear and peri-nuclear truths that gives the real dogmatic motive for conduct."[22] By 1939 Cooper was calling for a new field of theological research that he called "dynamic theology." This new field would examine the "motivating function of dogmas." "We have," he asserted, "libraries of books on what dogmas are, practically nothing theologically thorough and scientific on what they do."[23] This functional and pragmatic approach to doctrine (and truth), which reflected a continuity with earlier modernist themes and with the progressive education movement, clearly separated Cooper from the neo-scholastic approach to doctrine.

Cooper's approach to religion at the college level was in emphasis moral, pragmatic (action-oriented), functional, integrative, student-oriented, and focused upon the pre-scholastic forms of theological reflection. By the end of his teaching career he had become a forceful advocate for a return to the theology of the fathers, which for him was more spiritually and intellectually organic than what had developed since the scholastic era; and it was much more life-oriented than scholastic theology. He saw his own movement as a recovery and a restoration of theology in a new mode, but, given the reigning neo-scholastic view of theology, he called what he was doing religion and not theology.

William H. Russell (1895-1952), a priest of the Archdiocese of Dubuque, joined Cooper at the Catholic University in 1931 and until his death in 1952 he fostered the Cooper approach to theological education at the college level. Russell, however, modified Cooper's approach and changed Cooper's order of presentation. Rather than code, creed, cult, he preferred creed, cult, code. What this meant was that students were introduced first to the person of Christ (creed, he called his approach "Christocentric") and to the whole Christ (*totus Christus*) in the Mystical Body and in liturgical worship (cult) before they were introduced to the moral activity that should flow from such an understanding. And, the way to introduce students to the person of Christ was to introduce them to the gospels and the gospel stories, which would lead them to an identification with and appreciation of Christ's humanity and through his humanity to the divinity of Christ. What students needed to know was a person, not an abstract truth or dogma.

Much more than Cooper, Russell emphasized the centrality of the Bible (especially the New Testament) in the formation of Christian character, the aim of all Christian education—an aim that was congruent with the aims of progressive education. Russell, too, saw this emphasis as a recovery of the Catholic tradition that had become increasingly obscured since the rise of scholastic theology.

Russell's dissertation, published in 1934 as *The Bible and Character*,[24] was an historical overview of the use of the Bible in Christian education from the early church to the 1930s. He argued there for a recovery of "Bible reading" as an essential part of Christian education. Since the rise of scholasticism, and particularly since the Protestant Reformation, he argued, the use of Bible reading for Christian formation and theology had receded into the background. In the scholastic era the Bible became one of the elements in the disputed questions, and since the sixteenth century Catholics had used the Bible primarily as proof texts to resolve religious controversies with Protestants. "Actually, during this period the Bible was used by Catholics in a formative manner less than in any other period of history."[25] Russell wanted to revive Bible reading as the fathers and the monks read it— as a means of forming the Christian mind and heart. He called for an approach that would appeal to the ordinary reader who did not need "specialist equipment" in order to appreciate the moral and religious values in the Bible. For him the ultimate test for an authentic reading of the Bible was the Augustinian test: the increase of love of God and neighbor.

The Scriptures, he argued, "are a narrative record of God's revelation to man and of a plan for man. The Scriptures are story, drama, life, poetry, warning, heart-rending appeal, tales of sin and of spiritual heroism. Scripture is a personal, human-interest document. It is religion seen in the concrete."[26] A narrative approach to Bible reading similar to the method the fathers used, Russell maintained, should produce "a spiritual delight that pervades the whole personality of the reader." The object sought in Bible reading is the person of Christ, and the appeal of the person of Christ produces "a coordinate development of all the faculties of the individual—the intellect, the will and the emotions."[27] Such an approach to Bible reading, moreover, was democratic; all were capable of reading it in this way.

The English term Bible "reading," according to Russell, could not translate what the monks meant by *lectio divina*. The Latin *lectio* meant an earnest and deep study, but more importantly an affective and devotional reading that aroused the reader to a love of God.[28] *Lectio* implied study and resolution, but it was an intellectual grasp that was intended to generate love. It was formational more than merely informational. For the monks, the Bible was a *speculum*, a mirror. "The Bible was considered to be a book that would reveal the individual to himself and bring him to an understanding of his own problems." Gregory the Great clearly articulated this perspective when he wrote: "Sacred Scripture is put before the eyes of our mind as a sort of mirror that our internal face may be seen in it."[29]

The average Catholic (at least those who could read) in the Middle Ages "did not read Scripture to learn what to believe; he did read it to learn what to do." This spiritual and moral reading of the Scripture, however, need not condemn nor deny the value of contemporary scientific biblical scholarship. The prayerful reading of the Bible is not an "emotionalized religious experience," but a holistic spiritual orientation that is open to the scientific study of the Bible and that seeks such learning ultimately for the sake of love. Such an approach to Bible reading is more synthetic than analytic, but it uses the analytic to reach a synthetic understanding of the Christ to whom the Bible points.[30]

Russell's approach to college-level religious instruction was an American-style *ressourcement* tradition, precipitated to some extent by the experience of teaching, the progressive education movement, and the insights of functional or affective psychology. He wanted to return education to the earlier tradition of the fathers and the monks because such an education, he believed, was psychologically and pedagogically sounder than the scholastic and manual approach to abstract truth. And, the Bible was concrete, not abstract. Christ himself taught "virtue from life-situations; He went from the concrete to abstract."[31]

This American-style return to the sources was clearly voluntaristic in intention and orientation. College religion, Russell repeatedly asserted, should focus on the "desirability of God" and not just on the knowledge of God. The emphasis was placed upon the affective not the cognitive psychology of the student. For Russell, such an emphasis was rightly placed because, in his experience, most students were not intellectual and he believed that it was his aim as a teacher to reach all students. Even those 20 percent or so who had intellectual interests would be reached by this approach.[32]

The return to the Bible in college education was not for Russell simply an attempt to retrieve the past. It was clearly oriented to the needs of his American students. Like Christ, the teacher must correlate religion with real life situations. The teacher cannot live in the past. "The teacher must tie up religion with the familiar things of American background. . . . Sympathy with, and understanding of, all that is good in American life must needs be a trait of the teacher of religion if he is effectually to correlate modern life with God's plan of life." This meant that the religion teacher must indeed be familiar not only with American athletics, music, and culture, but also with contemporary science and other disciplines in the college.[33] Like Archbishop Ireland, whom he invoked favorably, Russell believed that it was better to know the twentieth century than the thirteenth if the teacher was to prepare students to live and struggle with present modes of thought that affect American students. Christo-Centrism was an effort to meet conditions peculiar to American circumstances.[34]

By 1952, the time of Russell's death, the religion program for undergraduates at the Catholic University had developed into a unique discipline that was self-consciously innovative, non-scholastic, voluntaristic, pragmatic and moral, student-centered, life-oriented, and Americanist. It was also an American-style *ressourcement* tradition that had some influence upon the development of college theology. How extensively the Catholic University program was used in American colleges, however, needs much further study.

The Manual-Catechetical Tradition in College Theology

It is clear that the religion program at the Catholic University in the early twentieth century was unique. A brief comparison to the religion program at Marquette University, which I believe was probably much more typical of what was happening in other Catholic colleges, points out just how innovative the Catholic University program was.

Marquette was established in 1881 and Jesuits taught religion to all Catholic students from the beginning. But, unlike the Catholic University, there was no specific department of religion until 1930, no full-time professors until the 1940s, no secretaries, no office, and no budget until the 1950s. Religion was taught part-time by Jesuits who were primarily assigned to other teaching responsibilities in the college. The college curriculum in religion consisted of courses called "Christian Doctrine" or "Evidences of Religion." The texts used were post-Vatican I abridged seminary manuals or adult level catechisms (such as Wilhelm Wilmer's *Handbook of the Christian Religion* or Joseph Deharbe's *A Complete Catechism of the Catholic Religion*) that focused on apologetics, dogma, and Christian morality. From 1881 to 1952 (when the department changed its name from Religion to Theology) there appears to have been little systematic reflection on the religion program and few signs that the Jesuits teaching in the program were even aware of the discussions on undergraduate religion that were going on at the Catholic University and other places prior to 1952. Religion at Marquette was languid as a specific college discipline, and Marquette was perhaps representative of the discipline in much of the United States. What had developed at the Catholic University was creative in comparison.

Battles over College Theology: 1939 to 1957

Marquette and most other Catholic colleges and universities in the nation were awakened to systematic reflection upon the undergraduate discipline by a 1939 National Catholic Alumni Federation symposium on "Man and Modern Secularism." That convention touched off a national debate on the nature of college theology that lasted for the next twenty years. It was clear from a number of papers delivered at the conference that there was great dissatisfaction with the discipline. Some asserted that it was not respectable in most places, that it was not given a place of prominence in the curriculum, and that many who taught were not qualified to teach. Fathers Gerald B. Phelan of the Pontifical Institute of Medieval Studies in Toronto, Francis J. Connell, CSSR, of Mount Saint Alphonsus, Esopus, New York (later of the Catholic University Theology Department), and John Courtney Murray, S.J., of Woodstock College agreed that current religion courses, whose sole aim apparently was to encourage students to fulfill their religious exercises, did not meet the academic aims of college education nor the needs of the modern Christian who lived in a secular world. These three speakers agreed that college theology should be scientific and should introduce students to the lay apostolate, which their incorporation into the Mystical Body of Christ postulated—in other words, theology at the college level should be a theology for the laity.[35] They differed, however, on what a scientific theology for the laity meant.

By "scientific" Phelan had in mind a Thomistic-Aristotelian notion of science and theology. It was clear that for him theology was not religion. Religion appealed to the will primarily; theology appealed to the intellect, and it was knowledge not desire that was the proper aim of education. Connell agreed with Phelan's general approach but added that college theology ought to be primarily apologetic, preparing students "to discuss religious problems intelligently with others."[36] Murray agreed that theology needed to be scientific and that it should be oriented toward the lay apostolate and Catholic action in the world. Catholic action, however, was not a polemic against modern errors or a defense of the faith; it was the result of reflection upon the social dimension of the Christian message. Influenced to some extent by Joseph A. Jungmann, S.J., Murray held that the formal object of college theology was "the livability of the Word of God as kept and given us by the Church; in other words, that our courses in theology must be wholly orientated towards life."[37] Such an object, of course, was consistent with the Cooper-Russell approach, and they indeed saw Murray's view as compatible with their own kerygmatic approach even though they continued to call what they did religion and not theology.

The conference's emphasis upon scientific theology would eventually carry the day. Increasingly, as at Marquette, undergraduate departments (except at the Catholic University) changed their names from religion to theology. Those who advocated scientific theology disapproved using diluted seminary manuals in college courses and using college courses exclusively to maintain or promote religious practices.

Although all at the conference called for a movement to scientific theology for undergraduates, all did not understand the aims of the theology in the same way. Between about 1939 and 1957, there were at least three different conceptions of the primary aim of the college discipline: (1) the Thomistic approach, stressing the intellectual grasp of the faith, dominated in the Dominican schools, in some Midwestern Jesuit schools, at St. Mary's College in South Bend, Indiana (where a new graduate program in theology for women was organized in 1944),[38] and at a few other places where the undergraduate program focused on the theology of Aquinas's *Summa Theologica*; (2) the Murray emphasis on the livability of the Word would be taken over by some Jesuit institutions in the East; and (3) the Cooper-Russell approach (or a modification of that approach) would continue at the Catholic University and a few other places.

For the Dominicans in particular, college theology aimed to communicate the intelligibility of the faith, and the *Summa* or some rendition of it was the most useful text for giving students an intellectual grasp of the faith. Walter Farrell's four volume *Companion to the Summa*, although not intended for college use, became a popular text for some undergraduate courses in theology. Farrell and others emphasized that the goal of undergraduate theology was the inculcation of divine wisdom, an acquired virtue that enabled students to see and interpret all things in light of the knowledge of God. Farrell and others also defended this approach to theology, particularly against the Cooper-Russell religion approach.[39]

The Murray approach was most fully developed in 1944 in two articles he entitled "Towards a Theology for the Layman."[40] These two articles, which were frequently quoted in subsequent years by his ardent followers and even by those who opposed some of his positions, focused on the finality of college theology, which he saw as the livability of the Word of God. Thus, the college course should prepare students to reflect upon Christ and the Mystical Body in ways that demonstrated the social dimensions of Christianity and the Christian responsibility to transform the world in accord with the Word.

After 1944, Murray no longer focused his work on the aims of college theology, but some East-coast Jesuits at Georgetown, Loyola of Baltimore, Fordham, and Le Moyne College created an integrated theological program that implemented his notion of the finality of a college course. The most famous of the Jesuit plans that emerged was the so-called Le Moyne Plan organized primarily by John J. Fernan, S.J., of Le Moyne College.

The fundamental purpose of the four-year Le Moyne Plan was to introduce students to their place in the divine plan of salvation. The course was thus organized around the master idea of the *totus Christus*. Fernan explained to an international audience that the program self-consciously carried the "Mystical Body from year to year" and tried to keep "a consciousness of the whole while studying the significance of the parts."[41] The focus of the course was upon the Bible, and primarily the New Testament, introducing students to the plan of salvation and the doctrinal implications of that plan. The courses followed an historical and literary approach rather than a logical or ontological one. Fernan argued that theologians at Le Moyne preferred the historical and literary approach rather than the philosophical because it was better adapted to the mentality of the students who had yet to study philosophy and because speculative theology itself depended for its validity and usefulness upon the revealed historical realities. Fernan had no difficulty with using Aquinas's theology but that theology needed to be placed in an historical rather than in a purely logical setting.[42]

The Le Moyne Plan was followed by a number of Jesuits because they believed it fit in more with the humanistic aims of college education than with the speculative or scientific aims of the Thomistic approach to theology. Gustave Weigel and others asserted that "humanistic contemplation" was the proper approach to college theology.[43] College theology as humanistic contemplation sought to impart a penetrating, unified, and "abiding [Christian] vision of the meaning of life and work" in such a way that "it will make one react to all of life in a Christian fashion." Such an approach looked to action not to static truth, and reflected the Jesuit ideal of contemplative action.[44]

John L. McKenzie also advocated the new approach, but he believed more strongly than others in the mid-1950s that the Thomistic synthesis could not be taught at the college level. The Thomistic approach, he asserted, did not correspond to the intellectual methods of the modern world. What he found lacking in the Thomistic synthesis and in speculative theology as a whole, he wrote in 1956, "are historical and critical methods and approach. In modern education and in the modern intellectual world these have a place in the training of the educated man which they did not have in the thirteenth century; our students will meet them in their humanistic disciplines." St. Thomas's historical and critical attitude "does not meet the standards of modern historians and critics."[45]

The Le Moyne Plan and method certainly had its supporters, primarily among the Jesuits, but it did not achieve the goal that Murray himself had set for college theology. Murray's focus on Catholic action, although indirectly present in the biblical-historical approach at Le Moyne, was not as central as Murray himself conceived it to be. In fact, the absence of the moral dimension in the Le Moyne Plan came in for some criticism.

The Cooper-Russell approach continued at the Catholic University from 1939 into the early 1950s, but this approach was clearly on the defensive, particularly after World War II when it came under mounting criticism, especially from the Thomistic school of college theology. Cooper and Russell had intended to correct weaknesses in the seminary manual approach, but in the process of doing so, some thought, they had developed a program that was without intellectual challenge or content.

Like Phelan, many criticized the Cooper-Russell approach because it tried to do what college education, by its very nature, was incapable of doing: that is, moving the will to the good. The Cooper-Russell approach was persuasion; it was, some critics charged, homiletic and catechetical more than it was academic. Theology was an intellectual discipline, an acquired virtue, and religious formation was only indirectly related to it. Roy Deferrari, graduate dean at the Catholic University of America in the 1930s and 1940s, was a constant critic of the Cooper-Russell approach because he believed they emphasized method over content and they appealed to the will, not to the intellect. Students, he asserted, complained about the lack of content in the courses. Almost every student, moreover, received a grade of "A" and was required to do little work or research outside of class—reinforcing the view that the religion approach was devotional and not rigorously academic and challenging intellectually.[46]

Even Gerard Sloyan, a member of the Catholic University's Cooper-Russell Department of Religion, who understood and was sympathetic with the "kerygmatic spirit" and aims of the Cooper-Russell approach criticized that approach. The Cooper-Russell approach, Sloyan argued in 1955, was "not emotion-prone or non-theological," as some unsympathetic critics charged, but its texts were outdated and its approach was geared toward a student body that was less sophisticated and less well-educated than those of the 1950s. Without subordinating truth to action, Sloyan claimed, the Cooper-Russell program used dogma "as a motivating force to virtue," but that approach tended to minimize the students' needs for solid theological education.[47] As we shall see, Sloyan gradually revised the Catholic University undergraduate theology program during the mid and late 1950s to include something of the old Cooper-Russell approach, the benefits of the Le Moyne Plan, and the doctrinal orientation of the Thomistic Plan (without following the ontological order so characteristic of the Thomistic approach).

The religion approach came under more severe criticisms from a few who saw in it Americanist and modernist tendencies. Joseph

Fenton, a member of the Catholic University's Theology Department, implied that the Cooper-Russell approach had leaned in the direction of Americanism by its emphasis upon the active over the passive virtues in Christ's life.[48] Bishop Aloisius J. Muench of Fargo saw undercurrents of modernism in the religion approach.

> In discussing texts and books useful for religious instruction one hears these days again and again the phrase, "religion is something that must be lived." The meaning of it, upon further explanation, is that religion has remained too doctrinal and that dogma has sterilized human conduct. Religion has been too much a thing of the head and too little a thing of the heart. It must become a religion of personal experience. The student of modernism detects an undercurrent of modernistic theology in this conception of religion. The modernism of three decades ago clothed its subjective conception of religion in theological language; today it speaks a popular language and seeks to make religion purely a matter of personal experience.[49]

Transition to a New Era: 1957 to 1964

From the late 1950s to the end of the Second Vatican Council the discipline of college theology was in a period of transition. Although the diversity of approaches to the discipline during the previous two decades continued, a new historical-critical approach emerged. The change and transition is most clearly evident at the Catholic University under Gerard Sloyan and at Marquette University under Bernard Cooke, S.J., both of whom became heads of their departments in 1957 and 1958 respectively.

Sloyan, a product to some extent of the Cooper-Russell approach, began to push the Catholic University Department of Religious Education in a slightly new direction that combined a life-centered approach to theology and a descriptive, historical, and doctrinal approach. The new element in the transition from the Cooper-Russell approach was emphasis upon historical-critical methods and some movement toward specialization in theology. He did not criticize the formational aims of college theology, but such aims were not foremost. For him, undergraduate theology was an academic reflection upon the Christian message, starting with an historical-critical examination of the biblical record—significantly missing from this approach was Russell's

"Bible reading" Christocentrism. Although for Sloyan the Bible was the primary focus of theological education at the undergraduate level, it was not studied, as with Russell, for its explicit potential to form Christian character. It was studied phenomenologically to acquaint students with its message in its historical context. In 1960, Sloyan justified the movement toward specialization in the discipline on the grounds that students had specialized courses in their secular subjects but only generalized courses in their study of religion. He asserted that the undergraduate curriculum should continue to serve the generalized needs of young adult Christians, but it should also respond to "the needs of those who by disposition and training think critically, historically, theologically."[50] Specialization was necessary in theology as in the secular disciplines and the courses should reflect the increasing specialization in theology.

The emerging historical consciousness was also evident at Marquette, where Bernard Cooke began to articulate a new approach to theology in 1957. Returning from the Institut Catholique in Paris, where he was one of the first Midwestern Jesuits to be explicitly trained for college theology, he brought with him the new non-scholastic, non-manual, historical, and kerygmatic theology to which he had been introduced in Europe. He began to change both the undergraduate and graduate curriculum to reflect an historical, not an ontological or scholastic or manual-tract, approach to theological education. He wanted undergraduate as well as graduate students to become acquainted with the historical development of revelation and Christian doctrine. He arranged the curriculum so that students started with an examination of Old Testament literature and traced out the historical evolution of the religious tradition, situating the student within the historical context of a developing tradition. This was a self-conscious break with the traditional seminary division of theological courses (which ordinarily would begin with a course "De Revelatione" and another "De Ecclesia"), as he told the dean of Marquette's graduate school.[51] By 1964, Cooke was looking forward to the development of a new kind of theology that would be worked out according to the precise needs of college students, a theology that would be scientific, integrated, contemporary, and vital to the life of the laity.[52]

Before the Second Vatican Council had ended, serious questions were being raised about all past approaches to the theological education of undergraduates. The undergraduate population itself had changed significantly since the mid-1950s and students themselves were raising new questions about the entire tradition. Brother Luke Salm, a theology professor at Manhattan College, reflected the revolutionary changes in a 1964 address to the Society of Catholic College Teachers of Sacred Doctrine. He questioned whether any of the past approaches to theological education at the college level could be effective with the new generation of students. Neither courses in scriptural, historical, scholastic, or kerygmatic theology, he argued, would meet the needs of contemporary students. College teachers, he asserted, needed to re-do theology in terms of a balance between a theology of questions and a theology of answers—a self-conscious attempt to see theology itself as a discipline that sought and questioned, more than one that simply provided answers. Students must be opened up to ways of thinking about the reality of their own experience, to the experience of non-Catholics, and to the genuine religious experience in literature outside of theology. College theology, like the Vatican Council itself, must abandon the "authoritarian and arbitrary forms that have driven away or kept away men of piety, intelligence and integrity."[53] The times were changing very rapidly by 1964 and Salm was only indicating something of the torrent of change that was about to overtake college theology in the mid-1960s.

Academic Study of Religion: 1965 to 1970s

In the midst of revolutionary changes in society and in the church following the Second Vatican Council, from 1965 to the early 1970s, a host of new issues arose that significantly altered the understanding of the undergraduate discipline. One of the major new developments was an extensive national advocacy of what was called the academic study of religion. Precisely what "academic" meant varied from person to person, as did the standards by which one judged what was academic. By the early 1970s the academic approach to the discipline had moved in two different directions: one in the direction of religious studies and the other in the direction of theological studies. But both approaches considered themselves rigorously academic. Religious studies saw the academic study of religious phenomena as neutral, objective, and descriptive. Theological studies saw the academic study of religion from the perspective of faith seeking understanding.

The theological as well as the religious studies approaches gradually moved away from what some were now considering the outdated pastoral functions of the college discipline. In 1966, Cooke argued

that the goals of deepening students' faith, promoting Christian behavior, and encouraging apostolic activities were not "proper academic
objectives of theology," yet he did not want to abandon these goals
entirely. These "pastoral or fringe objectives," he told an audience at
the National Catholic Education Association convention, can indeed
enter into "the strict academic endeavor, because of the fact that they
introduce into the psychological receptivity of the student the all important elements of the practical experience of Christianity."[54] Experience, he maintained, is as necessary to academic theology as it is to
other sciences. "Is not," he asked, "the experience of liturgy and the
experience of the Church in apostolic action as essential an experimental foundation for theologizing as laboratory work is for the speculation of the physical sciences?"[55] These statements, however, occurred
in the context of his argument for a strictly academic role for theology. Although Cooke could clearly distinguish the pastoral and academic roles, he could not yet fully separate them. But, that separation
would come very shortly.

By 1967, the Society of Catholic College Teachers of Sacred Doctrine changed its name to the College Theology Society, indicating by
the name change two desires the society hoped to accomplish. First, it
wanted to be recognized as an ecumenical, not simply a Catholic confessional organization. Second, it wanted to demonstrate its own academic, not confessional, allegiances. That same year, moreover, the
society endorsed "Religion as an Academic Discipline," a statement
of the Commission in Higher Education of the Association of American Colleges. The statement clearly indicated that theology or religious studies departments were "designed to promote understanding
of an important human concern rather than confessional commitment."[56] Religious studies or theology programs were concerned with
a universal human experience, not with a particular confessional orientation. Pastoral concerns, or concerns for the religious lives of the
students, became an obsolete relic of a now defunct system.

One of the chief characteristics of the academic approach was its
separation from spiritual formation. The complete separation of teaching (conceived of as an exclusively intellectual enterprise) from religious or spiritual guidance in the Catholic college became institutionalized in the late 1960s and early 1970s in a large number of Catholic
schools when campus ministry departments were established as the
proper place for fostering religious life. The theology or religious studies departments became the domain of intellectual development—one

separated from spiritual development. Theology became a phenomenological or humanistic or descriptive discipline that yearned for and sought academic respectability—a respectability that was built upon an understanding of academic theology as an exclusively rational enterprise.

To some, like Robert A. McDermott, to be rigorously academic meant to be exclusively neutral in examining religious phenomena. In 1968 he argued that religion as an academic discipline should be taught in the church-related schools as well as in the secular universities, and that this approach should replace the catechetical approach that was so much a part of college religion courses. And, for him, academic meant an empirical and comparative approach to the study of religion. Empirical meant disallowing any *a priori* judgment on what should be counted as religious, and comparative meant a critical study of religious experiences, ideas, and institutions in different traditions.[57] The attempt to gain academic respectability was clearly a movement away from concerns for the students' Catholic or even religious identity.

Not everyone went as far as McDermott, but even those who supported the theological approach had moved away from the strictly confessional and spiritual concerns of the previous generation in their attempts to justify the academic approach of theological studies. The justification of theology as a strictly academic discipline took place within the context of an attempt to make the theology course a universal requirement for graduation—that is, a graduation requirement for non-Catholic as well as Catholic students.

In the late 1960s, some Catholic colleges, like Webster College in St. Louis, completely abandoned theology courses as a requirement for graduation. Required courses were dropped and made electives in the curriculum because of the student movement toward freedom and elective choice and because these courses were conceived to be confessional in nature and therefore had been required only for Catholic students. Non-Catholic students had no theology requirements for graduation. So, the argument at Webster went, equity demanded that the theology requirement for graduation be dropped for all students, Catholic as well as non-Catholic.

Prior to the mid 1960s only Catholic students in most Catholic colleges and universities had to take theology courses as a requirement for graduation. Those who articulated the aims of college theology presupposed that what they were talking about was theology courses for Catholic students alone. Theology departments were clearly functioning within the context of the church's overall mission. There was no thought, for example, in speaking about a theology for the laity, as John Courtney Murray did in the 1940s, that he was imposing his aim upon non-Catholic students. He was talking, as almost everyone else was prior to the late 1960s, about college theology for Catholic students.

There were always, of course, large numbers of non-Catholics in Catholic colleges and universities. They were not required to take courses in theology because those courses were explicitly Catholic in orientation and it was generally felt that to impose such a requirement on non-Catholic students would be a violation of their religious freedom. By the 1930s, when many Catholic colleges began to require Catholic students to take credit-hour courses in theology for graduation, they also began to develop course requirements in "Foundations of Morality" or "Philosophy of Conduct" for non-Catholic students. Usually these required courses were offered as credits in philosophy rather than in theology, even though many times they were taught by professors who taught theology. Such courses were attempts to provide non-Catholic students with some rational grounds for an understanding of God, human nature and destiny, the spirituality of the soul, relations of science and religion, and foundations of morality—without specific reference to the Catholic theological tradition. College administrators and members of theology departments were never fully satisfied with this solution to a graduation requirement, but they saw themselves clearly in a dilemma. Either they require theology courses for all students, in which case they would be violating the non-Catholics' religious liberty, or they require it only for Catholics, in which case they would be sending the wrong message about the college's view of the importance of religion and morality in human life.[58] Thus, many colleges decided to require non-sectarian or philosophical courses on religion or morals for non-Catholics—courses parallel to those required courses offered in the theology department for Catholic students.

In the late 1960s some theological educators—those who opposed both the new movement to make theology courses purely electives and the older system of two separate graduate requirements, one for Catholics and another for non-Catholics—argued for a universal graduation requirement in theology, one for non-Catholic as well as Catholic students, on the basis that neither religious studies nor theology was inherently sectarian. They were academic disciplines and should be required of all students. The universal requirement was also justified by the fact that religious experience, being an experience of all cultures and all peoples, was a phenomenon worth studying in and of itself. A liberally educated person, so the argument went, could not be truly educated without considering the impact of religion on history, culture, and the personal lives of so many human beings. If theology courses were academic and not sectarian, if they did not promote Catholic identity and Catholic religious practices, if they were separated from religious or apostolic motivations, why should they not be required universally?

Those schools, like Marquette, that moved in the late 1960s and early 1970s to make theology courses a universal requirement for graduation did so on the basis of the above arguments. Yet, the arguments left two questions significantly unanswered. How could one call what was being done in the academic study of religion theology, and how was this approach Catholic?

Christopher Mooney, S.J., responded to these questions by suggesting a new configuration of the entire undergraduate discipline. He argued that theology courses be organized in such a way that all students would be required to take an introductory course that would examine universal religious experience, and all subsequent required courses would be electives that offered students the widest possible choice and professors the opportunity to teach courses in their own academic specialties. Such an approach created a link between religious studies, which examined "the ultimate religious values of mankind phenomenologically, as these have appeared and continue to appear in human life and history" and theology, which "is the study of ultimate religious values insofar as they have been embodied in a given tradition, whether Christian or non-Christian, and involve a commitment of faith." Such an approach was also Catholic in the sense that "To be Catholic [meaning, after Vatican II] means to be open."

This elective approach to the undergraduate discipline, it could be argued, destroyed any sense of theology as an integrated organic discipline. Mooney asserted, however, that the whole question of the unity of the discipline or of the integration of the discipline ought to be abandoned as a remnant of a medieval hope for some kind of organic unity in theology. "In fact," he opined, "there has been a fragmentation in the theological thinking which should naturally reflect itself in a certain fragmentation of the theological curriculum. . . . They [Catholic theologians] now think less in terms of synthesis than in terms of hypothesis, less about the possession of truth than about its quest."

Other than a general introductory course on universal religious experience, he believed that no other single course in theology should be required for graduation and that "no course in Catholic theology should be required of any Catholic student."[59]

Like Mooney, William Sullivan, S.J., a member of Marquette's Theology Department, argued that the requirement should be universal because the understanding of theology itself had been broadened to include an essentially descriptive, historical, or phenomenological approach as well as an approach that sought understanding on the basis of faith. Departments could offer two kinds of courses: those that were academically neutral, i.e., purely historical and descriptive, and those that were academically theological (or in his terminology "confessional"), where the dynamic of faith seeking understanding was operative. To be academic did not necessarily mean neutrality. Confessional truth claims could be rationally examined and explored from the perspective of faith especially in the Catholic tradition where reason and faith were not perceived in opposition to one another.[60]

Conclusions

The movement toward the academic study of religion, whether in its religious studies or theological incarnations, was an attempt to solve some real problems: for example, the needs of a new generation of students of the 1960s and 1970s, the need to justify a universal course requirement, and the desire for respectability within the academy. But, in the process of developing the academic approach, new problems were created—and we have inherited them.

Let me identify a few of the new problems that the academic approach has unwittingly created. First, in an attempt to be rigorously academic, the new approach divorced itself from the older formational approach and in effect separated theology from spirituality.

Second, the academic approach—in its attempt to be more objective, more neutral, more descriptive, and phenomenological than past approaches—overestimated, in my view, the possibilities of such objectivity. The academic approach, as some have understood it, made the intellect alone the object of education and the role of desire and will and emotions in the total educational process (as Cooper and Russell clearly perceived) has been sorely neglected. Can the educational process be more holistic without making it less academic? The educational relationship between the intellect, the will, and emotions needs to be re-addressed in the discipline at the college level. The academic approach has tended to become identified with an intellectualism that is devoid of voluntarism—and theology itself must examine and teach in such a way that the whole of the religious dimension is included in the examination and in the process of teaching.

Third, the academic study wanted to emphasize and support elective freedom in the curriculum in order to provide students with an opportunity to maximize their interests in the study of religion. But, the creation of a consumer variety of electives created a lack of integration in the discipline. Some in other college disciplines look at the incoherent theological curriculum and ask: what does the discipline do? What are the steps of its development in the curriculum? What is the discipline's content, method, and aim? What is it trying to accomplish in the college curriculum? The problem of the definition of the discipline is evident in the elective fragmentation that has arisen in the past twenty-five years.

Fourth, the academic approach claimed to be non-confessional, or ecumenical, or universal in its approach to the human phenomenon of religion in the world. For college theology or religious studies departments in the Catholic tradition such an approach created problems of identity. In the pre-conciliar era, undergraduate theology was almost exclusively a study of the concreteness of the Catholic tradition. In the post-conciliar period Catholicism was either studied phenomenologically as one of the manifestations of the universal religious phenomenon, or theologically in terms of its universal claims (e.g., the universal salvific will), or as an elective in a smorgasbord of courses. Such an approach made theological courses more inclusive, but it also created the anomalous situation of Catholic institutions providing elective courses in Catholic theology and to some extent ignoring (or in some cases rejecting) the publicly acknowledged concrete Catholic identity of the institution in which the theology or religious studies programs participate. Have we created a situation at Catholic institutions in which there is today little room for anything specifically and concretely Catholic in the curriculum because of the need to introduce students to the universality of the religious experience? How can we balance in the curriculum the need to be universal and the need to be concretely Catholic? This is a real problem for those of us who are striving to re-think what we are doing in college theology.

Fifth, the academic approach tried to meet the needs of rebellious and non-establishmentarian students of the 1960s. Those students were tired of the familiar and cramping Catholic culture in which they believed they had been raised. The students' needs are very different today. One does not have to be a Jeremiah to lament the general religious illiteracy among contemporary college students. Many teachers are aware that large numbers of students are innocent of the intelligibility and of the sources of fundamental Christian and Catholic doctrines. Most of our students today need to know the basic story line of the biblical and historical tradition of Christianity in some of its wholeness and concreteness before they can proceed to electives in the discipline. The new situation demands more emphasis upon fundamental issues.

It has been my own view for a long time now that we are in new circumstances today and that those new circumstances call for a re-examination of the aims of college theology. We need not agree on the national level about those aims (universal agreement was not a characteristic of the past). Why could we not have, as in the past, schools where specific Catholic emphases were followed: a Catholic University with one approach to college theology, a Le Moyne College with another, a Providence College with still another? Unity is not needed at the national level, but at the departmental and college level a great deal of consensus is needed to construct a theological curriculum that has intelligibility as a discipline within the college curriculum.

The history of the discipline indicates that it has experienced conceptual diversity and development as it tried to meet the changing needs of undergraduate students. What we need today is a new approach that will appropriate the values of the past while it meets the new circumstances of today. We need to re-think our discipline for the sake of all our students (Catholic as well as non-Catholic), for the sake of defining the discipline, for the sake of parents who send their students to Catholic institutions, and for the sake of administrators and colleagues in other disciplines who want some reasons to justify our prominence or place in the curriculum.

Notes

[1] In what follows I am dependent upon the historical studies of Rosemary Rodgers, "The Changing Concept of College Theology: A Case Study" (Ph.D. dissertation, The Catholic University of America, 1973), Pamela C. Young, "Theological Education in American Catholic Higher Education, 1939-1973" (Ph.D. dissertation, Marquette University, 1995), and Susan M. Mountin, "A Study of Undergraduate Roman Catholic Theology Education, 1952-1976" (Ph.D. dis-

sertation, Marquette University, 1994). Outside of these three dissertations there are, as far as I know, only a few other explicit historical studies of the discipline. Philip Gleason's *Contending with Modernity: Catholic Higher Education in the Twentieth Century* (New York: Oxford University Press, 1995) has some analysis of the discipline, but his focus is not explicitly on the development of the discipline.

[2] On Cooper, see William H. Russell, "John Montgomery Cooper: Pioneer," *Catholic Educational Review* 47 (1949):435-41. Cooper needs a biographer and much more analytical historical study than he has hitherto received in the history of American Catholicism.

[3] On Catholic University's leading role and on the general history of Catholic higher education in the twentieth century, see Philip Gleason's brilliant analysis in *Contending with Modernity*.

[4] On Cooper's appreciation of Shields, see Justine Ward, *Thomas Edward Shields: Biologist, Psychologist, Educator* (New York: Charles Scribner's Sons, 1947), p. 173.

[5] Ibid., p. 226.

[6] Shields, "Correlation in the Teaching of Religion," *Catholic Educational Review* 1 (January-May, 1911):420.

[7] Ibid., p. 425.

[8] Thomas Edward Shields, *Philosophy of Education* (Washington: The Catholic Educational Press, 1921), pp. 305-6.

[9] Ibid., p. 306.

[10] Ibid., p. 309.

[11] Shields, "The Method of Teaching Religion," The Catholic Education Association *Bulletin* 5 (November 1908):202-3.

[12] Ibid., p. 205.

[13] Yorke's response to Shield's "The Method of Teaching Religion," The Catholic Educational Association *Bulletin* 5 (November 1908): 235.

[14] John Dewey, *Moral Principles in Education* (Boston: Houghton Mifflin Co., 1909), p. 11.

[15] He also established in 1920 a specific department within the college for undergraduate religion, wrote a series of college textbooks from 1922 to 1938, and in 1930 created a graduate department at the Catholic University for the scientific training of religious educators at all levels from primary to college.

[16] Cooper, "Catholic Education and Theology," in *Vital Problems of Catholic Education*, ed. Roy Deferrari (Washington: Catholic University Press, 1939), p. 130.

[17] Cooper, "Religion in the College Curriculum," in *College Organization and Administration*, ed. Roy J. Deferrari (Washington: The Catholic University of America Press, 1947), p. 149.

[18] Ibid.

[19] "Catholic Education and Theology," p. 135.

[20] "Catholic Education and Theology," pp. 140-42.

[21] After 1926 the Catholic University required students to take religion courses two hours a week for four semesters.

[22] Cooper, "The Dogmatic Content of the Advanced Religion Course," *Catho-*

lic Educational Review 21 (1923): 80-93.

[23] "Catholic Education and Theology," p. 132.

[24] (Philadelphia: The Dolphin Press, 1934).

[25] Ibid., p. 162.

[26] "The Use of the Scriptures in the Teaching of Catechism," *Journal of Religious Instruction* 12 (1941-42): 521.

[27] Ibid., p. 38.

[28] Ibid., p. 49.

[29] Ibid., 46, quoting *Lib. Mor.* II, Cap. I, *PL* 75, 753-54.

[30] Ibid., 243, 244, 248.

[31] Ibid., 256.

[32] "Nature and Function of Christo-Centrism in the Teaching of Religion," *Journal of Religious Instruction* 12 (1941-42):847-48.

[33] "Religion and Correlation in Education," *Catholic Educational Review* 34 (1936):77.

[34] "Nature and Function of Christo-Centrism," p. 838.

[35] For Phelan, theology was "an intellectual discipline, and can be taught. Religion is a moral discipline, a virtue of will, and therefore cannot be, properly speaking, a subject in the curriculum although it can and must be fostered and developed by instruction as well as training." "Theology in the Curriculum of Catholic Colleges and Universities," *Man and Modern Secularism* (New York: American Catholic Alumni Federation, 1941), p. 129.

[36] "Theology in the Catholic Colleges as an Aid to the Lay Apostolate," *Man and Modern Secularism*, p. 145.

[37] "Necessary Adjustments to Overcome Practical Difficulties," *Man and Modern Secularism*, p. 152.

[38] Sandra Yocum Mize of the University of Dayton is working on a history of St. Mary's graduate program in theology.

[39] Farrell, "Argument for Teaching Theology in Catholic Colleges," National Catholic Education Association *Bulletin* 42-43 (August 1945-May 1947):239-44. See also, Joseph Fenton, "Theology and Religion," *American Ecclesiastical Review* 112 (1945):447-63; and Thomas C. Donlan, O.P., *Theology and Education* (Dubuque, Iowa: Wm. C. Brown Co., 1952). These critics saw the Cooper-Russell approach as homiletic or catechetical. Cooper's approach was rhetorical, not scientific and theological, according to Fenton.

[40] "The Problem of Its Finality," *Theological Studies* 5 (March 1944):43-75; "The Pedagogical Problem," *idem* (September 1944):340-76.

[41] John J. Fernan, "College Religion Course," *Lumen Vitae* 7 (1952):83.

[42] John J. Fernan, "The Historical, Scriptural Approach in College Theology," Society of Catholic College Teachers of Sacred Doctrine *Proceedings* (1955): 36, 39. See also Francis M. Keating, S.J., "The Finality of the College Course in Sacred Doctrine in the Light of the Finality of the Layman," Society of Catholic College Teachers of Sacred Doctrine *Proceedings* (1956):25-39.

[43] Gustave Weigel, "The Meaning of Sacred Doctrine in the College," Address delivered before the Fall Meeting of the Baltimore-Washington Section of the Society of Catholic College Teachers of Sacred Doctrine, November 1, 1955.

Paper in the Archives of the Woodstock College Library, Georgetown University.

[44] Weigel, "The Meaning of Sacred Doctrine in the College," in Gerard Sloyan, ed., *Shaping of the Christian Message: Essays in Religious Education* (New York: Macmillan, 1958), pp. 175, 179. See also Christopher F. Mooney, "College Theology and Liberal Education," *Thought* 34 (Autumn 1959): 325-46.

[45] John L. McKenzie, S.J., "Training Teachers of College Theology," *Jesuit Educational Quarterly* 19 (1956):101. See also *idem.*, "Theology in Jesuit Education," *Thought* 34 (Autumn 1959):347-57.

[46] For Deferrari's criticisms, see Rodgers, "Changing Concepts," pp. 206-08, 213, 219-20.

[47] Gerard Sloyan, "From Christ in the Gospel to Christ in the Church," Society of Catholic College Teachers of Sacred Doctrine *Proceedings* (1955):10-24.

[48] "Theology and Religion," p. 452.

[49] Foreword to James J. Graham, *Faith for Life* (Rev. ed., Milwaukee, 1944), v.

[50] "Undergraduate Studies in Sacred Doctrine at One U. S. University," *Lumen Vitae* 15 (1960):714-15.

[51] Cooke to John Riedl, October 12, 1958. Letter in Marquette University Archives, Academic Affairs, B63.

[52] "The Problem of Sacred Doctrine in the College," *Modern Catechetics*, ed. Gerard Sloyan (New York: Macmillan, 1964), pp. 267-90.

[53] C. Luke Salm, FSC, "The Status of Theology in the College," Society of Catholic College Teachers of Sacred Doctrine *Proceedings* (1964):45-46, 49.

[54] "The Place of Theology in the Curriculum of the Catholic College," National Catholic Education Association *Bulletin* 63 (August 1966):210-13.

[55] Ibid., p. 213.

[56] Rodgers, "Changing Concepts," p. 254.

[57] "Religion as an Academic Discipline," *Cross Currents* 18 (Winter 1968): 12.

[58] On the dilemmas faced by St. Louis and Marquette Universities, see Stephen J. Rueve, "Religion for Non-Catholics," *Journal of Religious Instruction* 6 (October 1935): 138-42; *idem.*, "Non-Catholics in Catholic Colleges," *Journal of Religious Instruction* 8 (1937-38):417-20; Patrick W. Carey, "Theology at Marquette University: A History," (unpublished, privately printed, second draft, 1996), p. 7.

[59] "The Role of Theology in the Education of Undergraduates," a privately distributed unpublished paper that Mooney delivered at the Jesuit Education Association workshop at Regis College, Denver, August 6-14, 1969.

[60] Sullivan argued his case in three articles: "Theology for Undergraduates," *America* (November 15, 1969):463-66; "Theology Should Be Required of All," *New Dimensions in Religious Experience*, ed. George Devine (Staten Island, NY: Alba House, 1971):301-13; "The Catholic University and the Academic Study of Religion," Council on the Study of Religion *Bulletin* 2 (December 1971):2-9.

CONTRIBUTORS

Frederick Christian Bauerschmidt, assistant professor of theology at Loyola College in Maryland, received his Ph.D. from Duke University in 1996. He has published essays on Julian of Norwich, Michel de Certeau, and the intersection of theology and social theory.

Michael J. Baxter, C.S.C, is visiting assistant professor in the theology department at the University of Notre Dame. He received his Ph.D. from Duke University in 1996. He was visiting research fellow at the Center for the Study of American Religion at Princeton University in 1995-96.

Gerald J. Bednar is associate professor of systematic theology at St. Mary Seminary and Graduate School of Theology in Cleveland, Ohio. He received his doctorate in contemporary systematic theology from Fordham University in 1990. He is the author of *Faith as Imagination: The Contribution of William F. Lynch, S.J.* (Sheed & Ward, 1996).

Una Cadegan is assistant professor of history and American studies at the University of Dayton in Dayton, Ohio. She received her Ph.D. in American civilization from the University of Pennsylvania. She has published articles on the history of American Catholic literary culture.

Patrick W. Carey is associate professor and chair of the Department of Theology at Marquette University in Milwaukee, Wisconsin. His books include *American Catholic Religious Thought* (Paulist, 1987), *People, Priests, and Prelates* (Notre Dame, 1987) and *The Roman Catholics in America* (Praeger, 1996).

Patricia Mary DeFerrari is a doctoral candidate in the Department of Religion and Religious Education at The Catholic University of America. She is writing a dissertation on the theologies of work in the U.S. Grail.

James T. Fisher holds the Danforth Chair in Humanities at St. Louis University. His books include *The Catholic Counterculture in America, 1933-1962* (North Carolina, 1989) and *Doctor America: The Lives of Thomas A. Dooley, 1927-1961* (Massachusetts, 1997).

Roberto S. Goizueta is associate professor of theology at Loyola University of Chicago. He is the author of *Caminemos con Jesus, Toward a Hispanic/ Latino Theology of Accompaniment* (Orbis, 1995).

Peter A. Huff is assistant professor of theology at St. Anselm College in Manchester, New Hampshire. He is the author of *Allen Tate and the Catho-*

lic Revival: Trace of the Fugitive Gods (Paulist, 1996) and co-editor of *Knowledge and Belief in America: Enlightenment Traditions and Modern Religious Thought* (Cambridge, 1995).

John F. Kane is professor of religious studies at Regis University in Denver. He is the author of *Pluralism and Truth in Religion* (Scholars Press, 1981) and publishes occasionally on matters of religion and public life.

Patricia M. McDonald, S.H.C.J., is associate professor of theology at Mount Saint Mary's College, Emmitsburg, Maryland. She received her Ph.D. in biblical studies from The Catholic University of America in 1989.

Elizabeth McKeown is an associate professor in the Department of Theology at Georgetown University. She is the co-author with Dorothy M. Brown of *The Poor Belong to Us: Catholic Charities and American Welfare* (Harvard University Press, 1997).

Sandra Yocum Mize is assistant professor of religious studies at the University of Dayton where she serves as director of the religious studies graduate program. She is currently at work on a history of St. Mary's Graduate School of Sacred Theology.

William L. Portier is professor of theology and department chair at Mount Saint Mary's College in Emmitsburg, Maryland. He is the author of *Isaac Hecker and the First Vatican Council* (Mellen, 1985) and *Tradition and Incarnation, Foundations of Christian Theology* (Paulist, 1994).

Jon H. Roberts is professor of history at the University of Wisconsin-Stevens Point. He has been visiting professor of history at both the University of Michigan and the University of Wisconsin-Madison. He is the author of *Darwinism and the Divine in America: Protestant Intellectuals and Organic Evolution, 1859-1900* (Wisconsin, 1988).

Anthony B. Smith received his Ph.D. in the Program of American Studies at the University of Minnesota in 1995. He is currently visiting assistant professor in the Religious Studies Department at the University of Pittsburgh. He has also taught in the Department of American Studies at the University of Maryland, College Park.

Michael F. Steltenkamp. S.J., received his Ph.D. in anthropology from Michigan State University. He is associate professor of social science and religious studies at Wheeling Jesuit University. For Spring 1997 he holds the Chair of Ecumenical Studies at Xavier University, Cincinnati, Ohio. He is the author of *The Sacred Vision, Native American Religion and Its Practice Today* (Paulist, 1982) and the award-winning biography *Black Elk: Holy Man of the Oglala* (Oklahoma, 1993).

David S. Toolan, S.J., is associate editor of *America* and the author of *Looking West From California Shores, a Jesuit's Journey into New Age Consciousness* (Crossroad, 1987). He is a frequent contributor to journals such as *Cross Currents* and *The Way.*